WITHDRAWN

ANSELM AND TALKING
ABOUT GOD

ANSELM AND TALKING ABOUT GOD

BY

G. R. EVANS

CLARENDON PRESS · OXFORD

1978

Oxford University Press, Walton Street, Oxford OX2 6DP

OXFORD LONDON GLASGOW
NEW YORK TORONTO MELBOURNE WELLINGTON
KUALA LUMPUR SINGAPORE JAKARTA HONG KONG TOKYO
DELHI BOMBAY CALCUTTA MADRAS KARACHI
IBADAN NAIROBI DAR ES SALAAM CAPE TOWN

British Library Cataloguing in Publication Data

Evans, G R
    Anselm and talking about God.
    1. Anselm, *Saint*   2. Theology, Catholic
    I. Title
    230'.2'0924   BX4700.A58   78-40314

ISBN 0-19-826647-2

Printed in Great Britain by
Western Printing Services Ltd., Bristol

For Sir Richard Southern

PREFACE

THE reader of St. Augustine or of John Donne comes away from every encounter with him with a sense of the contradictoriness and complexity of the man, an impression of unresolved war in progress between a passionate nature and a powerfully rational intellect. St. Anselm had as lavish an endowment of intelligence and sensibility as Augustine or Donne; his capacities and energies were as large as theirs. But his reader rarely finds him at war with himself. He possessed a single-mindedness which is not in evidence in either of these men, and which is his distinguishing mark as a thinker. He differs from Augustine and Donne not so much in his gifts as in the unity he made of them.

He concentrated his powers on the task of distilling out the essence of each thought and each sensation until he could express his view of it once and for all. He found no need to revise his opinions in later years. The result, perhaps surprisingly, is that his writing has not a laboured, but a freshly-minted quality. He seems to see everything new. His writings are attractive and approachable because he had spent many years of effort in keeping what he had to say simple and easily comprehensible. Anselm's thoughts are often exciting, but rarely disturbing. For the most part he stirs, not confused sympathies with his failings and his strivings, but a happier sense of recognition of the conclusions to which he comes. It is still an enjoyable experience to read him, as it undoubtedly was for his friends and pupils.

For the sustaining interest and limitless kindness which has helped me in the writing of this study, I should like to thank many friends, but in particular, the Very Revd. Dr. H. Chadwick, Dr. D. P. Henry, Sister Benedicta Ward, and Sir Richard Southern. This book is dedicated to him in gratitude for the generous friendship to which it owes its beginning.

Reading G.R.E.
June 1977

CONTENTS

ABBREVIATIONS

AB   R. W. Southern, *St. Anselm and his Biographer* (Cambridge 1963).

CCCM   Corpus Christianorum Continuatio Medievalis.

CCSL   Corpus Christianorum Series Latina.

JH   J. Hopkins, *A Companion to the Study of St. Anselm* (Minneapolis 1972).

LA   D. P. Henry, *The Logic of St. Anselm* (Oxford 1967).

MA   *Memorials of St. Anselm*, ed. R. W. Southern and F. S. Schmitt (London 1969).

PL   J. P. Migne, *Patrologia Latina*.

S   *Anselmi Opera Omnia*, ed. F. S. Schmitt (Rome/Edinburgh 1938–68), 6 vols.

VA   *The Life of St. Anselm by Eadmer*, ed. R. W. Southern (London 1962).

A BIBLIOGRAPHICAL NOTE

A comprehensive bibliography up to 1972 is given in J. Hopkins, *A Companion to the Study of St. Anselm* (Minneapolis 1972), and brought up to date by him in the fourth volume of his series of translations of Anselm's treatises, *Anselm of Canterbury* (New York 1976). An alternative translation of the *Proslogion* may be found in M. J. Charlesworth, *St. Anselm's Proslogion* (Oxford 1965), with accompanying Latin text and commentary, and another in Sister Benedicta Ward, *The Prayers and Meditations of St. Anselm* (London 1973), together with translations of all the Prayers and Meditations. D. P. Henry includes a translation of the *De Grammatico* in his *Commentary on the De Grammatico* (Dordrecht 1974). A few of the letters have been translated by Paschal D. Honner, 'Letters of St. Anselm to his monks at Bec', *American Benedictine Review*, 14 (March 1963), 138–63, and 'Letters of St. Anselm to the Community of Bec, II', ibid., 14 (June 1963), 319–40, and by Anselm R. Pedrizetti, 'Letters of Saint Anselm and Archbishop Lanfranc', *American Benedictine Review*, 12 (December 1961), 430–60.

SOME DATES

Anselm was born in 1033 in Aosta. He left Italy when he was twenty-three years old, spent three years wandering in Burgundy and France, and came at last to the Abbey of Bec in Normandy in 1059. He stayed to hear Lanfranc, and to teach in the school at Bec. By 1060 he had entered Bec as a novice. In 1063, Lanfranc went to Caen, and Anselm took his place as Prior of Bec. He remained Prior until 1078, when Herluin, Bec's first Abbot, died, and Anselm succeeded him as Abbot. Eleven years later, Lanfranc, now Archbishop of Canterbury, died in his turn and after an interval, Anselm was appointed his successor. From 1093 to 1109 Anselm was Archbishop of Canterbury, spending his time partly in England and partly in exile abroad.

The Prayers and Meditations were composed at various times, but by far the greater part of them were finished early in Anselm's career as a writer. The *Monologion* was written about 1076, the *Proslogion*, 1077–8. The *De Grammatico*, the *De Veritate*, the *De Libertate Arbitrii* were composed between 1080 and 1085, and the *De Casu Diaboli* within the following few years. The *De Incarnatione Verbi* occupied the years 1092–4, the *Cur Deus Homo*, the years 1094–8. The *De Conceptu Virginali* was written between 1099 and 1100, the *De Processione Spiritus Sancti*, based on Anselm's words at the Council of Bari in 1098, in 1102. The *Letters on the Sacraments* belong to 1106–7, and the *De Concordia* to 1107–8.

INTRODUCTION

i: *The Appeal to Understanding*

SAINT ANSELM'S thought has a persistent charm which it owes in large measure to the fact that it is easy to understand. He himself went to a good deal of trouble to make sure that it was so. It also possesses qualities which lift it from the local context of time and place in which it was written down, and give it an immediate appeal to readers of a very different era.

These are not necessarily the qualities which give Anselm's thought its greatness; his 'universality' also has something to do with his habit of stripping a problem of its incidental details so that it stands revealed as a common problem, a problem which anyone can recognize, even if he has not thought of it in quite that way before. When Anselm writes about the Atonement, he says that he intends to do so, *remoto Christo*,[1] without taking the revealed and historical details of Christ's Incarnation as 'given'; but he also avoids dwelling upon names and places, familiar elements of the Gospel narratives, which might have been expected to give his contemporary readers a comfortable sense of knowing where they were.

Instead, he attempts the much more difficult task of discovering common notions which all his readers will recognize and understand when they read of them, whatever the range of their reading or the scope of their education. Anselm attempts, in other words, to speak to the common core of knowledge of self-evident truths which he firmly believed that all men shared.[2] His success may be measured by the fact that a modern reader may still experience some of the moments of personal illumination which Anselm evidently expected his contemporary readers to enjoy.[3]

---

[1] S 2.42.12, in the Preface to the *Cur Deus Homo*.

[2] Cf. *Monologion*, 10, S 1.25.12, where Anselm says that the *naturalia verba*, the common notions, which approximate to the ideas in the mind of God, are common to all races of men.

[3] S 1.93.20–1, S 2.48.8–9.

But a considerable part of the study of Anselm's works, which began in earnest in the thirteenth century, has tended to concentrate upon the specific theological and philosophical questions he attempts to answer; in the light of the greater technical developments of later centuries, it has often been customary to question his views, to point out technical weaknesses in his arguments. Those who have read him since the days of Aquinas have frequently been inclined to disagree with him. To take issue with the conclusions of so much sophisticated and informed discussion is not my intention here, not least because it would only take us a stage further from the resolution of the principal question I should like to consider: what was Anselm's own view of the scope and force of his arguments?

Perhaps there is something to be said for going back to Anselm's own starting-point—as far as it is possible to do so—and trying to read him as he expected and hoped to be read, with a willingness to be convinced. Anselm asked his readers to approach what he had to say with an open mind of a very particular kind; it was to be an open mind conditional upon agreement with the doctrinal truths of the Catholic Church: 'For no Christian ought to debate about how that which the whole Church believes in its heart and confesses with its lips may *not* be so; but holding firmly to that same faith in love, and living humbly according to its tenets as well as he can, he may seek the reasons why it *is* so.'[1] Such an exercise will tell us nothing of general usefulness about the ultimate soundness of Anselm's theological conclusions. But it may enable us to see more clearly the kind of force his arguments possessed for himself and his pupils.

It would be agreeable to pay him a second compliment, too. His works have not always been read as a whole. Single arguments have been discussed in isolation—particularly the argument, or arguments, of the second, third, and fourth chapters of the *Proslogion*.[2] From the days of Aquinas, the study of St. Anselm has almost always been a patchy and piecemeal business.[3] Yet, to judge from their intimate connection with

[1] S 2.6.10–7.4.

[2] In the bibliography collected by J. Hopkins in JH, articles on the *Proslogion* argument alone match in number those on all other topics put together.

[3] The notable exception to this rule in recent years has been R. W. Southern's *St. Anselm and his Biographer* (Cambridge 1963).

one another, Anselm must have hoped that his treatises might be read as a group—perhaps even in order.[1]

In this study of the treatises I have tried to do two things: to look at that part of Anselm's work in which he examines the problem of talking about God more or less in the order of its writing, and to search for the evidences Anselm himself provides as to the journey he was making in his own understanding. The treatises represent the sustained effort of a life-time spent in talking about God, in conversation and in writing. They are orderly in the way they go about this, settling one set of problems remarkably tidily before going on to look at another, developing or adapting methods where a different kind of subject-matter seems to require it, adopting a variety of forms. The very changes of subject-matter and means of expounding it provide evidence of Anselm's own changing perception of the problems he considers.

Anselm still possesses the power of attracting devoted pupils. He does so precisely because he reveals so much of his own process of discovery in the course of his expositions. It is still possible for his readers to feel that they are engaged with him in pursuing his investigations. This disarming openness has a more than literary grace about it; if we simply look at what Anselm says he is doing, he will tell us a good deal which is not to be attributed to the demands of conventions of expression of the day.[2] The value of the attempt lies perhaps chiefly in the possibility that it may allow the personal qualities of the man to colour his arguments once more. They certainly did so for the pupils who knew him.

Throughout his treatises Anselm was writing a form of intellectual autobiography, characterized by the freshness and individuality of his view of contemporary theological problem-solving and his own unpretentiousness. There is nothing of the almost self-indulgent desire to share his own emotions which

---

[1] There is, however, no evidence that Anselm attempted to see that the treatises were copied and bound in order. He was meticulous about the copying of prefaces and introductions with the individual treatises to which they belong, and perhaps if he had lived to finish the last work he had in mind, he might have begun to make some orderly collection of his works.

[2] That is, the convention of protesting one's unworthiness to write, to which Anselm does give way in the *De Incarnatione Verbi* (S 2.5.7), and similar devices in current use which he does not permit himself to use.

sometimes mars Augustine's revelations about himself. Anselm explains how he feels, for the most part, because he wants his readers to see quite clearly how he has arrived at his conclusions and why he feels them to be convincing. He is simply testing his arguments on his own pulses. This is a necessary part of the exercise of writing for him, if he is to avoid the repetition of old arguments and the plain borrowing from established authority which would have saved him so much trouble. He is steering a narrow way between the old and the new, and every inch of the distance he travels has had to be examined with care. Anselm was always scrupulously careful and conscientious in showing his readers why he feels it proper to proceed. Thus he clarifies for himself the process by which he has arrived at a given point, and often perceives a new direction along which he may move further.

Eadmer told the story of Anselm's life admirably. But most of what he knew was, of necessity, to do with its outward circumstances. Only Anselm himself could describe the development of his thought, and that he has done—almost certainly quite inadvertently—in his treatises.[1]

ii: *Sources and Influences*

This is not the place to say anything at length about the circumstances of Anselm's life; that has been most evocatively described in *St. Anselm and his Biographer*, where Anselm is to be met in every mood and engaged in every kind of activity,[2] and in Eadmer's own account.[3] But the tracing of such an intellectual autobiography as Anselm seems to have written for himself must take into account the influence of ordinary events. However rich and full a life Anselm may have lived in his mind, he was, it is evident, subject to discouragement and irritation when things went badly, and he was always responsive to the encouragement of other men's affection and interest. That is not to suggest that his contemporaries were not—equally—

---

[1] On reflection, he instructed Eadmer to destroy the *Life* he had begun. He certainly did not mean to write anything similar to the *Confessions* of Augustine, which his younger contemporary and friend, Guibert of Nogent, imitated in his *De Vita Sua* (ed. G. Bourgin, Paris 1907).

[2] AB.

[3] VA.

vulnerable human beings, but they rarely display so much of their changing feelings. Anselm is unique in providing both copious evidence as to the development of his thought, and such a full description of the effects upon him of the events and changes of his life.

At Bec, Anselm wrote the *Monologion* and *Proslogion* and the earlier Prayers and Meditations, in a very different atmosphere from that in which he began, even upon the *Cur Deus Homo*, and certainly in a situation strongly contrasted with that in which he found himself in the later years of his Archbishopric. But whatever effect personal satisfaction or unhappiness may have had upon the frame of mind in which he wrote, it is clear that the line of development of Anselm's thought runs steadily on decade by decade. Sometimes topics were forced upon him, as in the case of the *De Incarnatione Verbi*; sometimes, more acceptably, they were suggested to him by friends and pupils. There was, almost always, the prompting of others behind Anselm's decision to begin on a treatise. Yet, again, he makes a conscious and purposeful use of these external influences. He governs their effect on him, just as he incorporates the new insights given him by the events of his life into the steadily unfolding sequence of his thought. It is the purposefulness and orderliness of this process in Anselm which distinguishes him from others, and which makes it possible to retrace some of these developments even now.

A certain scope and a specific direction of development was laid down by the questions Anselm had set out to answer when he first began to write for publication. It would not be true to say that the arguments of the *De Concordia* are all implicit in the *Monologion*. But it rapidly becomes plain, if we read Anselm's treatises in order, that there is no perceptible break in the orderliness of his progression through the consequences of his first statements and explorations, to their full explication in later treatises. In the *De Veritate*, if not before, we begin to find hints of definitions adumbrated, subject-matter touched upon, problems to be considered, which are handled more fully in the later treatises. We are forced to conclude that the momentum of Anselm's thought carries him along with a sureness of direction which is not appreciably diverted by any event in his life, however upsetting, or by any task of explanation pressed upon

him, however alien it seemed to his interests when he first set
to work on it.[1]

Much the same can be said for the question of Anselm's debt
to his reading, of Scripture, the Fathers, and the textbooks of
the secular arts.[2] These have posed questions for him, particularly Augustine, whose writings on the Trinity and on free will
yielded many points of enquiry—although they seem singularly
to have failed to present Anselm with answers which would
satisfy him. A most striking instance is Augustine's declaration
in the *De Libero Arbitrio* that he proposes to show that God not
only exists, but is 'obvious' (*quomodo manifestum est deum esse*),[3]
and to discuss whether all goods take their goodness from him:
utrum ab illo sint quaecumque in quantumcumque sunt bona.[4] This at
once recalls Anselm's declaration at the beginning of the
Proslogion that he intends to show that God truly exists, and yet
there are important differences between *manifestum* and *vere*[5]
and Augustine has by no means hit upon a form of the ontological argument in the discussions which follow. Nor, when
Anselm looks at the relation between the Supreme Good and
ordinary created goods in the *Monologion*,[6] does he go about it
in the same way as Augustine. The 'outside circumstances' in
this case involve reading, not the influence of people and
events, but they remain 'outside' Anselm's inner stream of
thought. His borrowing from Augustine is always highly selec-
tive, and it is, for the most part, questions, not answers, which
prove most useful to him in Augustine's writings.

Anselm's sources have of course presented him with methods
of argument. Such technical skills were to be learned, formally,
in the textbooks of grammar and dialectic. D. P. Henry has
made clear a good deal of the nature of Anselm's debt to
Boethius especially.[7] But Augustine, too, frequently employs
Aristotelian terms and principles, and he explains in Book IV of

---

[1] It is, however, possible that Anselm might have begun work on his treatise on
the origin of the soul after he had completed the *De Conceptu Virginali*, if he had not
been obliged to write the *De Processione Spiritus Sancti*.

[2] A number of Anselm's sources have been identified by F. S. Schmitt in footnotes. See, too, the *indices* of S 6, AB, p. 17, JH, pp. 16–36.

[3] *De Libero Arbitrio*, II.iii.7.20.   [4] Ibid.

[5] S 1.93.7.   [6] S 1.14.5–18.

[7] D. P. Henry, *A Commentary on the De Grammatico of St. Anselm* (Dordrecht 1974)
gives references to the same author's earlier works.

the *De Doctrina Christiana* how Scripture may be reckoned to contain devices of rhetorical argument. Cassiodorus had made the same point in his *Introduction* to the Psalms. Bede's *De Schematibus et Tropibus* was written with a similar application to Scripture in mind. The greater part of Anselm's reading would have confirmed his impression that formal schemes and methods of reasoning were universally applicable, and that there was nothing intrinsically improper in applying them to theological matters. But again, Anselm has selected what he needs from the resources at his disposal. He introduces a technical term or a technical expression only here and there, where it is especially pertinent to the needs of a young scholar still close to his elementary textbooks. A notable exception perhaps is Anselm's extensive use of definition, not only as a method of clarifying the problem under discussion, but also as a means of carrying the argument on. Repeated division and subdivision, and careful definition of the resulting principles, often helps him to see where the argument should go next. Anselm's adoption of this device in particular is an indication of the importance of order and progression in his thought. He is happiest where he can show most plainly how one truth implies another; no technical skill available to him was so helpful in this connection as that of definition.

Anselm's perception of the nature of the problems he has set himself—or accepted for consideration from among the many set for him by others—carries with it a markedly clear sense of the ways in which such problems may most profitably be resolved. Naturally, Anselm's view of methods of problem-solving were to some extent those of his age. He was not to add substantially, as Abelard was to do, to the range of formal technical skills he inherited, although he exploited them more fully than any of his predecessors. But his methods were also very much his own because they were subordinated so firmly to an overall plan of argument. Technicalities are no more than an aid to demonstration of philosophical principles which Anselm often seems to have perceived without their assistance. His independence of convention is so integral to his thought that he comes close to Aristotle in his power of hitting upon forms of argument which possess a direct appeal to every man's mind, whether trained or innocent of technical knowledge. It is clear from the early chapters of the *Cur Deus Homo* that this was exactly the kind of universality of appeal at which Anselm was aiming.

Anselm's recognition of the possibility that an argument could be made, not so much technically sound—though he valued technical soundness highly—as universally acceptable, marks him off firmly from almost every one of his contemporaries. This it is which makes him, not the 'Father of Scholasticism' he has often been claimed to be, but that rarity, a philosopher for all times, a man who perceives some of the common factors of human understanding. And paradoxically he does so because he devotes himself to talking, not about man, but about God. Contemporary thinkers were working along much the same lines as Anselm in their choice of topics for discussion. It is often illuminating to compare their handling of the same questions with his. But Anselm, unlike the majority of his contemporaries, always saw each issue independently for himself, and he rarely comes by the same route to the conclusions they share about God.

This may go some way towards explaining the failure of the treatises to capture the interest of twelfth-century scholars. The disappearance at Anselm's death of that continuing personal influence which always won his pupils' hearts in the end[1] is also of considerable importance, but that alone cannot account for the comparative neglect of Anselm's treatises for the best part of a century. The creative energies of twelfth-century scholars largely went into improving technical skills; those of the thirteenth-century scholars were directed again towards the kinds of problem to which Anselm had given fresh thought. Newly equipped with an armoury of technically sharp weapons, these scholars were less free than he to test their ideas on their own powers of immediate, unguarded 'appreciation' of the truth. But the modern reader may be able to respond to Anselm spontaneously, as his pupils did, and to recognize the immense attractiveness of much of what he has to say. It is still possible to take as it was intended to be taken, Anselm's appeal to his readers' willingness to consent to his views, and to enjoy him as his friends so evidently did.

---

[1] Eadmer describes how Anselm won over the difficult young Osbern, VA, pp. 16–20. I, x.

iii. *St. Anselm's Theology*

'In Spurgeon's day, we know, people found theology interesting, but I find it boring.'[1] For the nineteenth-century
Spurgeon we might substitute 'Anselm' and find ourselves in
much the same difficulty over this sentiment which J. I. Packer
puts into the mouth of modern man. Anselm himself never
paused to question the interest of his readers in his subject-
matter. How could he be expected to do so, when almost
everything he wrote was composed at the pressing request of
friends who wanted a permanent record of what he had to say?
Yet he is able to speak for himself even to the modern reader
and he needs no apologist. His own confidence that the topics
with which he dealt were interesting and important tends to
override apathy and to gather the reader up and carry him
along with the enterprise in hand. Nevertheless, it is unlikely
that anyone will give him a first hearing today out of general
interest; those who study Anselm's writing come to him as a
rule with an existing interest in philosophy or theology or
history. That is a pity, because Anselm himself certainly did not
write for the specialist. He wrote for anyone who wanted to
read, about matters of common interest to everyone he knew.
It is important that we should try to see his theologizing in that
light, or we shall begin by seriously misunderstanding him.

If Anselm's works were in their day immediate bestsellers
within his own circle at least, that does not mean that everything he said met the ultimate criteria of theological acceptability. His explanations have not been acceptable *ubique,
semper, et ab omnibus*; they were not received everywhere, at
every time, and by everyone, even in his own day. Yet it is surprising how often he envisages a difficulty not to be raised again
perhaps for centuries, and provides a working solution. He still
appears remarkably right-minded at points where he had made
a special effort to work from first principles in ways he found
most people could follow. There is little he has to say which is
quite unacceptable now, for that very reason. Anselm had a rare
gift for expressing himself in ways which do not appear dated.
This makes his theology clear, easy to follow, and attractive
because it is comprehensible and expects no special expertise
in the reader. If we disagree with his conclusions that is not

[1] J. I. Packer, *Knowing God* (London 1973), p. 14.

because the steps by which he has arrived at them are in any way
doubtful or hard to follow; it is only by querying Anselm's first
principles that it is possible seriously to question his conclusions.
He has generally been careful to travel the distance between the
two step by step with the slowest of his pupils. On the whole—
and exceptions are to be found, of course—it is at the level of
Anselm's assumptions about God that his theology can be
attacked, rather than in his exposition.

In many cases, those assumptions constitute not only the
points of departure for the arguments, but also the *terminus ad
quem*, the final statements towards which Anselm is arguing. He
clearly felt that doctrinal fundamentals would bear stating
twice—indeed his philosophical method required that his conclusions should be kept in view from the beginning, and that he
should argue towards them. This brings us to a further aspect
of Anselm's readership. It does not follow from the fact that
most people found theology interesting that most people shared
Anselm's expertise on the subject. It is plain that few of his
friends and pupils did. He answers, sometimes with mild exas-
peration, what he describes as very simple questions, as well as
profoundly difficult ones. A widespread conviction that
theology is important and interesting does not imply a generally
high level of theological knowledge among laymen. Anselm's
first principles of theology have had to be stated with a plainness which would not seem appropriate if he were writing to
meet the needs of men as well-grounded in essentials as himself. When, for example, he states the main points of the
doctrine of the Trinity at the beginning of the *De Processione
Spiritus Sancti*, he is not merely rehearsing what everyone knows,
but laying down firm guidelines, showing exactly where Greeks
differ from Latins, and helping his readers to see where they
are to begin in their own thinking.

Some, even of the better-educated of Anselm's readers, seem
to have been surprisingly unsure of doctrinal fundamentals—or
at least to have approached them in a remarkably cavalier
manner. It has been pointed out that in the last hundred years
philosophy has become increasingly interested in questions of
method, and theologians in problems of biblical exegesis.[1] That

---

[1] A. Macintyre, J. Macintyre, Foreword to K. Barth, *From Rousseau to Ritschl*,
tr. B. Cozens (London 1959), pp. 8–10.

was exactly the position in Anselm's day. Some of his pupils, and others to whom his treatises were addressed, were well-grounded in dialectic, but still apparently prepared to question the doctrine of the Trinity at a level which would make nonsense of its first principles. They were sophisticated philosophers but naïve theologians. The developments in logical method of Anselm's day consisted chiefly in refining the understanding of the ways in which individual terms could be linked together into propositions, and of the ways in which these propositions could be linked together into argumentative sequences. There is nothing in this which is reminiscent of the 'dynamic' methods of thinking about change and movement and development to which Torrance refers.[1] Equally, the methods of biblical exegesis current in Anselm's day[2] would seem dated if they were to be employed in exactly the same way now. But Anselm's time and our own century have this in common: there was a consciously-felt tension between the methods and purposes of philosophy and theology, and there were many who felt that philosophical method possessed an intellectual respectability which theology lacked. Anselm encountered an increasingly vocal body of young scholars who felt that philosophy made nonsense of certain points of doctrine, and some at least of these were men who knew rather more about logic than they did about theology.

Anselm's own theology is, perhaps deliberately, limited in its scope. He never attempted to look systematically beyond the doctrines of Trinity, Incarnation, Atonement, grace, free will, predestination and the foreknowledge of God, and the nature of sin—with a brief look at the Sacraments, which he seems to have taken only because he was pressed to do so. This must have been to some extent a self-imposed restriction of subject-matter. Other writers in Anselm's day explored a much larger field. Anselm's topics are, broadly speaking, those of the Latin Fathers; they are also chiefly those with which the Creeds are concerned. They are the central themes of the faith. The fact that he has almost nothing to say about the Church or the Last

---

[1] T. F. Torrance, *God and Rationality* (Oxford 1971). Cf. E. J. Fortman, *The Triune God* (London 1972), p. xxiv.

[2] On biblical exegesis, see B. Smalley's classic, *The Study of the Bible in the Middle Ages* (Oxford 1952), and H. de Lubac, *Exégèse médiévale* (Paris 1959–64), 4 vols.

Things, for example, may make his theological system incomplete in comparison with the work of others, but that does not detract from the consistency it gains from Anselm's policy of going back to first principles, beginning with essentials, and working out the implications of a few doctrinal statements thoroughly. What emerges is a strong impression that Anselm possessed a sure sense of what is sound doctrine and what is not. The provisions of the Creeds are firmly rooted in his mind and he allows himself to explore no solutions of problems in which these are not the ultimate data. They are taken as axioms, and as in all the most elegant systems of thought, the fewer the axioms, the firmer the texture of the proofs.

Theology, then, is for Anselm not only interesting and important, but also intellectually satisfying, challenging his powers of winning and sustaining interest among his readers to the limit, even in an age when his readers came to him willing and even eager to hear what he had to say. He produced a theology perfectly tuned to the needs of an age when fashions of thought were in a state of change. He did so by keeping to a few simple principles and never overworking or over-complicating his explanations. He considered first what everyone would enjoy and understand, without making compromises with what he saw to be the straightforward truth. That is why, even in an age when theology is not an immediately attractive subject to everyone, and when fashions of thought are again in a state of change, he still has much to say that is full of interest, and which conveys its own sense of its importance and relevance.

PART I

WHAT CAN WE SAY ABOUT GOD?

AT the beginning of the *De Magistro* Augustine asks his son a question: 'What does it seem to you that we wish to do when we talk?' Augustine could take it for granted that his question would be of immediate interest to every reader of his own time, much as Anselm could be sure of a ready readership for his theological writings. It does not occur to Augustine to question or to attempt to justify the philosophical importance of thinking about language, because he had been educated in a tradition which gave prominence to the arts of language. Anselm's education did so, too, although with a different emphasis. As a result, both writers are always conscious of the function and of the elegance of the words they use. Some of their concerns are of current interest to modern linguistic philosophers and literary critics. Others are, for the moment, out of fashion. But most have aroused interest in subsequent centuries and few, if any, of the questions they raise can be said to have been resolved in any permanent form.

Anselm's primary question is rather different from the one posed by Augustine in the *De Magistro*, although it is closely related to it. When Anselm asks, not the general question, 'What do we do when we talk?' but the specific question, 'How is it possible for us to talk of God and what can we say about him?' he begins on the task in the belief that since God is the author of human language, and himself the very Word, no study of language can profitably be approached in any other way. That is his first assumption, and for all its self-evidence to him and to Augustine, it may now appear an uncertain candidate to bear the philosophical load which he places upon it.

The differences of emphasis between the two writers are not perhaps very crucial. Much of what Augustine has to say in the *De Magistro* has its echoes in Anselm's work. What is of greater interest is the fact that, although the subject of language in general is so close a concern of Anselm's, he never attempted to consider the question of what we are doing when we talk in a single comprehensive work, as Augustine does in the *De Magistro*. Yet the ramifications of Anselm's thinking upon the subject are so extensive that there is scarcely a treatise which does not bear some signs of it. If the problems raised by the attempt to talk about God cannot be said to give Anselm subject-matter for complete and self-contained treatises, it may be that the reason for this lies in their very penetration into the furthest corners of his thought. A nexus of related ideas on the subject reinforces and gives coherence to much apparently very varied material in the early treatises. Perhaps it constituted a unifying principle for Anselm himself quite consciously, but if it did he does not say so.

What we must concede him is the allowance that what he has to say about talking, and in particular about talking about God, is probably worth saying only if it is allowed to rest upon the prior assumptions he makes: that God is the Word, and that language is a working possibility only because of the way in which the Creator has built a capacity for the use of words into every rational creature. It follows that the study of language will tell us something about God, and that the study of God will make us aware of the functions and purpose of language.

I

THE *MONOLOGION*

i. *The writing of the book*

IT would be misleading to suggest that the *Monologion* is exclusively, or even principally, concerned with the question of talking about God. As Anselm says in his preface, it is about a number of questions which come to the minds of those who meditate on the being of God.[1] He continued to see it in the same light, as a book about many things, when he looked back on it from the distance of a year or two at the beginning of the *Proslogion*.[2] If we were to take a single topic in isolation from one of the later treatises we might be doing a disservice to Anselm's intentions, but we shall not do so here. At this stage of his life, Anselm was not so much concerned with the fashioning of a comprehensive system of explanations of divine mysteries as with answering single questions which were put to him, or which arose in his own mind. That led him soon enough into examining related questions, and the complex of explanations rapidly became increasingly comprehensive. But when he says to the reader of the *Prayers* and *Meditations* that he is at liberty to begin where he likes, and wherever he finds it most helpful to do so, he is saying something which might equally have been said to the reader of the *Monologion*.[3] He does in fact indicate that his brothers had wanted him to write a work which would be of practical help as a working manual as well as of spiritual usefulness to them.[4] Although the chain of arguments in the *Monologion* is closely linked, so is the sequence of thought in the *Prayers*, and yet all these more or less contemporary writings would allow some flexibility in use.

The book was written about 1076, while Anselm was still Prior of Bec, for reasons which he himself explains in the Preface. His brothers had begged him to write down for them, in simple language, his account of certain theological matters which caused them difficulty during periods of meditation.[5]

[1] S 1.7.2–4. [2] S 1.93.5. [3] S 3.3.8–12. [4] S 1.7.14–15. [5] S 1.7.3–5.

Among them are some of the primary questions of the Christian faith. In the effort to make himself clear and to illuminate profound problems by writing about them simply, Anselm made of the book something strikingly fresh in conception, although he had not yet shaken himself quite as free of the support of Augustine's arm as he claims in his Preface that he has tried to do.[1]

When the work was ready, he sent it to his old master, Lanfranc, now Archbishop of Canterbury, with a pretty compliment and a serious request for his opinion. It is, he says, best to ask advice before one does anything,[2] and he has been encouraged to publish the work so that a wider readership than the monks of Bec may have access to it.[3] It is clear from the letters Anselm wrote about this time that a lively interchange of books and discussion went on among the monasteries of Normandy; perhaps some of his correspondents were asking for copies of the book. Lanfranc seems to have been slow to reply. Anselm prompted him with a letter in which he raises some points which have evidently occurred to him since he sent the manuscript. What, for example, is he to do about providing the piece with a title? He has not felt it proper to give it one until he has Lanfranc's approval.[4] He tries to arrange for his ex-pupil Maurice, who is now at Canterbury with Lanfranc to see the book, with Lanfranc's permission.[5]

Lanfranc's answer, when it came, was evidently not what Anselm had expected. He seems to have commented unfavourably on Anselm's failure to base his writing on the authority of Scripture or the Fathers. The letter he wrote is lost, but Anselm's reply conveys some bewilderment and distress.[6] He tries hard to thank Lanfranc for his advice, as politeness and respect required. He has looked at the copy he has kept by him, and he cannot see that it contains anything which goes against Augustine or against Scripture.[7] He concedes that he might have expressed himself better.[8] But on reflection, his view of the work as already finished must have reasserted himself, for the book was published and it seems unlikely that Anselm altered it greatly. He certainly did not change it to meet Lanfranc's objections.

---

[1] S 1.7.7–11.   [2] S 1.5.6–8.   [3] S 1.6.7–9.   [4] S 3.193–4 (Letter 72).
[5] S 3.195–6 (Letter 74).   [6] S 3.199–200 (Letter 77).   [7] S 3.199.18–20.
[8] S 3.200.30–1.

Curiously enough, it may be that Lanfranc put his finger on a serious weakness of the work, and that Anselm himself perceived another. When Lanfranc said that it did not rest foursquare on Scripture and the Fathers he meant that he wanted Anselm to support what he said openly by quoting authorities. As it stands, the work rests upon the hidden authority of Augustine, particularly upon the *De Trinitate*. Because this influence is not openly identified at every point it is not always immediately apparent that it provides Anselm with a series of undefended assumptions which have become self-evident axioms in his mind. He borrows Augustine's imagery of memory, will and understanding, for example, without apparently pausing to ask himself what kind of a statement this makes about the relationship between the mind of man and the Trinity. In such respects, although it is refreshing because it makes the *Monologion* easy and uninterrupted reading, the complete absence of patristic quotation or of direct reference to sources may constitute a limitation of the work.

Anselm himself saw the *Monologion* as unsatisfactory because it contained a chain of arguments and because it lacked the conceptual unity he was searching for when he wrote the *Proslogion*. As a result, the book is chiefly of interest because it raises a series of issues which are important in themselves, but not because it settles any of them finally for Anselm himself. Methodologically speaking it is an exploration. The 'chain of arguments' has a different look about it when we meet it again in the *Cur Deus Homo*, for example. The form was not one which Anselm used again without considerable amendment. The procedure of arguing independently of quoted authorities is again only being tried out here, although it was to be a technique Anselm perfected rather than abandoned later.

When Anselm found that he could not rewrite the work as Lanfranc suggested, he perhaps discovered several things of importance to his later development as a thinker.

ii. *Talking about God*

'All our speech about [God] is creaturely and cannot be cut loose from its creaturely context without ceasing to be human speech altogether, but it is not for that reason false as if it could have no authentic relation to the reality and intelligibility of

God.'[1] Anselm would have met this point of Torrance's by saying that it seemed to him self-evident that language of every kind and at every level has an 'authentic relation to the reality and intelligibility of God'. But that does not mean that he would have regarded the issue as unworthy of consideration. In fact this is the very issue he confronts in the chapters of the *Monologion* which deal with language, but he is interested in demonstrating what follows from his belief in the existence of that 'authentic relation' rather than in questioning its existence. Here we have, at the outset, a case in point of Anselm's taking as an axiom a view of things which present-day thinkers require to have proved valid for them.

Torrance links the problem of talking about God with the problem of the relation between God's reason and the reason with which man is familiar through the workings of his own mind.

Here we are up against one of those ultimate boundaries in thought such as we reach when we ask a question as to the rationality of the universe: not only do we have to assume that rationality in order to answer the question, but we have to assume it in order to ask the question in the first place. We cannot meaningfully ask a question that calls into question that which it needs in order to be the question which is being asked.[2]

Here he identifies two aspects of the problem of language with which Anselm is much concerned. Anselm's assumption that God's rationality is the same in kind, though not in degree, as the rationality of man makes possible a good deal of discussion which would otherwise be philosophically, if not theologically, impossible. Secondly, Anselm is well aware of the problem of circularity in attempting to discover a point of reference for such discussions.

The first issue does not present Anselm with any serious problems at all. It is built into his view of things, as we shall see, that such goods as will, beauty, rationality, all participate in the Supreme Good. When Torrance asks: 'How are we to conceive the relation between the transcendent rationality of God independent of space-time and the rationality immanent within the space-time structures of this world?',[3] Anselm would answer him by pointing out that all reasonable things are

---

[1] T. F. Torrance, *Space, Time and Incarnation* (Oxford 1969), p. 53.
[2] Ibid., p. 53.   [3] Ibid., p. 61.

ultimately reasonable in the same way. Thus the words we use for such concepts, crude and unsatisfactory though he acknowledges them to be, are perfectly serviceable. We can hold some sort of useful discussion about the attributes of God, his reasonableness among them.

The second issue is mentioned by Anselm in the *De Veritate*. 'For when I said, "When was there a time when it was not true that something was going to exist?", I did not say that that saying was itself without a beginning . . . or that that Truth was itself God.'[1] In the *Monologion* itself, with a similar anxiety at the back of his mind, he asks whether there may be infinite gradations with no identifiable beginning or end within the natural world.[2] Conceptually speaking, the problem of infinite regress did present Anselm with problems of some magnitude. Contemporary logical training was not designed to help with such metalinguistic exercises as 'talking about talking' involves. Anselm developed methods of his own for handling such difficulties, some of which are to be met in his later works. They all depend upon the possibility of limiting the circularity, avoiding situations of perpetual circling, and speaking of no more than two or three layers of language. But in conceding, as he often must, that language is not functionally all one, he discovers a fruitful source not only of logical distinctions, but also of theological reflections.

Hugh of St. Victor raises much this question, in rather less testing terms, in his *De Verbo Dei*:

If God's word is believed to be one, how is it that many words are attributed to him? But we must recognize that God speaks in one way through the mouths of men and in another way through himself. . . . Therefore he speaks many words through men and one Word through himself. But he himself is one Word in all the words which he speaks through the mouths of men and they are all one in that one Word. Without that Word they cannot be spoken at any time or in any place. Let us recognize therefore that there is a great mystery in this.[3]

Hugh is content to worship what he cannot understand here. Anselm strives to stretch his understanding of the matter as far

---

[1] S 1.190.15–17.   [2] S 1.17.5–10.
[3] Hugh of St. Victor, *Six opuscules spirituelles*, ed. R. Baron (Paris 1969), p. 60.8–13. I have looked at some aspects of Anselm's 'metalinguistic' efforts in 'The "Secure Technician"; Varieties of Paradox in the Writings of St. Anselm', *Vivarium*, 13 (1975), 1–21.

as it will go, before he gives himself up to worship of the mystery. It is necessary for him to do so if he is to say anything further about human language and its workings, but it seems that he also felt it to be necessary to do so if he was to do justice to his God-given reason and use language for its highest and most important purpose of talking about God. In this way it seems that we might regard Anselm as building his general theory of language upon a special theory of divine language. If this is the case, the two cannot be considered separately without doing violence to Anselm's own view of their dual nature.

Anselm himself cannot be credited with the discovery of the fundamental ideas about language he propounds. He is heavily indebted to both Augustine and Boethius. But he has tested Augustine's account introspectively upon his own mind, and what he describes—although it accords closely enough with Augustine's views—has been drawn directly from his own experience of the operations of language. Despite his respect for Augustine, Anselm was a thinker of a very different cast; their common practice of examining the workings of their own minds in order to discover truths which they feel to be common to the experience of all human minds, reveals one of the few areas of natural sympathy between the two. Their single purpose is to attempt to glimpse something of the working of the divine mind upon which they believe the human mind to be modelled.

Anselm has done more than borrow the habit from Augustine. He would have been encouraged to do so in any case by Augustine's description in the *De Trinitate* of the resemblances between the Holy Trinity and the 'trinity' of memory, understanding and will in the mind of man. What Augustine has to say there about language would have been helpful, too. In Book VIII.vi.9, for example, he looks at the forming of images in the mind and their connection with words; in Book X.i.2 he argues that the natural curiosity in man to know the meaning of an unfamiliar word is a good thing, because it represents an urge to perfect the God-given faculty of speech. But there can be little doubt that it came naturally to Anselm to think in this way. When he reflects upon his own experience of remembering and upon what he knows of reasoning and imagining and so on, he makes additional discoveries of his own.

Anselm's debt to Boethius is of another kind. Boethius had

enlarged his view of the technical principles upon which language operates, according to the rules of formal grammar and dialectic. He had, following Aristotle, gone back to the first principles of the arts of language and looked at the way words are constructed mechanically out of sounds; but the whole direction of this account of language is different from that of Augustine. It has to do with the imparting of a technical knowledge which is essential as a preliminary to the carrying out of a sequence of correct argumentation. It is Boethius' influence which gives Anselm's account of language those qualities which make it possible for D. P. Henry to say that his work, 'exhibits, quite self-consciously, that artificialization of the Latin language for technical purposes which . . . is characteristic of Scholasticism'.[1] A certain tension between these two accounts of language is often apparent. Anselm certainly found it stimulating.

He first enters upon the discussion of the origins of language early in the treatise. He has been considering the question of Creation, and he has come upon a paradox. Nothing can have an existence independent of God; there can have been no pre-existing stuff for the Creator to use; so everything must have been created from nothing. But in some way, Anselm feels, created things must have had an existence in God's mind before they appeared in the natural world, because we must assume that God thought out his creation and planned and intended to make things as they are. Yet, since God himself is eternal, every thought in the mind of God must be eternal too, and created things are manifestly not eternal. This view of the matter raises all sorts of questions into which Anselm does not go at this point. He is interested for the moment in the implications of this idea for the theory of language.

His description of the process of creation is couched in terms which are of some importance for the later development of his 'special theory' of language. He draws a parallel with the mind of a 'maker' and says, 'Unless there was already in the maker's mind, as it were, an example, or perhaps it would be better to say a "form" or a "likeness" or a "principle" of the thing to be made,'[2] nothing could be made. Thus, 'It is clear that before

[1] LA, p. 12.   [2] S 24.13–14.

all things came to be made there was some thought in the
mind of God as to what, and what kind of thing, they were to
be.'[1] Anselm's choice of words here includes *exemplum*, *forma*,
similitudo, *regula*, for the idea or principle with which the maker
begins, and *ratio* for the seat of (creative) ideas, which lies in the
reasoning part of the mind where language, too, belongs. It is
difficult to recognize the image or principle as a word, at this
stage of Anselm's argument, but he shows what he feels to be
the connection between word and image more clearly as he
goes on.

Unfortunately these terms were in far too common use in
both the secular and non-secular sources of Anselm's reading
for it to be possible to draw any helpful conclusions from his
exact choice of words. In order to talk about 'words' and
'language' and 'speaking' and 'thinking' so as to make ordinary
expressions accommodate technically unusual meanings, Anselm stretches the resources of his technical and non-technical
language to the limit. It is not surprising that it should sometimes be difficult to be sure of his exact meaning. One thing
does, however, stand out. Anselm believes that thoughts in the
divine mind, and in human minds, too,[2] may concern what we
should call images, rather than conventional words, and
thinking need not, in his view, necessarily involve the use of
language in the ordinary sense of the word. Such images, which
are here used for making things, but which need not necessarily
be 'creative' images,[3] are at least one stage removed from conventional words. What we may call 'primary language', then,
is that power of thinking directly in images which Anselm
believes to exist in both God and man.

He goes on in Chapter 10 of the *Monologion* to make the difference between these images and conventional words perfectly
clear:

> Mentis autem sive rationis locutionem hic intelligo, non cum
> voces rerum significativae cogitantur, sed cum res ipsae vel
> futurae vel iam existentes acie cogitationis in mente con-
> spiciuntur.[4]

---

[1] S 1.24.14–16.
[2] S 1.24.26. Anselm uses *faber* for a human craftsman. The reference to a 'maker'
already quoted may refer to God alone.
[3] S 1.25.2–4.   [4] S 1.24.27–8.

('I understand this "talking" of the mind or the reason to take
place, not when the words for the things are thought, but when
by the penetration of intuition the things themselves are
directly beheld in the mind, whether they are present or to
come.') This passage poses a variety of problems of translation
and interpretation, but for our purposes, the important distinction is that which Anselm makes here between thinking of
the 'thing' itself directly and thinking of the word for the thing.
The same distinction appears in the *Proslogion*:

> Aliter enim cogitatur res cum vox eam significans cogitatur,
> aliter cum id ipsum quod res est intelligatur.[1]

('Something is thought about in one way when the word which
means that thing is thought of, and in another way when the
thing itself is understood.') In both cases the term *vox* is used in
preference to *verbum*, and in both cases it is linked with signification. A 'meaningful sound', a *vox significativa*, is the commonly-
used expression of Anselm's day for a word in the ordinary
sense of 'word'. In both cases the proper verb for use in references to thinking with words appears to be *cogitare*. The verb
used for thinking in the sense of perceiving directly is, in the
Monologion passage, *conspiciuntur*, in the *Proslogion* passage, *intel-
ligitur*. Anselm seems to find it far more difficult here to settle
on a single form of expression, just as he has difficulty in Chapter
9 of the *Monologion* in finding the right word for an image. The
technical language available to him, in the writings of Boethius
and in contemporary dialectical usage, furnished him adequately with a means of describing the operation of thinking
with conventional words. His knowledge of the terminology
seems to have encouraged him to make a clear distinction between the use of language (in the usual sense of the word) in
thinking and the use of mental images in thinking of quite
another kind and at a level much closer to the way God may be
supposed to think.

But two anomalies require closer examination. At the beginning of the passage quoted from Chapter 10 of the *Monologion*, Anselm introduces the idea of 'talking' (*locutio*).[2] In
succeeding chapters we often find thinking and speaking
apparently being used interchangeably. In the *Proslogion*, too,
Anselm remarks that *dicere in corde*, 'to say in one's heart', is

[1] S 1.103.18–20.   [2] S 1.24.25.

the same as *cogitare*.[1] In *Monologion* 31 we have, *mente dicimus, id est cogitamus*[2] ('We say in our minds, that is, we think'). In *Monologion* 48, *Rem etenim cogitare . . . hoc est mente eam dicere*.[3] ('For to think about a thing . . . is to speak of it in the mind').

One passage in particular, in *Monologion* 63, suggests a close association in Anselm's mind between talking and thinking:

Nihil autem aliud est summo spiritui huiusmodi dicere quam quasi cogitando intueri, sicut nostrae mentis locutio non aliud est quam cogitantis inspectio.[4]

('For when the Supreme Spirit "speaks" in this way, it is the same as when he perceives by thought, just as the "speaking" of our own minds is nothing but the act of reviewing our thinking.') Here, it seems, thinking is envisaged as something more than a still activity, in which we simply contemplate the object of thought; and *locutio*, too, involves some sort of movement, a reviewing of thought, a process perhaps of bringing it into focus. The exact sense is by no means clear, but there can be no doubt about the closeness of association between the two in Anselm's mind. When God expresses himself by speaking his thought, he creates: 'So that I may consider, if I can, his speaking, through which all things were made' (*ut de eius locutione, per quam facta sunt omnia*);[5] 'There is one Word, through which all things were made' (*est unum verbum, per quod facta sunt omnia*).[6] It is plain enough, then, that thinking and talking are closely allied activities for Anselm and almost always when he mentions either activity in the *Monologion*, he considers both their human and their divine application. What he has to say about 'thinking' about God will tell us a good deal about his view of the problem of 'talking' about God, even if it leaves us uncertain of Anselm's own view of the difference between the two.

Secondly, it rapidly becomes clear that Anselm's apparently tidy distinction between thinking in words and thinking in images is not as precise as it seems, nor perhaps as clear in his own mind when he tried to develop it as it was when he first perceived its philosophical possibilities. In Chapter 10 of the *Monologion* he remarks that there are in common usage three

[1] S 1.103.15–16.   [2] S 1.48.19.   [3] S 1.63.20–1.   [4] S 1.73.10–12.
[5] S 1.47.6.   [6] S 1.48.9 and 12.

ways of speaking of something.[1] We speak in the language of bodily signs or signs perceptible to the senses (which seems to include spoken words),[2] or we may 'speak' to ourselves by thinking of those same signs without physically seeing them or perceiving them. Or else we may contemplate the images of these things directly and speak them to ourselves inwardly.[3] This would seem a very singular usage of 'speaking', since neither the second nor the third mode of *locutio* involves actual talking. Talking in any manner which allows communication with others must be rather different from this introspective communication of the mind with itself, which Anselm describes in close imitation of his picture of God's own *intima locutio*[4] with himself. Actual vocalization of sounds may not be pertinent to thinking, and it is unnecessary to postulate anything of the kind when we describe God's utterances, but Anselm's failure to remark on the anomaly here is curious. In real life he did not place talking for purposes of communication so low down on the ladder of language as this would suggest. We can, in a perfectly ordinary sense, talk with words. We can, to a limited extent, talk with other kinds of signs. But it is impossible to communicate the quality of those images which Anselm tacitly assumes to be present in every man's mind, and which he evidently considers to be closest to the thoughts of God himself.

Nowhere does Anselm consider how we know that all our mental images are alike; the first principles of his theory of language entail the view that they must be alike, if they are all in some sense resemblances of the ideas of God. They may be conveniently referred to by means of *voces significativae*, but there is neither need nor any possibility of communication of these *verba* in the sense of passing on an understanding of them from one mind to another, because every man already possesses a knowledge of them. 'Talking' in such images, even if it were possible, thus appears an unnecessary refinement of the use of language. Yet the need to try must occasionally have caused Anselm to be aware that he was being driven to violence in order to write about universal language at all. His development of the point is disappointingly slight. This is one of the factors

---

[1] S 1.24.29–30.   [2] S 1.24.30–25.1.   [3] S 1.25.2–5.   [4] S 1.26.28.

which helps to set Anselm outside the main stream of the thinking of his own generation and the succeeding generation on the problem of universals.

Perhaps the key to Anselm's train of thought in the *Monologion* lies in his introduction of the term *verbum*: 'These three kinds of speaking all have "words" of their own sort.' (*Hae vero tres loquendi varietates singulae verbis sui generis constant.*)[1] The *verbum* seems to be the general term for *signa, voces significativae,* image—the 'words' of every mode of speech or thought. Those 'words' of the third kind, the direct images of things, are common to all races.[2] They are 'natural words' (*naturalia verba*) and they are universal. Their existence has made possible the invention of all other words of lower orders, including the humble *voces significativae: alia omnia verba propter haec sunt inventa*[3] ('All other words were invented because of these [*natural words*].') Anselm goes on to propose the view that these are in every way the 'best' words, and that if it were possible to use them and no others it would be desirable to do so.[4] He does not point out explicitly that man is thrown back upon *voces significativae* for purposes of conversation, because he is concerned here only to show why these supremely excellent *verba* are ultimately like those in the mind of God. But this is the only interpretation which can be put upon the fact that men do not converse in *naturalia verba* but in *voces significativae,* ordinary meaningful words, and which is in tune with what Anselm has been saying. Again, it might be argued that the very single-mindedness of Anselm's analysis has led him to neglect an aspect of the question which might have provided a helpful clarification.

Anselm's identification of universal words with the 'images of things' he has been describing so far ought to cause us to review the claim of these *formae* or *similitudines* or *exempla* or *regulae* to be called images at all. Some of them may indeed possess the character of visual images; a *res,* if it is a solid object, can be visualized in the mind easily enough. But Anselm also uses the word *conceptio.*[5] The craftsman has in his mind before he begins to work a conception of what he is about to make. If Anselm wants his universal words to refer to anything of an

[1] S 1.25.10.   [2] S 1.25.11–12.   [3] S 1.25.12–13.   [4] S 1.25.15–27.
[5] S 1.24.26–7.

abstract kind, he must in some sense see them as concepts. Unfortunately the examples he gives deal consistently with solid objects. The image of a man is, he says, the 'word' for that man: *Quae imago eius verbum eius est.*[1] The craftsman in whose mind the *conceptio* lies is planning to make a concrete object. Whatever extension Anselm may have wished to make to the idea—and he does extend it in the *De Casu Diaboli*, as we shall see—it seems that he found it more helpful for the moment to refer to cases where his *naturalia verba* are recognizable images rather than more strictly abstract concepts. That is perfectly in keeping with his habit of beginning with the simplest first principles and moving on to more difficult issues later.

It follows from the assumption that *naturalia verba* are universally understood that no man can invent an entirely new image or concept for himself; he can only fashion his images and ideas from those which are already present in his mind. Some of those ideas he can draw from observation of the created world in which he can see God's ideas given physical form. Others he can know only intuitively. These are understood by man only because they can be recognized by comparison (in some undefined manner) with the archetypes in the mind of God. All universal principles comprehensible to man are already in the mind of God. All this is, of course, Platonic in flavour, although Anselm's immediate source is Augustine.

Anselm finds himself in some difficulties because he has no words for 'idea'.[2] When he attempts to describe the ways in which the human mind makes its images, he is clearly struggling for suitable terms:

Faber vero penitus nec mente potest aliquid corporeum imaginando concipere, nisi id quod aut totum simul aut per partes ex aliquibus rebus aliquomodo iam didicit.[3]

('A craftsman cannot envisage by an act of imagination any object which he has not already learned of in some way either as a whole or piecemeal, through a variety of things.') The

---

[1] S 1.52.23–8.

[2] Cf., among many instances in the twelfth-century commentaries on Boethius' *opuscula sacra*, *The Commentaries on Boethius of Thierry of Chartres and his School*, ed. N. M. Häring (Toronto 1972), pp. 168, 169, 176, 270, 275, where the word *idea* is used freely.

[3] S 1.26.9–11.

image he has in mind seems again to be that of a solid object,
rather than an abstraction, but even so, he is obliged to fall
back on verbs which describe the act of conceiving because he
has no technical term for the idea conceived (*imaginando concipere*). His use of pronouns (*id; aliquid*) would also appear to
suggest that he is trying to avoid the use of nouns. This same
difficulty seems to have arisen throughout the chapter:

> nequaquam tamen hoc facere valet, nisi componendo in eo
> partes, quas ex rebus alias cognitis in memoriam attraxit.[1]

('Nor can he do this except by composing it of parts which he
has brought into his memory from things he already knows.')
God himself requires no such sources for his ideas:

> quod illa nec assumpta nec adiuta aliunde, sed prima et sola
> causa sufficere potuit suo artifici ad suum opus perficiendum.[2]

('[The Divine *locutio*], without help and without borrowing from
elsewhere, was able, as the first and only cause, to bring its
work to perfection for its[elf the] Creator.') Again, Anselm
avoids the use of terms for the images or concepts themselves.
This lack of an adequate technical terminology helps to distinguish his account of the *naturalia verba* from the more familiar
Platonic theory of Ideas. Anselm's images are, essentially,
verba; they underlie all conventional human languages, and
they provide him with a foundation, not only for his theory of
knowledge, but also for his theory of language.

Anselm comes up again and again in the *Monologion* against
the special difficulties this raises when we try to talk about God
himself. There is simply no means, in the resources of language
available to man, of devising a system of expression apart from
God, by means of which we can talk about him. God can, quite
literally, be described only in his own terms. In Chapter 15,
Anselm asks the question, 'What can be said about the Supreme
Being?' (*Quid possit aut non possit dici de illa substantialiter*).[3] His
precise question is framed with a view to making it moderately
conventional and familiar to his readers. Augustine himself had
looked at the 'theological categories' of substance and relation
in the Godhead;[4] and the larger question of which of the ten
Aristotelian categories can be predicated of God was of current

---

[1] S 1.26.14–16.   [2] S 1.26.18–20.   [3] S 2.28.2.
[4] *De Trinitate*, V.iii.4–V.v.6; V.viii.9; XV.v.8.

contemporary interest.[1] But Anselm is asking a rather different question here: not, 'What categories can be predicated of God?' but, more simply and directly, 'What can we say about God which will have any reference to his inmost being (*substantia*)?' He finds the question impossible to answer in quite these terms.

Anselm is acutely aware in this chapter of the difficulties inherent in the attempt to turn words back upon their source, and ask them to describe their inventor—especially in view of the fact that the words he has at his disposal are *voces significativae*, themselves far removed from the directly-perceived images which are the closest man can come to the actual ideas in the mind of God. 'I should be surprised,' he acknowledges, 'if among the nouns and verbs which we use of things created from nothing, there were to be found any words which can properly be used of the Creator of the substance of all things':

> Quamquam enim mirer, si possit in *nominibus* vel *verbis* quae aptamus rebus factis de nihilo reperiri, quod digne dicatur de creatrice universorum substantia.[2]

There can be no doubt that Anselm viewed these 'nouns' and 'verbs' as *voces significativae*, not as *naturalia verba*. He says as much in the *De Grammatico*:

> Cum enim in definitione nominis vel verbi dicitur quia est vox significativa,[3]

('For when it is said in the definition of a noun or a verb that it is a meaningful sound . . .'). The words Anselm must use in writing about God are, then, the words of ordinary language, not the great universal *verba*, and thus his task is made even more difficult.

His attempt to answer his question begins along conventional lines. Perhaps it did not occur to him to question the helpfulness of principles drawn from the *Categories* here. We accept, he argues, that a word applied relatively to something cannot tell us anything about the substance of the object under discussion. Augustine had put forward the view that nothing which is said of God implies that he has 'accidents', because accidents are incidental, and nothing which is true of God is incidental to

---

[1] It seems to be an exercise of this kind which underlies Roscelin's challenge of the assertion Anselm refutes in the *De Incarnatione Verbi*. S 1.282.28–283.6.
[2] S 1.28.5-7.   [3] S 1.161.16.

God; but he had maintained that some things may be said of God relatively, that is, when we describe the relation of the three Persons to one another.[1] Anselm is interested in another aspect of 'relation'. If we say that God's nature is 'greater than' (*maior*) or 'the highest' (*summa*),[2] we are saying nothing about his substance.[3] Such a statement implies that there are other existing things 'than which' God is greater. But it is essential to the definition of God that if nothing but God had ever existed, his nature would still be—absolutely, not relatively—highest of all (*summa omnium*).[4] In saying anything relatively of God the normal rules do not apply; there are no reciprocal relatives in God, since the Father is absolutely Father, the Son absolutely Son, and their relationship cannot be viewed as a mutually interdependent one.[5] Thus Anselm rapidly discovers that the conventional technique of employing the categories to distinguish one substance from another by its accidents is no help at all in speaking of God.

In the course of his demonstration Anselm has, however, slipped from talking about words into to talking about actual properties:

> Illis itaque quae relative dicuntur omissis, quia nullum eorum simpliciter demonstrat alicuius essentiam, ad alia discutienda se convertat intentio.[6]

('Setting aside those things which may be said relatively, for none of them directly refers to the essence of anything, let us turn our thoughts to the discussion of other things.') It is remarkable that Anselm avoids the use of terms to do with words or speaking or concepts or images throughout the chapter, once he has explained his initial doubts about the applicability of ordinary words to the discussion of God. He works his way, instead, towards a statement of his notion that the nature of God is that-than-which-nothing-is-better (*Illa enim sola est qua penitus nihil est melius*).[7] He has, for the time being, set aside the problems posed by trying to talk about God, for another set of problems to do with conceiving of God in relation to known human experience. His 'solution' touches only obliquely upon

---

[1] *De Trinitate*, V.v.6.   [2] S 1.28.14.   [3] S 1.28.9–10.   [4] S 1.28.20.
[5] Cf. S 2.202.9–15.   [6] S 1.28.24–5.
[7] S 1.29.20, cf. *Proslogion*, II, S 1.101.13–14, with the important difference that there God is described as 'that than which nothing greater can be thought'.

the problem he has posed. We have, as he shows, working words
to describe huge abstractions such as those listed at the end of
the chapter:

> Quare necesse est eam esse viventem, sapientem, potentem,
> et omnipotentem, veram, iustam, beatam, aeternam, et quid-
> quid similiter absolute melius est quam non ipsum.[1]

('Therefore it is necessary for that nature to be living, wise,
powerful and all-powerful, true, just, blessed, eternal, and
whatever like these it is absolutely better to be than not to be.')
These, surely must approximate to the abstract concepts
Anselm does not explicitly discuss when he is considering the
nature of direct human perceptions of *res* by images or *naturalia
verba*. But nowhere does Anselm acknowledge that he has
passed from image to concept, from words for objects to words
for ideas. And nowhere does he tie up the conclusions of this
chapter with his special theory of language used for talking
about God.

Disappointing as this chapter of the *Monologion* is, it does not
contain Anselm's last word on language in the treatise by any
means. Further aspects of the difficulties he perceives in talking
about God open up as we go on. In Chapter 17 he raises a
question he might have posed at the end of the chapter on what
may be said of the substance of God. If so many words are used
to describe so many different goods, must we conclude that
there are several goods in the Highest Good, and that that Good
is therefore composite (*composita*)?

> an potius non sunt plura bona, sed unum bonum, tam pluri-
> bus *nominibus significatum*.[2]

Anselm has already provided himself with a way out of this
difficulty. There can be no more than one *naturale verbum*, a
single image in the mind, for a single *res*. But there may be un-
limited variants among the *voces significativae*. In speaking of
nomina and *significare* here, Anselm makes it plain that he has
voces significativae in mind, and that the difficulty arises only in
connection with the secondary words of ordinary language. A
similar but more testing problem like that raised by Hugh of
St. Victor is posed in Chapter 30. In God's mind there are
many universal *verba*, spoken or thought by God himself. But
there can be only one Word of God: Anselm asks whether this

---

[1] S 1.29.29–31.   [2] S 1.31.14–15.

locutio consists of many words, or of one Word (*utrum haec locutio in pluribus verbis an in uno verbo consistat*); he is anxious to assert that there are not many words, but one Word through which everything is made (*unum verbum per quod facta sunt omnia*).[1] He reminds us that when we think by using the best kind of words available to us, we think in images:

    similitudines et *imagines* sunt rerum quarum verba sunt.[2]

Such images are more or less true, depending on how closely they approximate to the *res* they imitate.[3] God, we have already established, is Truth itself, and so the Word of God must be wholly true. We also know that Truth is single, not many. And so the Word of God must be one Word, not many. The apparent plurality of the images by which we approach an understanding of that Word arises from the fact that we cannot understand it as a whole. In working out this demonstration, Anselm has recourse to much of his earlier thinking about language, but more importantly for our purposes, he looks at language as it is used of God. He shows that the ultimate purpose of all talking is talking about God:

    sed omnem creatam naturam eo altiori gradu essentiae
    dignitatisque consistere, quo magis illi propinquare videtur.[4]

He asserts that every created nature ascends the ladder of Being as it approaches more closely to the Word. To talk about God in his own 'terms' is to come closer to God.

Elsewhere, Anselm looks at several difficulties which arise when we compare God's use of language with out own. We have already seen that a man who speaks merely reviews in his mind the ideas that God has put there. A man's speaking could not be creative even if he had the power to put his thoughts into action, because he cannot invent anything entirely new; he can be a craftsman only. Again, when God speaks, he speaks 'to himself', or he may be said to 'speak himself':

    quod summus spiritus seipsum dicat coaeterno verbo.[5]

There is no comparable mode of *locutio* in man. For God, to know is to speak:

    Denique haec ipsa locutio nihil aliud potest intelligi quam
    eiusdem spiritus intelligentia, qua cuncta intelligit.[6]

---

[1] S 1.48.8–12.   [2] S 1.48.19–20.   [3] S 1.48.20–1.   [4] S 1.50.12–13.
[5] S 1.50–15. Either translation would seem to be possible.
[6] S 1.47.20–1.

('Then that speaking cannot be understood to be anything other than the understanding of the same spirit, by which he understands everything.') Once more, human experience has no exact parallel for this.

Anselm raises, in addition, numerous large questions to do with language. We might enquire, he suggests, whether the Word would ever have existed if God had never spoken,[1] how God's speaking to himself differs from the speaking which creates natural objects, if indeed there is a difference,[2] what use we are making of language when we speak indirectly or improperly or inexactly, in rather the way we see things in a glass, not directly but indirectly.[3] We might ask what is the number of possible words.[4] When a man thinks of several objects there are as many words in his mind as there are objects thought of:

Item si unus homo cogitet plura aliqua, tot verba sunt in mente cogitantis, quot sunt res cogitatae.[5]

Throughout the *Monologion*, then, Anselm is raising issues which have to do, not only with his theory of language in general, but with the special theory of language which is appropriate for the task of talking about God.

By raising such issues, and giving what is often a very brief analysis of the ways in which they may be resolved, Anselm achieves two things essential to the later development of his thought. Firstly, he makes it unnecessary for himself ever to discuss the roots of language again in quite this way in any later work. Most of what he has to say about the use of language later has to do with the technical refinements of grammar and dialectic and with the problems they pose in their turn.[6] Secondly, he has laid a foundation in these discussions which helps him, not only to develop his ideas about language itself, but also to make progress in areas of difficulty which, in later works, appear to have little or no connection with the theory of language. Yet, as we have seen, in the *Monologion* they are intimately connected with it. In Chapters 9 and 10 of the *Monologion*, for example, Anselm first enters upon the discussion of language because he is puzzled about the mode of creation of

---

[1] S 1.50.27–9. [2] S 1.51.22–3. [3] S 1.76.15–18. [4] S 1.72.8–9.
[5] S 1.72.12–13.
[6] These aspects have been comprehensively discussed by D. P. Henry in a series of works to which reference may be found in his *Commentary on the De Grammatico* (Dordrecht 1974).

all things from nothing, and about the relation between God's first conception of created things and their ultimate appearance in the natural world. He has so fully satisfied himself on this point that he never again questions the actual mode of creation. When he raises the question of the possible creation of new angels to replace those who have fallen, in the *De Casu Diaboli* and the *Cur Deus Homo*,[1] nothing is said about the mechanics of God's making; the discussion turns entirely on the rules which must govern any such attempt, and the reasons why such fresh creations would not solve the problems of fallen angels or of fallen man.[2] Similarly, although Christ is later referred to as the *Verbum Dei*—in the *De Incarnatione Verbi*, for example,[3]—the precise nature of that Word as a word never seems to Anselm to require further comment.

In the *Monologion* Anselm had laid down modified Augustinian principles, from which he never later departs. But although he never feels the need to reopen discussion of the fundamentals of language, he has cleared the ground for two positive developments of the ideas of the *Monologion* which evidently owe something to the thoughts about language he has explored there. In the *De Grammatico* and its companion works[4] he looks at length at *voces significativae* and their peculiar problems of meaning. And in the *Proslogion* argument he is able to move from the *Monologion*'s view of God as the best that can exist of every sort of goodness[5] to the principle that God is the best that can be thought.[6] He is able to do so only because he has already worked out carefully, if only in outline, a view of the relation between thought and reality in the *Monologion*. What we can think of or speak of by using the language of *naturalia verba*, or universal ideas, comes as close as it is possible for us to come to reality. But reality itself always lies a step beyond, except for God himself, for whom words are realities. The importance of this set of principles to an understanding of the force of the *Proslogion* argument for Anselm himself cannot be overstated.

Anselm ultimately concedes, in the *Monologion*, that God is *ineffabilis*, beyond speaking of.[7] The admission follows perfectly

---

[1] S 2.75–6.   [2] Cf. S 2.52.14–24.   [3] S 2.32.15–19.
[4] i.e., the *De Veritate*, the *De Libertate Arbitrii*, the *De Casu Diaboli*.
[5] S 1.29.29–31.   [6] S 1.101.14.   [7] S 1.75.18.

consistently from his earlier arguments. Only God possesses command of a language in which it is possible to speak fully and accurately of himself. But nevertheless, for all practical purposes, Anselm finds it perfectly possible to talk about God. God is, in fact, the centre of interest in most of his treatises. The words of Scripture give him material for analysis, and a precedent for the practice of talking about God at large. Anselm is happy to examine the exact sense of the words of the Bible, the use of tenses there, and so on. Secular sources, patristic writings, and the work of contemporary scholars demonstrated on every side that, even if we cannot talk about God with perfect comprehension, there is much to be said of a more 'approximate' kind, of value and interest to the enquiring Christian. Indeed, Anselm came to adopt the view that, since man's reason had clearly been given him to help him understand about God as well as any creature could, no means of discussion allowed to mankind should be neglected. The use of language clearly falls into the category of divine gifts especially provided to help man approach an understanding of God. So much Anselm never questions in the *Monologion*, and indeed much of what he has to say there depends upon this assumption and enlarges its scope of application. The strong impression of God's inaccessibility which pervades Anselm's devotional writings[1] is entirely in keeping with the view that it was, in Anselm's view, in the very nature of language that it should be used to work towards a knowledge of God, but that it is, in the end, impossible to talk about God as he is, because the words themselves, whether *verba*, or *voces significativae*, do not permit us to do so.

iii: *The Problem of Language*

'If our aim is never to succumb to falsehood, it would be prudent for us to abstain from using language altogether.'[2] In his *The Problem of Knowledge*—a book remarkable for its lack of recourse to solutions involving God as a special case or as an ultimate explanation—A. J. Ayer takes a stand at some distance from Anselm's position. He asserts that only 'such things as statements or propositions' which are capable of being expressed in language may be true or false. In the *De Veritate*

---

[1] See, especially, the first chapter of the *Proslogion* itself, S 1.98.1–15.
[2] A. J. Ayer, *The Problem of Knowledge* (London 1956), p. 52.

Anselm puts forward the view that truth may be predicated of a great many other things besides statements in words—of thought, will, action, sense, for example. The difference lies in this: for Anselm language is something more than a device for making statements about reality. It possesses a reality of its own which sets it on a level with other *res* created by God. It is both a vehicle of understanding and an object of understanding, a means to the end of knowing itself, which might also be described as a means of knowing God by knowing God. Thus the use of language ought to lead not to falsehood, tautology and paradox but to a clearer view of the truth. Anselm was not so naïve that he did not perceive a great many of the difficulties which have dogged philosophers who have tried to discuss language age by age. But he approached them optimistically because he believed that these problems could be resolved, that it was only his own failure to see clearly which made them appear to be problems at all. Often enough, when he had thought for a while, he found an explanation which satisfied him.

What he thought he was doing is what Copleston describes Aquinas as doing: 'His insight . . . is the result of reflection on data of experience and of insight into those data which are in principle data of experience for everyone, whether he is a philosopher or not.' In this way 'the philosopher makes explicit what is implicitly known by people in general.'[1] It is because Anselm works from such first principles of observation of ordinary phenomena of mind and of sense-perception that he speaks so directly to his readers. But he differs from Aquinas in one crucial respect. Aquinas had doubts about what sort of account of reality can be constructed from such common data, because, unlike Anselm, he was not convinced that we can know them to be identical in all men's experience. Anselm's view of language excludes the possibility that, 'in so far as one uses words to refer to the content of one's experiences, they can be intelligible only to oneself'.[2] That does not make Anselm altogether a realist, but he would have had some sympathy with the position of Ayer's naïve realist who says that he knows whatever he knows

---

[1] F. C. Copleston, *Aquinas* (London 1955), pp. 40–1.

[2] Ayer, p. 206, cf. M. Schlick, *Allgemeine Erkenntnislehre* (Berlin 1918) and R. Carnap, *Der Logische Aufbau der Welt* (Berlin 1928) on this principle.

by intuition or direct acquaintance.[1] That is exactly what
Anselm has claimed to be his position in the chapters of the
Monologion which deal with *naturalia verba*, universal words and
images, directly perceived by all human minds. Anselm moves,
then, to the assumption that he can make himself understood
by appealing to common human experience, from the deeper
assumption that all human experience of reality is ultimately
common.

The acceptability of his view rests on two things: the belief
that concepts are comprehensible and recognizable to all
rational beings, if they are recognizable to any rational being at
all, and the belief that this general comprehensibility is the
direct result of the creation of rational beings by a rational God
who is himself the Word, the ultimate source of both concepts
and ordinary language. In other words, Anselm's notion of
language makes sense only if God is allowed to enter into it; it
is a theologian's view not strictly that of a philosopher, even
though it is unlikely that Anselm would have made any distinction between the two.

Can Anselm's theory of language still be held as he proposed
it? A great deal depends on what we take it he was trying to do.
He provides a mere outline of a general theory and a special
theory. In the sketch included in the *Monologion* Anselm does
not pursue his definition of natural, universal words very far,
nor does he explain exactly where an abstract concept differs
from an image. He does not explain how talking may take place
inwardly, nor what is the exact relation between talking and
thinking. He does not discuss the mode of knowing: how we
know what we talk about. He touches on a number of large
questions of linguistic philosophy to which he gives no satis-
factory answers. We must not assume, then, that Anselm has
given us a full study of the problem of language, or that he had
even worked out his own ideas thoroughly at this stage. What
he has done is to take up a position. He has made a statement
about the interdependence of the things of the mind and the *res*
of reality, without which he could not have formulated the
Proslogion arguments. He has demonstrated his willingness to
take as axioms certain principles so fundamental and ultimately so wholly unsusceptible of proof, that it is impossible to

---

[1] Ayer, p. 82.

get behind them and demonstrate their truth or falsehood. He has made a choice with which every thinker is still presented. When we say that he makes assumptions, it would perhaps be more accurate to say that he declares where he stands.

2

MONOLOGION AND *PROSOLOGION*

i. *The Writing of the* Proslogion

THE *Monologion* and the *Proslogion* are the only works of
Anselm's which he himself came to regard as a pair.[1]
When he chose their final titles, he suggested two Greek
expressions which he must have intended to indicate to the
reader that the two works were related to one another.[2] Yet he
did not, as far as we know, envisage the writing of the *Proslogion*
when he set out to compose the *Monologion*. In fact he says that
it was only after he had finished the first book that he conceived
the idea of writing the second work.[3] There cannot be more
than two years or so between them,[4] and this alone would
suggest that some energy carried over from the first has prompted the writing of the second.

Nothing else in the pattern of Anselm's work in later years
quite matches this. Other treatises may have been composed in
quick succession, or in groups. The *Cur Deus Homo* has an
appendix in the *De Conceptu Virginali* and a companion meditation in the *Meditation on Human Redemption*, but the relationships of these works are quite different; the *De Conceptu Virginali*
cannot be said to transcend the *Cur Deus Homo* in the way that
the *Proslogion* transcends the *Monologion*. The three treatises
'pertaining to the study of Holy Scripture' were written, as
Anselm notes, 'at different times'[5] and only later arranged in
their final sequence. Closely argued though their sequence
seems, their relationship is again distinct from that of the
Monologion and the *Proslogion*. Only here did Anselm have so

---

[1] Others were 'grouped', however. See the Preface to the *De Veritate*, S 1.173.2.
[2] See Letter 109, to Hugh, Archbishop of Lyons, S 3.242.10–11.
[3] S 1.93.2, S 1.94.12–13.
[4] Anselm first mentions the *Monologion* in Letter 72, before he became Abbot of
Bec; the *Proslogion* is first mentioned in Letter 100, when Anselm was already
Abbot. The problems of dating which arise in connection with Anselm's writings
have been discussed by F. S. Schmitt in his *ratio editionis* to Vol. 1 of the *Opera
Omnia*.
[5] S 1.173.3.

persistent a nagging sense of work unfinished that he could not
rest until he had satisfied himself. In the *Proslogion* he has done
more than follow up a fresh line of thought which has occurred
to him in the course of his teaching, or complete a portion of
argument neglected in a former work.[1]

What Anselm himself has to say about their relationship at
the beginning of the *Proslogion* is familiar enough. When he
thought about the *Monologion* he realized that there he had
strung together a chain of many arguments:

> considerans illud esse multorum concatenatione contextum
> argumentorum.[2]

Some sense of the untidiness of this perhaps suggested to him the
idea of writing a treatise which would be built upon *unum
argumentum*,[3] a single argument; this was to be a self-evident
truth which would allow a series of demonstrations to be derived from it, so as to display all the attributes of God. But, if
only by implication, Anselm says something else: he wrote the
Monologion at the request of his brothers.[4] The *Proslogion* he
wrote for his own satisfaction (*coepi mecum quaerere*).[5] His own
sense of dissatisfaction was the mover here, not his brothers'
requests for another treatise like the first.

The finding of his argument cost him an intellectual and
spiritual discomfort which is nowhere evident in the *Monologion*.[6] In his attempt to meet a central need of his own
Anselm shows us something of the nature of that need—both its
emotional and its intellectual aspects. It was a driving force set
in motion by the writing of the *Monologion*. Only by writing the
Monologion had Anselm cleared his mind of a number of detailed discussions of problems to do with his knowledge of God,
and put himself in a position to perceive what he saw as the
central problem—and to see it as a whole.

That there was an emotional component in this process is
beyond dispute. Not only does Anselm—whose account is confirmed by Eadmer[7]—mention the distress in which he found
himself while he was trying to hit upon his solution, but he also
expresses his great joy in finding it. That is not merely a per-

---

[1] S 1.173.2–8 emphasizes the teaching context of the 'Three Treatises'. Cf.
S 2.126.5–19 and S 2.139.6–8 on *Cur Deus Homo*'s unfinished task.
[2] S 1.93.4–5.   [3] S 1.93.6.   [4] S 1.7.2, S 1.93.3.   [5] S 1.93.5.
[6] S 1.93.10–19.   [7] VA, pp. 30–1.

sonal relief at the relaxation of tension; it is a pleasure which he thought others would feel, too:

> Aestimans igitur quod me gaudebam invenisse, si scriptum esset, alicui legenti placiturum,[1]

('Thinking, therefore, that what it had given me such joy to find would, if it were written down, please whoever read it . . .'.) Anselm had found for himself, and for others as he thought, a means of recapturing the moment of illumination when he had grasped the idea of God. A little like Wordsworth, he wanted to be able to recollect emotion in tranquillity, to be able, in times of meditation, to feel that first sensation again. Wordsworth's sister provided him with conscientiously-kept notes to enable him to recapture his earlier emotion. Anselm provides his readers with a plan of thought. It would perhaps be misleading to speak of this as a conversion experience, but it has something of the quality of Augustine's description[2] of how he spent a long period of thinking and exploring—just as Anselm did in the *Monologion*—and how he resisted the insight which was pressing itself upon him—as Anselm did in the case of the *Proslogion* argument.[3] Such moments require both an intellectual, and a spiritual-and-emotional preparation. In Anselm's writing of the *Monologion* there is some record of his undergoing a similar process of 'making ready'.

When he wrote the *Proslogion* he deliberately attempted to prepare his readers for a similar experience. It is to be supposed that when Augustine described his own conversion in the *Confessions*, he meant to help others to recognize similar experiences in their own lives. Anselm's aim is rather different. He wants to help his readers to share his own experience directly by handing it on to them intact. He saw the *Monologion* as a meditation.[4] He set the portions of argument in the *Proslogion* within passages of devotional writing. Both works are more than plain treatises. But in the *Proslogion* in particular Anselm seems to have wanted to create a mood of heightened spiritual awareness in his reader before he presents him with his delightful argument. He tries to help the reader by a shorter route into that state of preparedness which he himself had had to reach before the argument became clear to him. The *Monologion* is a

---

[1] S 1.93.20–1.   [2] Especially *Confessions*, Book VIII.
[3] S 1.93.15–16.   [4] S 1.7.3–4, S 1.93.2.

discursively argued sequential meditation. Anselm has done a good deal to give unity to the book, even though his relatively recent reading of Augustine has made it difficult for him to free himself altogether of the Augustinian habit of pursuing digressions.[1] But in the *Proslogion* the contrast is striking. We find Anselm dwelling intensely on the single thought of God, and there is no escaping the force of his intention that others should see what he has perceived, feel what he has felt and share his new certainty of faith.

ii: *The Central Argument*

All this has little or nothing to do with the much-debated matter of the validity of the ontological argument. Those who find it compelling still are frequently prepared to concede that it has more force for believers than for Anselm's hypothetical Fool. That is what we should expect to be the case if the underlying rules of thought which have determined Anselm's theory of language should turn out to govern his thinking in other areas, too. We must, in other words, believe something about the relation between words and realities which Anselm himself believed, if we are to find the argument convincing. Yet its dogged persistence as a subject for philosophical debate must be due to something more universally recognizable than its effect upon the faith of a man who comes to it prepared to be sympathetic. Anselm himself thought it could do more than merely heighten existing faith.

Charles Hartshorne has remarked that,

it proves possible to reconcile, in surprising degree . . . the contentions of Anselm and Kant, or of Descartes and Russell. This often happens with new perspectives, and is one sign of their probable superiority . . . Anselm and Descartes were rather simple-minded in their claim to have found a clear and obvious logical connection, scarcely open to intelligent dispute, between their 'idea' of divine perfection and the existence of something perfect. But have opponents of the argument been less simple-minded in proclaiming a clear, obvious and non-controversial lack of connection?[2]

---

[1] It is clear that Anselm had spent the years at Bec before he began to write his treatises in reading; until he had written the *Monologion* at least, the influence of Augustine was not entirely digested, and his teaching is relatively near the surface of Anselm's mind.

[2] C. Hartshorne provides a summary of the main objections to the argument in *The Logic of Perfection* (Illinois 1962), pp. 44–7. For this comment, see ibid., pp. 29–30.

Two things might be said about this. The ontological argument itself has the quality of a 'new perspective'; it was constructed out of ordinary materials fashioned into an extraordinary new form. It is possible to reconcile the claims of Anselm and his supporters with those of their opponents in some measure only because the argument itself possesses such powers of anticipating and encompassing objections. Hartshorne implicitly concedes a 'probable superiority' to the argument itself. Secondly, the 'simple-mindedness' of Anselm's assumption that there is a connection between thought and reality in the special case of God must surely be inescapable. Intuitive perceptions, such as Anselm experienced when he hit upon the argument, always have an air of simplicity about them at the moment when they are understood. It is because it depends upon a single direct insight into what Anselm regarded as the nature of things that the argument involves so 'simple-minded' an assumption. Nothing but an assumption of this kind or of this level would have done. The argument itself is simple. Anselm grasped it in an instant. Its implications are not. Anselm's achievement lies, not only in the making of the discovery, but in describing it in plain language and in making use of no technical terms. To keep the argument simple in its presentation was the work of magnificent philosophical skill; it gives the argument a quality which has helped to preserve its attractiveness for succeeding generations of thinkers. But it is important that we should not confuse the inspired simple-mindedness to which Hartshorne refers, with the simplicity and clarity of exposition which gives the argument its classic Anselmian form.

Questions to do with the argument's ultimate validity must approach it at the level of that first insight. It is not my intention to attempt to do anything of the kind here. But if we look at the *Proslogion* as a whole, and at its connections with the *Monologion*, perhaps something may usefully be said about the place of that insight in the scheme of Anselm's thought about words and things. It may, too, be worth-while to examine the apparent simplicity of Anselm's method of presentation of the argument, which is dependent upon the very 'simple-mindedness' of his first assumption for its philosophical force.

It may be convenient to give the argument of Chapter 2 of the *Proslogion* here:

We believe that God is something than which nothing greater
can be thought.

When an unbeliever hears this he understands it, and what he
understands exists in his mind.

But what exists in the mind and in reality too must be greater
than what exists in the mind alone.

So that than which nothing greater can be thought cannot be
that which exists only in the mind.

So that than which nothing greater can be thought must
exist in the mind and in reality, too.

So God must exist in reality.

In Chapter 3 Anselm goes on to elaborate:

What cannot be thought not to exist must be greater than
what can be thought not to exist.

By a similar sequence of argument it follows that God cannot
be thought not to exist.

This necessitates the giving of some account of how the Fool
thinks what cannot be thought, in Chapter 4:

To think of the word for a thing is not the same as thinking of
the thing itself.

The Fool can think the words of the statement that God does
not exist, but he cannot do so unless he distorts or ignores
their meaning. He cannot think their true sense or apply to
them their true meaning, because such a thought is impossible.

Anselm says he had searched for a single argument (*unum
argumentum*). He took several of the topics treated in the *Monologion* and handled there by more usual contemporary methods
and looked at them again from a new point of vantage in the
hope of finding a single principle which he could apply to them
all. He discovered a mode of demonstration which can almost
be called Euclidean, and which he must presumably have found
for himself, since there is no evidence whatsoever that he knew
any part of Euclid's work'[1] This 'axiomatic method' is not,
however, quite the same as that of Euclid. Nor is it indebted, as
was the renewed interest of twelfth-century scholars in the self-

---

[1] On the background to this problem, see M. Clagett, 'The Mediaeval Latin
translations from the Arabic of the *Elements* of Euclid', *Isis* 44 (1953), 16–42, and
my article, 'The Sub-Euclidean Geometry of the Earlier Middle Ages up to the
mid-Twelfth Century', *Archive for History of Exact Sciences*, 16 (1976), 105–18.

evident axiom, to the study of Boethius' *opuscula sacra*.[1] In the
De Hebdomadibus Boethius proposes to use a series of axioms as a
basis for the arguments which follow.[2] He then lists his axioms
and proceeds to test his arguments 'against them. There is
nothing in Anselm's writings to suggest that he knew the
Theological Tractates of Boethius—all that he has to say about
the doctrine of the Trinity could have been derived by his own
reflections from Augustine's *De Trinitate* without any reference
to that of Boethius. The works were not much read in Anselm's
day as far as we know. In any case, Anselm's use of the axiom
in the *Proslogion* differs significantly from that of either Euclid
or Boethius, in that Anselm provides only a single axiom, not a
series. The essence of Euclid's axioms is their plurality: they
allow of the development of the theorems only because more
than one principle may be brought into play. Anselm's desire
was to find a single axiom which, applied to all the Augustinian
notions of God's attributes, would yield demonstrations of all
that we believe about God:

> *unum argumentum quod nullo alio ad se probandum quam se solo*
> *indigeret*,[3]

('a single axiom which would need no proof but itself').

Boethius distinguishes two kinds of axiom, that which is
immediately comprehensible to everyone: *quam quisque probat*
auditam, and that which only the initiated understand: *alia vero*
est doctorum tantum.[4] The latter type are based upon and derived
from the former, and they are in fact still self-evident, but only
to those who know upon what prior assumptions they rest.
Anselm's axiom is of the former kind. He intends it to be immediately acceptable to everyone who hears it, just as the
naturalia verba are understood by all men. He had said in the
Monologion that he wanted what he had to say to be grasped
even by those of limited powers of thought (*si vel mediocris*
ingenii est).[5] He has thus set himself a task at which Boethius and
Euclid had balked: that of building upon one axiom, and that a

---

[1] See my article, '*More geometrico*: the place of the axiomatic method in the
twelfth-century commentaries on Boethius' *opuscula sacra*', *Archives internationales*
d'histoire des sciences, 27 (1977), 207–21.

[2] Boethius, *The Theological Tractates*, ed. and tr. H. F. Stewart and E. K. Rand
(London 1946), p. 40.16–17.

[3] S 1.93.6–7.   [4] *Theol. Tr.*, p. 40.18–24.   [5] S 1.13.10.

communis animi conceptio.[1] And as far as we can tell, he had conceived the idea independently.

It is perfectly clear from Anselm's other writings that he had an easy mastery of the methods of argument available in his own day to students of formal logic. In the *De Grammatico* he employs syllogisms[2] and analogies[3] in a manner which he intends to be strictly formal, since the purpose of the treatise is to introduce beginners to the study of dialectic. Anselm did not perhaps enjoy so comprehensive a training as Abelard,[4] but he would have been familiar with the idea that a major premiss must be acceptable to both parties in a dispute and that it must therefore be self-evident or supported by hard evidence.[5] The methodological originality of the *Proslogion* argument lies in the attempt to use a single generally acceptable notion, on its own, as the basis for a series of demonstrations where it may be employed in any formal scheme of argument. In using it in this way, Anselm seems to conceive of its function rather as Euclid thought of his axioms, or as Boethius envisaged his 'common concepts'. The axiom is a touchstone for a variety of demonstrations.

The content of Anselm's distinctive single axiom poses some difficulties of identification. A case might be made out for the view that it is not the principle, already adumbrated on several occasions by Augustine, that God is that than which nothing greater can be thought.[6] That may be regarded as being merely the first statement of the argument's application. The axiom itself seems to amount to the idea that God is in some sense 'more than' whatever we can conceive of as a good. It could be stated crudely as the principle that, for whatever a we can imagine, God is $a + x$. This axiom is never explicitly stated by Anselm, but it underlies every piece of demonstration in the *Proslogion* in a way that 'God is that than which nothing greater can be thought' does not. He remarks in Chapter 5 that God is

---

[1] *Theol. Tr.*, p. 40.18.   [2] S 1.151.1–10.   [3] S 1.159–61.

[4] Peter Abelard provides a systematic account of the modes of formal argument with which he was familiar in his *Dialectica*, ed. L. M. de Rijk (Assen 1956). Most of them are to be found in use in Anselm's day and earlier.

[5] Garlandus notes the point in his *Dialectica*, ed. L. M. de Rijk (Assen 1959), p. 87.11, and it is implied in Lanfranc's *De Corpore et Sanguine Domini*, PL, 150.417.

[6] S 1.101.8. This statement has tended to capture the attention of students of the *Proslogion*. Cf. JH, p. 19 on some Augustinian parallels.

whatever it is better to be than not to be. He goes on to show that since it is better to be omnipotent, merciful, incapable of suffering than not to be so, God must be all those things. Given that certainty, he tries to show, for example, that there is no conflict between God's omnipotence and the fact that there are many things he cannot do (Chapter 7), by demonstrating that doing what is unworthy of God involves a negative act; it involves, not a power, but a lack of power. He shows how God can be both merciful and incapable of suffering, even though that would seem to imply that he feels no compassion (Chapter 8). At each point the absolute '$a + x$-ness' of God is taken as the fundamental *datum*.

In the ontological argument itself it is the '$a + x$-ness' of God which enables us to see that if it is better to be in reality than to be in thought alone, God must exist not only in thought but also in reality (Chapter 2); if that whose non-existence is inconceivable is necessarily greater than that whose non-existence is conceivable, the axiom of God's '$a + x$-ness' will again demonstrate that his non-existence is inconceivable and that he must therefore exist. It might be objected, particularly at this point, that all this presupposes the existence of God; it has often been suggested that that is precisely what the ontological argument does do. If Anselm had applied his axiom only after he had formulated an independent proof for the existence of God, its force in the arguments of successive chapters would be far less debatable. But we cannot escape the plain statement he makes at the outset that he has found a single argument (*unum argumentum*).[1] If he thought that argument applied only to part of the work, or that the proof for the existence of God rested upon a special argument, then it is difficult to account either for the preliminary setting of Chapter 1, or for the writing of Chapter 5 to the end. The task Anselm performs in Chapters 2–4, to his own satisfaction, if not to that of his subsequent critics, is merely the first of the three tasks he sets himself in the *Proemium*. He has shown that God truly exists (*quia deus vere est*),[2] but not that he is the highest Good, needing no other to make him so, nor that all the other things we believe about the

---

[1] Some of the recently published articles dealing with the question whether Chapters 2–4 contain more than one argument are listed in the bibliography of JH.
[2] S 1.93.7.

divina substantia are true.[1] All these demonstrations are to have the primary axiom, the *unum argumentum*, applied to them. It cannot be the case, as has sometimes been implied, that the proof of the existence of God in itself constitutes the *argumentum*. It would have been far more natural for Anselm to use the term *argumentatio* if he had meant to refer to the whole sequence of proof. Anselm's own declaration of purpose must be allowed to stand.

This view of the *unum argumentum* as an axiom does, however, have a direct bearing upon the question with which we are chiefly concerned: Anselm's view of the ways in which we can usefully employ language in talking about God. Hegel notes in his *Lectures on the Proofs of the Existence of God* that, 'If we prove a geometrical proposition every part of the proof must in part carry its justification within itself.'[2] That, *mutatis mutandis*, is very much the problem which confronts us in trying to identify the axiom which Anselm believed carried within it the proof of the existence of God. The axiom only makes sense if we grant the existence of God in formulating it. To say that God is that-than-which-nothing-greater-can-be-thought, or that he is that-which-it-is-better-to-be-than-not-to-be, is to make a statement about God which has no meaning at all unless we accept that God exists. Arguably, what Anselm does in Chapters 2–4 of the *Proslogion* is simply to unfold the implications of his axiom and show that what strikes the reader from the first as self-evident contains within it a demonstration of the necessary existence of God. To quote Hegel again: when we talk about God,

we start by unfolding the meaning of the notion or conception of God . . . The notion [of God] . . . apart altogether from the question of its reality, brings with it the demand that it should be true in itself as well . . . The second thing, accordingly, is to show that this notion exists, and this is the proof of the existence of God . . . [But] the product thus reached does not answer to the fullness of the idea of God, and we have accordingly a third division of the subject, in which we treat still further of the attributes of God and of his relations to the world.[3]

This threefold process corresponds remarkably closely with Anselm's declared intention in the *Proslogion*. The whole

[1] S 1.93.8–10.
[2] Hegel, *Lectures on the Proofs of the Existence of God*, Lecture 2 in *The Philosophy of Religion*, tr. E. B. Speirs and J. B. Sanderson (London 1895), Vol. III, p. 166.
[3] Ibid., p. 204, Lecture 7.

demonstration rests upon a single assumption about the nature of language without which Anselm could say nothing at all about God. As Hegel puts it in another of his lectures: 'On God's part there can be no obstacle to a knowledge of him through men.'[1] However obscurely we grasp what we are saying when we talk about God, because of the way in which God himself gives rise to language, we are bound to be saying something which has a bearing on the nature of God in the very act of speaking of God, provided we are using language with that correctness which for Anselm is also truth. Therein lies the simplicity of Anselm's conception, and therein lies its weakness, if we are not prepared to accept his view of the divine origin and function of language.

iii: Monologion *and* Proslogion

If we set the *Monologion* and the *Proslogion* side by side, the contrasts between the approach Anselm makes to the study of the divine attributes in the first, and his special method of argument in the second, fall more clearly into place. His sequence of exposition in both works follows the overall pattern of his writings throughout his life—that is, he moves from a consideration of God at his most abstract (the highest good) to consider God's attributes in detail, and then he goes on to look at God's dealings with man and man's attitude to God. Both the *Monologion* and the *Proslogion* end with a series of reflections on the nature of the blessedness a man may hope to enjoy if he fulfils the purpose for which he was made, and loves God.[2] In the *Monologion* the emphasis is upon the wretchedness of estrangement from God.[3] In the *Proslogion* Anselm dwells lovingly upon the *gaudium plenum*, the fullness of heavenly joy, and the many good things of body and soul which await the believer.[4] But in both he brings home to his reader the direct application of what he has been saying about God to the concerns of his own soul. With this more or less common subject-matter Anselm constructs two treatises whose methods of exposition give them altogether different directions.

In the *Monologion* we begin with the notion that something must occupy the supreme position above all existing things, and

[1] Ibid., p. 194, Lecture 5.
[2] *Monologion*, S 1.78 ff., *Proslogion* S 1.118 ff.
[3] S 1.81–2.
[4] S 1.118–22.

that that is the highest thing of all. Anselm encourages his readers to examine their own experience of the good things of life. Then they are to look upwards, placing one good above another, until they can see that, unless we are to postulate an infinite series of goods, one good must occupy the topmost place. The underlying conception here is not new; it goes back at least to Plato. But Anselm tries to help those readers who have no special bent for abstract thought to use their own experience so that they can understand the argument.

Then he explains that because the ultimate good is at the very top of the pile, it cannot depend upon any good above it to give it character or definition. It must therefore derive its goodness, not from other goods, but from itself. 'Since there are so many goods, whose great variety we both experience through our senses and discern in our minds by reason, must we not believe that there is one good through which all other goods are good?'[1] This good differs in kind from all other goods because it does not derive its goodness from outside itself (*et ipsum solum per seipsum*).[2] The same principle can be applied to the notions of greatness and of the greatest being.[3] The idea that God is that than which nothing 'greater' can be thought comes in almost as an afterthought, after a much more lengthy discussion of the view that he is that than which nothing more good can be thought. Presumably Anselm had not yet seen how much more helpful the notion of greatness would ultimately prove to be when he came to work out the exposition of the ontological argument, but it has already taken its place with 'goodness' in his thinking about God.

So, too, has the germ of the idea that it is through thinking about God that we come to understand his 'position' in relation to the created world. Already Anselm has the ingredients for the statement that God is, 'that than which nothing greater can be thought'. But for the moment he is content to try to find a method of approach to the concept of God which all his readers will easily be able to grasp. To begin with something everyone understands—the idea of a good thing—and to climb an ascending scale with his readers up to the topmost level where God stands would seem an altogether less demanding

---

[1] S 1.14.5–8.   [2] S 1.15.6–7.   [3] S 1.15.15–23.

process than to expect his readers to grasp the notion of God's supremacy directly, and then to work downwards and outwards from it in the demonstration of what follows. In the *Proslogion* that is exactly what Anselm does. It would have been a help to any reader to have read the *Monologion* first, both for the groundwork it lays and for its easier 'reversed' approach. Anselm is still recommending a method of patient ladder-climbing in the *De Incarnatione Verbi*. The *Proslogion* method was not one he found more generally applicable.

In his *The Logic of Perfection*, Hartshorne might be said to beg a considerable question. He speaks of God in a way that Anselm never does except by implication, as the perfect being. It is true that since all God's attributes are one in God, it cannot make any difference to the soundness of Anselm's *Proslogion* proof which attribute he chooses to concentrate upon for the purposes of argument. The sum of those attributes, or any single one of those attributes, by definition must constitute perfection in the case of God. But the idea of greatness was chosen by Anselm in preference to the idea of goodness—or blessedness or justice or mercy or omnipotence, or any one of a dozen other possibilities mentioned by him in the *Monologion*. It may be that the reason for his choice lies in the particular properties the idea of magnitude possesses in the *Categories* tradition. Anselm shows that he has the category of quantity in mind in Chapter 2 of the *Monologion*, where he explains that when he says that God is the *summum magnum*, the ultimate greatness, he means, not magnitude of bodily or spatial dimension, but greatness of another kind. We call God great because he is 'better' or 'more worthy', rather as we might speak of 'greater wisdom'; it is an evaluative greatness which is intended here.[1] There he leaves it in the *Monologion*, but when he comes to formulate the argument of Chapter 2 of the *Proslogion* he returns to the idea that God is *maius*, greater than anything else. Despite his assertion that it is not a quantitative notion of magnitude he has in mind, it seems that his idea of magnitude has not been entirely freed from the context of the *Categories* teaching. One of the issues discussed in the *Categories* commentaries is whether 'greatness' or 'smallness' or 'equality' can be predicated of any given

[1] S 1.15.19–20. Cf. Abelard, *Dialectica*, on the category of quantity in connection with 'bodies' and 'spaces', pp. 56–60.

category.[1] Anselm argues in the *Proslogion* from the notion that 'greater' implies 'greater than' something. God is of course absolutely 'great', just as the Father is absolutely Father and not merely Father in relation to the Son.[2] But for the purposes of the argument we must envisage him as being 'greater than' anything else we can think of. The idea of magnitude thus lends itself more graphically and more readily to the hierarchical arrangement which Anselm proposes as a model, than does any other attribute of God. Here again, the *Monologion* can be seen to have provided Anselm with space to try out this principle. He seems to have concluded that the idea of magnitude which takes second place there is in fact a more helpful one in an argument of the *Proslogion* type, where the reader must attempt to grasp the idea of God from another angle of view.

In the *Monologion* Anselm moves on to look more closely at the idea that whatever stands at the head of its 'kind' must possess its special properties of itself, *per se*. By definition, it cannot derive them from any other source. This is a notion which is entirely in keeping with Anselm's view of God as the author of human language, but himself the very Word, the ultimate and universal language from which ordinary speech is derived. Similarly, it allows him to see God not only as the source of the existence of all created things, but as the source of the very idea of existence and of the words for existence which rational beings have in their minds. Accordingly, we could not think about existence unless God himself existed, and we certainly could not think about the existence of God unless God existed. That is the burden of the *Proslogion*'s central argument and its force rests largely upon the assumption that the highest good is good *per se*, with all that follows from that. In the *Proslogion* the point is not raised until Chapter 5, where Anselm mentions it in passing, as though it were something already settled beyond dispute: 'But what are you but that highest of all things, which alone exists through itself, and which has made all things from nothing?'[3] Here again, the *Monologion*'s preliminary discussions have cleared the way for a brief statement in the *Proslogion*.

---

[1] For example, Boethius on the *Categories*, PL, 64.257–8, and 221.

[2] The example of father and son is retained by Boethius in discussing the category of *relativa*, PL, 64.222 (after Aristotle).

[3] S 1.104.11–12.

In both works a conceptual leap is demanded of the reader. He must be led to accept that not only is there a supreme 'best' which is the source of all other goods of the same kind, but that this 'best' is the same source of all goods of every kind. The problem is stated in Chapter 3 of the *Monologion*: 'That through which all things which exist have their being is either one or many.'[1] Three possibilities present themselves, if we try to argue that the 'best' is different in each case. Perhaps all these specific individual 'bests' themselves depend upon some single entity through which they, in their turn, all exist. Perhaps these many 'bests' all exist individually *per se*. Perhaps they exist through one another.[2] The first possibility may be dismissed quickly. If indeed many 'bests' exist through one single 'best', then they do not exist individually *per se*, but through something else. If we argue that they all exist individually *per se*, then they have in common that property of existing *per se* and that property itself becomes the common principle through which they exist. The *natura existendi per se*,[3] the quality of existing through themselves, becomes the 'one thing' through which they all exist.[4] If, thirdly, we try to regard them as existing through one another, it seems that something must be giving existence to the source of its own existence, which is impossible. Anselm is perhaps drawing here upon the teaching of the *Categories* in his discussion of relatives, and of what it means to exist in relation to or through something (*ad invicem* or *per invicem*).[5] But the formulation of the demonstration is his own. The point is crucial to the statement of the *Proslogion* proof. We must be able to accept that whichever way we climb the ladder of being, in imagination, we shall arrive at the same concept of God at the top, and that whichever way we turn when we climb downwards from the idea of God, we shall find that everything Anselm wants to prove follows from the fact of God's existence. From all the varied manifestations of God's attributes which a man may see in the world around him, a single generalization must be made if Anselm is right: whatever we

---

[1] S 1.16.1–2.   [2] S 1.16.2–4.   [3] S 1.16.7.

[4] This is a little reminiscent of some of the ramifications of Bertrand Russell's 'class of all classes' paradox.

[5] S 1.16.10–15. These expressions are used widely by Boethius, Abelard, and others in discussing the *Categories*.

can recognize as the best of its kind, God's unique exemplifi-
cation of its perfection begins at exactly the point where our
understanding fails us, and stretches unimaginably beyond that
point in total unity with every other possible good.

A further question presents itself to Anselm's mind in the
Monologion. He asks himself how the highest good is related to
this chain of goods, since God is not only the head but also the
source of every one of them. The question of modes of proceed-
ing was not to occupy his mind fully until many years later,
when he was asked to write the *De Processione Spiritus Sancti* in
order to demonstrate the soundness of the Latin doctrine of the
Procession of the Holy Spirit against the view of the Greeks.[1]
Here he confines himself to the question of the mode of creation.
If God occupies the topmost place, and is the source of all that
is, it follows that there can be nothing outside himself 'from' or
'out of which' he could form creation. The only possibility is
that he made things from nothing. The difficulty lies, not so
much in envisaging how God could create 'through' himself, as
in accounting for the stuff of creation, the material he used, the
materia universorum.[2] 'Nothing' would, it seems, have to become
'something' in order to compose matter. Anselm has no resort
to the discussion of matter and forms which was to be so topical
in the next century.[3] Instead he turns, as Augustine had done,
and as he himself was to do again, to the problem of 'nothing',
'but a problem arises in connection with nothing.'[4] The problem as he sees it, involves the difficulty of thinking about
'nothing'. In Anselm's scheme of things it ought to be impossible
to conceive of 'nothing', let alone to think about its properties,
since no human mind can grasp what God has not made a
'something'. Further, since so much of his argument in both the
Monologion and the *Proslogion* rests upon proofs from what can be
thought, *nihil* cannot but present him with a worrying anomaly:

[1] Anselm's design in writing this was shaped by his encounter with the Greek
viewpoint when he was in exile in Italy. AB, pp. 234-5.

[2] S 1.20.24.

[3] This, too, is a topic which was to be brought into discussion by the study of
Calcidius' on Plato's *Timaeus* and of Boethius' *opuscula sacra*. N. M. Häring has
edited a number of commentaries, including those of Gilbert of Poitiers (Toronto
1966), Thierry of Chartres, and his school (Toronto 1971).

[4] S 1.22.13. Cf. *De Casu Diaboli*, S 1.246-51 and Letter 97, S 3.224-8. Augustine
looks at *nihil* in the *De Magistro*, II.3, and the Carolingian scholar, Fredegisus, had
examined the problem in his *Epistola de Nihilo et Tenebris*, PL, 105.751 ff.

'What therefore is to be understood by nothing?'[1] he wonders in Chapter 8 of the *Monologion*. He is anxious to leave no aspect of the question unexplored in his meditation, however foolish the possible objections seem (*vel paene fatuum*).[2] He did not in fact satisfy either himself or others. When he came to write the *De Casu Diaboli* in which he takes up the problem of 'nothing' again, he did so partly at least at the request of friends, and its first drafting left out any account of the Fall of Satan in favour of a treatment of the abstract problems of the existence of evil and 'nothing'.[3] But Anselm was sufficiently content with his thinking out of the problem in the *Monologion* to pass over the question of 'nothing' very briefly indeed in the *Proslogion*. There, in Chapter 5, he merely remarks that God made everything which exists from nothing.[4] The problem of the way in which things proceed from God is never directly confronted at all in the *Proslogion*. Anselm had simply got his anxieties out of the way for the moment, as he does so frequently throughout the *Monologion*, so as to clear the way for the formulation of the *Proslogion* arguments.

It is beginning to seem as though the relationship between the *Monologion* and the *Proslogion* has something of the character of a mirror image. In the *Monologion* we look upwards towards the idea of God, and in the *Proslogion* we begin with the idea of God and move downwards and outwards. Anselm himself may have had some notion of the kind in mind. In the course of his discussion of Augustine's imagery of the mind of man as a small-scale Trinity, in the *Monologion*, he remarks that the mind may be regarded as something like a mirror, reflecting the image of God.[5] It is not impossible that he saw his *Proslogion* as a mirror of his earlier work, in which those who could not 'see' God from one angle of view might be able to see him from another. Those who found talking about him in one way, difficult, might find talking about him in another, helpful. Either must be equally valid if all language is designed to aid those who want to talk about God.

The repetition with modifications of the Augustinian image of the craftsman in the *Monologion*, in the image of the painter in the *Proslogion*, shows clearly enough that Anselm was going over

---

[1] S 1.23.3.   [2] S 1.23.4.   [3] See Letter 97, S 3.225.18–19.
[4] S 1.104.12–13.   [5] S 1.77.27.

previously-covered ground in his mind, and looking at it again
in the light of his earlier thinking. In the *Monologion* we are
introduced to the *factor*,[1] in the *Proslogion* to the *pictor*.[2] What
the craftsman or painter has in mind before he begins work is
not the word for the thing he is going to make but a picture of
it, or a conception of it, a *mentis conceptio*.[3] In the *Monologion*
Anselm uses this image as a basis for the discussion of the relation between words and the things they signify; in the *Proslogion* it provides an analogy for the differences between thinking
about something which exists only in the mind, and thinking
about something which exists in reality, too.[4] Its flexibility as
an image is clear enough; Anselm shows how closely related is
his thinking in these two works by adapting it to his needs in
both. Typically, it is in the *Monologion* that he goes to the
trouble of showing in exactly what respects the mind of the
human craftsman differs from that of God the creator; the
human craftsman can make nothing for which he has no
pattern in the physical world, but God creates his own designs.[5]

Anselm allows the two works to complement one another
again and again in their subject-matter. Occasionally, the
Proslogion's treatment is fuller than that of the *Monologion*. The
discussion of God's justice and mercy, for example, which occupies so many chapters of the *Proslogion*, is touched upon more
briefly in the *Monologion*.[6] There, in Chapter 16, Anselm lists
the attributes in which God is supreme: he is the highest being,
life, reason, well-being, righteousness, wisdom, truth, goodness,
greatness, beauty, immortality, incorruptibility, immutability,
blessedness, and so on.[7] Some of these attributes are taken up
and discussed thoroughly in the *Proslogion*, but not all.[8] Where
he does consider them, Anselm looks at them, not as attributes
to be established as belonging to God, but rather as attributes
we already know to belong to God in the highest degree, just as
$a + x$ is more than a in every case. Anselm perhaps never
finished his analysis of these attributes to his own satisfaction;
iustitia in particular is still being discussed in later works, particularly in the three treatises 'pertaining to the study of Holy

---

[1] S 1.24.26.   [2] S 1.101.11.   [3] S 1.24.26–7.   [4] S 1.101.12–13.
[5] S 1.26.9–14.   [6] S 1.30–1, cf. S 1.106–10.   [7] S 1.31.3–8.
[8] The notions of God's being *sensibilis, omnipotens, misericors, impassibilis, incir-
cumscriptus, aeternus,* in particular.

Scripture'.[1] But he had said enough about them in the *Monologion* to show how they stood in relation to God himself, and that is all he needed to do before he could write the *Proslogion* accounts of them. He found no need there to demonstrate their relation to the Godhead; he merely states it.

God's independence of time and place is a topic covered largely in both works. Again, the *Monologion* shows how time and place are limitations from which God is free, and the *Proslogion* builds upon that principle.[2] Once more, the *Categories* tradition is in evidence; it has formed Anselm's view of time and place as being possessed of dimension. He could, certainly, have found much the same teaching in Augustine, but even for Augustine a view of time and place based upon Greek dialectic was a paramount influence.[3] Anselm's educational background, in other words, encouraged him to take some things for granted, and to feel it necessary to explain others. He lays the groundwork in the *Monologion*, and in the *Proslogion* he is free to consider the implications of what he has said: how, for example, can God alone be limitless and eternal when other spirits are limitless and eternal, too?[4]

Another borrowing from the *Categories* tradition occurs in Chapter 15 of the *Monologion*, where Anselm returns to a thought he has touched on earlier—that of the 'relative' nature of greatness. When he begins to look at the *substantia* and *relativa* of the divine nature, it is natural enough for Anselm to do as Augustine had done, and to employ principles of discussion drawn from the *Categories*. The idea, for example, that relatives are normally paired, but that in the case of God himself, the Sonship of the Son and the Fatherhood of the Father are absolute, not relative to one another (as would be the case with any human father or son) can be found in a number of contemporary and near-contemporary contexts, as well as in the sources of Anselm's reading.[5] He had no need to think about

---

[1] S 1.191–6, for instance.   [2] S 1.32–42, S 1.110–11.

[3] Augustine's discussions of time and place are widespread, but the topics are particularly well covered in Book XI of the *Confessions*. In dialectic these subjects come up in the treatment of the topic of continuous quantity in all the *Categories* commentaries.

[4] S 1.110–11.

[5] Here again, the twelfth-century commentaries on Boethius' *opuscula sacra* are important; the use of father and son in discussions of *relativa* has already been noted in writing on the *Categories*.

such problems afresh in the *Monologion*; he falls automatically into the habit of pairing. He says, for instance, that he proposes to restrict himself to such *relativa* as, *corpus et non-corpus, verum et non-verum . . . et his similia.*[1] Substance is not relative, and God's possession of his attributes is not in any way relative to the possession of modified forms of those attributes by any of his creatures. The divine attributes, unlike the 'qualities' of created things, are themselves aspects of God's substance.

Even though Anselm makes very much his own uses of these principles in the *Monologion*, the familiarity which they would have had for him through his reading makes them a starting-point for further thought, rather than problems to be settled from first principles. In the *Proslogion*, these dialectical under-pinnings are never conspicuous at all. Anselm simply asserts, in Chapter 5 and the chapters which follow, that God is whatever it is better to be than not to be, that is, he is just, truthful, blessed:

Tu es itaque iustus, verax, beatus, et quidquid melius est esse quam non esse.[2]

We have here a three-tiered process of development of Anselm's thought: his early training has given him a firm platform upon which to construct the *Monologion* arguments, and from there he has a clear view of what all his preceding discussion amounts to. That allows him to express profundities with great simplicity in the *Proslogion*—and also with commendable brevity.

The same might be said for Anselm's discussions of the nature of the existence of the highest good in the *Monologion*.[3] God's existence may be regarded as that of a substance, but it is unique among existences and compared with it, no other substance exists in its own right. Some aspects of this issue were matters of current debate[4] and had been raised by Augustine and other sources of Anselm's reading. The way in which God's existence differs from the existence of all created things was to be a question which would engage the interest of Aquinas and later scholastics far more extensively. Indeed they were to add considerably to the technical vocabulary available for dis-cussing 'being' and to set in train the analysis of several con-

---

[1] S 1.28.28–9.   [2] S 1.104.15–16.   [3] S 1.44–6.

[4] In Letter 83 there occurs a brief discussion of the difference between Greek and Latin terminology, S 3.208.12–20.

siderable philosophical issues. All that Anselm wants to do is to turn over in a few chapters of the *Monologion* the aspects of the question which were of current contemporary interest. But the magnificent generalization about the existence of God which he expresses in the ontological proof could not have been made unless he had first got these matters out of the way.

iv: *The Trinity*

A large part of the *Monologion*'s discussions would seem at first sight to have no parallel at all in the *Proslogion*. In Chapter 12 Anselm had promised to return to the topic of talking or *locutio* in the special sense in which it refers to the Son, as the Word of God. 'I do not think,' he says, 'that this problem of "utterance" should be passed over lightly, but before we can discuss it adequately . . .'.[1] Now at last, in Chapter 29,[2] Anselm returns to the subject. This chapter and those which succeed it contain by far the most striking differences of subject-matter between the two works. Anselm here appends to the material covered in both a study of the Trinity, to which this forms the introduction, and to which the *Proslogion* has no direct parallel.

Anselm was to take up Trinitarian questions again in several of his works, and it might be fruitful to examine their relation to these chapters of the *Monologion* if space here allowed. But none of these works can be 'paired' with the *Monologion* in quite the way that the *Proslogion* can, and Anselm's reasons for leaving so much out of account in the *Proslogion* would seem to require some explanation. This constitutes not a small portion of the *Monologion* but a quite considerable section of the whole work. If this part of the *Monologion* were removed, the two works would be much more nearly comparable in length. And Anselm says at the beginning of the *Proslogion* that he intends his ex-planation—his single *argumentum*—to cover all that we believe about God, as well as demonstrating his existence. His exact words are: *quaecumque de divina credimus substantia*,[3] and here perhaps lies the explanation. Augustine had long ago pointed out that some of God's attributes are proper to the divine sub-stance, and others to the three Persons individually.[4] There were, in other words, two 'classes' of attributes of God.[5] Anselm

---

[1] S 1.26.31–2.   [2] S 1.47 ff.   [3] S 1.93.9–10.
[4] Augustine *De Trinitate*, Book V.ix–xv in particular.   [5] Ibid.

has simply chosen to concentrate in the *Proslogion* upon those which are attributes of God's substance, such as his omnipotence and his immutability, rather than upon his Fatherhood or Sonship.

This would seem to have been forced upon him in any case by his determination to link all that he has to say to a single axiom. If Anselm had wanted to demonstrate those things which we believe of the three Persons individually, he would have been obliged to employ other methods of argument. As it is, he makes only one concession, in Chapter 23 of the *Proslogion*, where he describes how the highest good is equally Father, Son, and Holy Spirit:

Quod autem est singulus quisque, hoc est tota trinitas simul.[1]

('What each is individually, the whole Trinity at once is, too.') Here, although he refers to the Son as the Word, and the Spirit as the Love of Father and Son, he does not attempt to distinguish between them. The burden of the chapter is their unity in goodness. Elsewhere in his writings, where he does look at the Persons of the Trinity individually, Anselm is indeed driven to adapt his methods of argument to suit the problems of discussing three related items at a time. His habit there is to discuss the Persons two at a time (*bini considerentur*), and so to demonstrate for one 'pair' of Persons what must follow for any combination of two, or for all three.[2] But here he wants to restrict himself to what can be made plain by using a single axiom. If that axiom is indeed something like '$a + x$ is greater than a', then it is easy enough to see why it could not be extended to encompass demonstrations of the distinctions between the Persons.

Here may lie the answer to an important question which the mode of argument in the *Proslogion* arises: why, if Anselm has here discovered for himself a wholly original method of demonstration, does he not develop it in later works, and apply it to other problems? It may be that he felt that he had formulated, not a universally applicable principle, but—as he clearly

[1] S 1.117.16–17.
[2] I have looked at some examples of the way in which Anselm does this in 'The use of technical terms of mathematics in the writings of St. Anselm', *Studia Monastica*, 18 (1976), 67–76.

states—a principle which would enable him to show three things: that God exists; that he is the highest good, and needs nothing else to make him so; that he is whatever else we believe about the divine substance. It is, in other words, an axiom of limited but precise application which Anselm has in mind, and he does not envisage the development of a whole axiomatic method from it. This is entirely in keeping with his feeling that he had made a 'discovery', something unique in his own experience and, of its essence, not something which could be modified or extended. And yet again, it would seem very probable that the writing of the *Monologion* had helped Anselm to find his own way through Augustine's thoughts on the 'trinity in the mind of man', so that he was free to look at the singularity of God in the *Proslogion* unencumbered by undigested reflections.

Augustine's advice in Book X of the *De Trinitate* is to examine one's own mind, so as to find in it pointers to thoughts about God. We have already seen how Anselm does exactly this in the *Monologion*. He calls the mind a mirror of God:

in quo speculetur ut ita dicam imaginem eius,[1]

('in which is seen, so to speak, his image'). The closeness of Anselm's view to that of Augustine is evident enough at several points in the *Monologion*'s treatment of the Trinity.[2] The Word, *locutio*, and the Love of God, especially, are central to Anselm's discussion. In omitting discussions of Trinitarian doctrine in the *Proslogion*, Anselm might seem to be cutting himself off from further consideration of these notions which he found so helpful in his attempts to reach some understanding of the mind of God. But both *locutio* and *amor* have a place in the *Proslogion*, in the devotional passages. There Anselm himself speaks directly to God, and in this way he presents his own mind to him, face to face. In the chapters on the fullness of joy which awaits the Christian soul, Anselm speaks of loving and understanding as natural concomitants of that joy:

Utique tantum gaudebunt, quantum amabunt; tantum amabunt, quantum cognoscent. Quantum te cognoscent, domine, tunc, et quantum te amabunt?[3]

[1] S 1.77.27–8.
[2] S 1.63–4, cf. Augustine *De Trinitate*, Book X, and parts of Book IX, for a slightly different image.
[3] S 1.121.9–13.

('Then indeed they will rejoice as they love; they will love as
they understand. How well will they then know you, Lord, and
how much will they love you?') He has set the imagery of the
memory, understanding and love, which in man imitates the
divine Trinity, in the context of prayer. Trinitarian meditation
in the *Monologion* has not, then, simply been left out of the
Proslogion; but it has been transferred from the realm of argument to that of prayer or meditation proper.

This is entirely in accord with the shift of emphasis between
the writing of one work and the writing of the other. In the
Monologion, Christ himself is looked at as *intelligentia* or *locutio* or
verbum, the intellectual principle, and the Father as *memoria*,
and the Holy Spirit as *amor*.[1] The reader is encouraged to look
up towards God, even if he can do so only by looking at the
mirror in his own mind. But in the *Proslogion* the intensity of
the inward meditation is heightened. The reader is to attain a
far more direct view of God by looking harder at the principles
of his own understanding, and by doing it in a mood of passionate love and longing brought about by the preliminary meditation. And because, in the *Proslogion*, the reader is to build
upon his own understanding and his own power of feeling, it is
not surprising that *memoria* has a far greater place in the *Monologion*, and virtually no place at all in the *Proslogion*. It is
through the Son and the Spirit that God comes to man, and it
is perfectly logical for Anselm to encourage his readers to use
those powers of understanding and love which he feels represent
these two Persons of the Trinity, in order to approach the Father
who cannot be so directly experienced in himself. Throughout
the *Proslogion*, in fact, he addresses himself to God (the Father
especially, perhaps) through the twin powers of understanding
(in the passages of argument) and love (in the devotional
passages), which he discovers in himself. Such a rationalization
of his explorations in the *Monologion* gives not only a literary
unity to this blend of stylistically distinct elements, but also a
conceptual unity of a kind Augustine would have recognized,
embracing both thought and feeling.

We are coming close to the question of the balance between
faith and reason which has so often been raised in connection
with the *Proslogion*'s *credo ut intelligam*.[2] If we set the *fides quaerens*

---

[1] S 1.63-4 ff.   [2] S 1.100.18.

intellectum of the *Proslogion* beside what the *Monologion* has to say on faith, there would appear to have been some alteration of emphasis before the writing of the *Proslogion*. In Chapter 64 of the *Monologion*, Anselm gives an account of the way in which he thinks faith should operate upon divine mysteries:

Videtur mihi huius tam sublimis rei secretum transcendere omnem intellectus aciem humani.[1]

('It seems to me that so sublime a thing is hidden beyond the reach of the utmost keenness of the human intellect.') Anselm pleads that a man should be satisfied if his reason will bring him to the point where he is sure of the truth of his belief, even if he cannot see how it may be so:

Sufficere namque debere existimo rem incomprehensibilem indaganti, si ad hoc ratiocinando pervenerit ut eam certissime esse cognoscat, etiamsi penetrare nequeat intellectu quomodo ita sit.[2]

By the use of his reason a man is to come up, as it were, against the 'underside' of the fact of the highest good. As Anselm himself points out, nothing is so incomprehensible as that which is 'above' the level of everything else:

Quid autem tam incomprehensibile, tam ineffabile, quam id quod super omnia est?[3]

Reason has gone as far as it can, and faith must take the last step of acceptance. But in the devotional passages of the *Proslogion* faith sets the pace and gives a sense of direction, and reason is driven before it until it does arrive at 'understanding', in some measure. Yet even here, the *altitudo*—quite literally the 'height' of God—is a repeated theme.[4] It would be a distortion of Anselm's intention to suggest that he felt that by this means he would come to understand fully what he sought to grasp. Yet faith does seem to play a more active part in the process of investigation in the *Proslogion*; its contribution is at any rate more freely acknowledged.

Anselm has here, yet again, looked in the *Proslogion* at something he has already said in the *Monologion*, and he has, again, given it pride of place in a way that the *Monologion*'s treatment does not allow him to do. That which is higher than all things lies at the boundary of our understanding. So we cannot fully understand it, and we must be content to know that it is there.

[1] S 1.74.30–1.   [2] S 1.75.1–3.   [3] S 1.75.6–7.   [4] S 1.97–100.

But that boundary itself provides Anselm with the central thought of Chapters 2–4 of the *Proslogion*. Its very existence provides us with a means of describing, even of defining, the idea of God. Anselm sees no reason to elaborate an explanation of why we can, mentally, reach up just to touch the idea of God, but not to embrace it, and why we can just touch the idea, rather than fall just short of it. Either alternative, as Anselm so often demonstrates in other arguments-by-elimination, would be improper. If the idea of God were partly within our grasp, he would not be 'above' everything. If anything lay between God and the ordered hierarchy of goods the human mind can recognize, something[1] would exist which did not proceed directly or indirectly from God. Even though Anselm does not state this argument explicitly, it can be reconstructed from the earlier arguments of the *Monologion*.[2] It is therefore essential to our powers of understanding that God should be regarded as coming to meet us precisely at the limit of our understanding, and that we should recognize that where understanding ends, God is to be found. Anselm did not envisage this as a thought too abstract for any of his readers. Those of 'limited ability'[3] may arrive at it by climbing up the ladder of their experiences of what is good or excellent. Some may find it more helpful to look directly at the implications of the idea that 'God is that than which nothing greater can be thought', as Anselm leads them to do in the *Proslogion*, beginning, in a sense, from the other end.

To say that the *Monologion* and the *Proslogion* are complementary is not to suggest that one cannot be read without the other. But if we regard the *Monologion* as presenting a 'keyed' surface, with some tall excrescences and some short, we shall generally find that the companion surface of the *Proslogion* has interstices which match it exactly. They make, when put together, a distinct whole. What, then, was it that Anselm felt that he had to add to the *Monologion* to complete the task he had begun there? It was certainly not material to meet Lanfranc's objections.[4] The *Proslogion* would seem rather less likely to have

---

[1] Even if that were a 'nothing'.
[2] The method and the substance of some of these have already been given.
[3] S 1.7.9–12.
[4] Anselm's Letter 77, S 3.199–200, is a reply to Lanfranc's objections.

pleased him than the *Monologion*, except perhaps for the devotional passages. Nor was Anselm left with the kind of feeling of dissatisfaction which led him to take the *De Incarnatione Verbi* apart and reconstruct it with additions, rather than write a fresh defence, when he found that the first version had not silenced Roscelin.[1] Perhaps what Anselm felt when he had finished the *Monologion* was a sense of loss because he had finished a book which it had given him pleasure to write. This was his first book. It would be natural enough to look about him for a new project, while running over the old one in his mind, reviewing it, bringing together strands of thought which he had not seen in juxtaposition before. As his understanding of what he had discussed there matured, Anselm perhaps reached a point where he felt that he could, indeed, write the *Monologion* again and recapture his former pleasure in it; but in doing so, he does not repeat himself.[2] He reconsiders the subject-matter of the *Monologion* from a completely fresh angle of approach. Matters which had required demonstration in the *Monologion* could now be taken as 'given', and Anselm was able to discover the single unifying principle he sought because he was now in a position to see a whole series of statements about the divine nature as self-evident, or at least as principles based upon what is self-evident.

The *Proslogion* is partly at least an exercise in generalization from the particular and detailed arguments of the *Monologion*. It is certainly an expression of Anselm's new degree of emancipation from his sources—an emancipation he could perhaps have hoped to achieve only by writing the *Monologion* first. Afterwards, when in later works he returns to borrow something from Augustine or from his secular studies, he does so as one returning to a well-organized repository; in the *Monologion* the influence of Augustine and the *Categories* tradition in particular seems far more recent.

Anselm nowhere indicates that he wished the *Monologion* to be destroyed, or that copies of it should be withdrawn from circulation—although he does express anxiety lest it be mis-

---

[1] The two versions (there may have been more) are edited separately by Schmitt, S 1 and 2.

[2] Anselm's capacity for avoiding repetition of matters established in his earlier works is a marked feature of his writings.

understood.[1] He evidently regarded it as more than a preliminary exercise, personally necessary to his own development. It succeeds not only in making the drift of Anselm's ideas plain to himself, but also, as he hoped, in being of use to others, too, especially if they were to derive the greatest possible illumination from the *Proslogion*. Though he mentions only the *Proslogion* to Hugh, the Hermit of Caen, he sent both works to Hugh, Archbishop of Lyons.[2] They are bracketed together in the *De Incarnatione Verbi*.[3] It was the *Monologion*, not the *Proslogion*, which furnished material for further discussions in later works.[4] The *Monologion* is far from being an apprentice-piece. But in the interest it aroused in contemporaries and in almost every subsequent century, the *Proslogion* takes precedence over it.

Anselm himself saw the two works as a pair. That is beyond dispute. But it seems that he may also have seen them as forming a single whole, to be read as he wrote them, in order. His reader, like Anselm himself, finds the way being cleared of those necessary but digressive discussions of which Augustine is so fond, so that it becomes possible to look with a less clouded vision upon the object of Anselm's own gazing and striving. Anselm himself evidently felt that at last, in the *Proslogion*, he had finished his task, and that his insight would take him no further.

The temptation to accede uncritically to his arguments becomes the greater if we attempt, as we have been doing, to enter into Anselm's own mind. There everything has been agreeably arranged. Yet Anselm himself urged his readers to withdraw into their own minds and not to accompany him into his. He expected his arguments to be equally convincing to others because they would find the furnishings of their own minds much the same. This was a first principle of his thought at an abstract level, but in practical terms it was one he was forced to modify in later years. He would have found it impossible to write the *Proslogion* in the 1090s, partly because he himself had changed and developed, but also because he had learnt that other men's minds did not always accord with his.

[1] In Letter 100, to Hugh, Archbishop of Lyons, for example, S 3.231.11–19.
[2] Letters 100, 109, 112.   [3] S 2.20.16–21.
[4] S 1.176.6–19, 190.13–15, in the *De Veritate*, the debt is explicitly acknowledged.

3

THE REPLY TO THE FOOL

i: *The Form*

ANSELM had in Gaunilo, the author of the *Reply on behalf of the Fool*, not a dissenter from the fact of God's existence, but a philosophical opponent who made just the kind of attack on the validity of the argument which so many later scholars have made. Yet Gaunilo freely concedes the value of the work as a whole. His objection is to be found at the end of an appreciable proportion of the manuscripts of the *Proslogion*.[1] It was placed there on Anselm's own instructions.[2] The very fact that it was preserved only as an *addendum* in this way indicates that Anselm himself may have felt that the value of his *Proslogion*, taken as a whole, was in no way diminished by the fact that it was possible for the validity of its central argument to be challenged. Admittedly he did not accept that Gaunilo's challenge had any force; but in arranging for the response and his own reply to be copied with the *Proslogion* he conceded that the attack might be made again, and that the validity of the argument, if not the argument itself, might require defence.

This distinction between value and validity which is implicit in Gaunilo's reaction to the work, recalls Ritschl's remarks on the special problems of epistemology raised by 'religious knowledge'. 'We have . . . to distinguish between *concomitant* and *independent* value-judgements.'[3] His point is that theology has to do, inescapably, with knowledge that involves the knower personally, while, broadly speaking, philosophy is concerned with disinterested knowledge. As a philosopher, Gaunilo could attack the validity of the ontological argument, while as a theologian he was prepared to accept its value.

It is worth asking why Anselm allowed Gaunilo's objections to be preserved. He could simply have suppressed his quibbles,

---

[1] See the *sigla* to Schmitt's edition of the *Objection and Response*.

[2] VA, p. 31, I, xix.

[3] A. Ritschl, *The Christian Doctrine of Justification and Reconciliation*, tr. H. R. Mackintosh and A. B. Macaulay (Edinburgh 1900), p. 204.

once he had satisfied himself that they possessed no force. The general tenor of his reply is that he has already, in the arguments of the first chapters of the *Proslogion*, blocked those objections at exactly the points where they seek to gain entry. Yet he went to the trouble of making sure that they survived, in a way which would guarantee that they would last as long as the *Proslogion* itself.

It may be that Anselm was delighted to discover that he had a reader who had so thoroughly grasped what he had said that he had been able to formulate objections which met his points at a level which did them justice. Gaunilo's remarks have a character of their own. No one else whose conversations with Anselm have been recorded could match him. It is doubtful whether even Boso could, unaided, have conceived such weighty objections. His understanding had been developed in discussions with Anselm himself, while Gaunilo appears to have thought out his point of view independently. There is a meeting of minds here. In replying to this able spokesman for the Fool, Anselm has replied to one of the most forceful objections which could be put in the terms available to his contemporaries. He may even have added the objection and response with a certain pride in the reaction his work had caused. He was sufficiently pleased to thank Gaunilo both for his praise and for his criticism at the end of his own reply.

This picture of Anselm pleased and flattered by the attention his treatise has received remains attractive, but something he himself says perhaps carries more weight. In later works it becomes increasingly common for him to provide explanations for points which cause special difficulties. In the *Cur Deus Homo* he begins by listing the objections of the unbelievers and replying to them.[1] In the *De Conceptu Virginali* he inserts a short digression to meet a common difficulty.[2] Here, in the reply to the Fool, he says that he will meet some of Gaunilo's objections because some readers find them forceful, and are therefore likely to be misled by them, although for Anselm himself they carry no weight at all:

Qualia vero sint et alia quae mihi obicis pro insipiente, facile est deprehendere vel parum sapienti, et ideo id ostendere supersedendum existimaveram. Sed quoniam audio

---

[1] S 2.50–9.   [2] S 2.147.10–11.

quibusdam ea legentibus aliquid contra me valere videri, paucis de illis commemorabo.[1] ('It is things like this, and others, that you propose to me as objections on behalf of the Fool. They are easy for even a man of little wisdom to put aside, and so I should reckon it unnecessary to show how. But since I hear that they seem to some of those who read them to carry some weight against me, I will say a little about them.') It is interesting to speculate as to the route by which Gaunilo's objection had reached Anselm, and as to the identity of these 'others' who had been reading the objections and finding them valid. They may have been Anselm's own monks at Bec. Whatever their identity, they provide Anselm with his only stated reason for having Gaunilo's words and his own reply copied at the end of the *Proslogion*; Anselm wanted to be sure that no one was misled, so he incorporated the objection into the original work. He thus made it impossible for it to circulate separately in any form which might be damaging to the less well–informed reader.

But that 'incorporation' takes a very singular form. In the *Cur Deus Homo*, Anselm anticipates as many *objectiones infidelium* as he can, but even so, he is obliged from time to time to integrate a *discursus* into the sequence of his argument.[2] The structure of the work as a whole is sufficiently flexible to permit such additions. In still later works, an objection and its counter-argument usually falls into place without Anselm's feeling any need to explain that he thinks a special place must be made for it, as he is still careful to do in the *Cur Deus Homo*. In the *De Concordia*, for example, Anselm merely remarks that he anticipates an objection at a certain point, and deals with it as he goes along.[3] There, is, in other words, a steady and perceptible change in Anselm's methods of integrating objection and response into the course of his arguments. In the *Proslogion* only has he chosen to leave an objection standing awkwardly outside the treatise, and to allow his own reply to stand, equally obtrusively, as an appendix to the work.

This was of course an objection raised after the completion of the work, whereas the objections which are taken in in the

---

[1] S 1.134.20–4.   [2] e.g. S 2.74–84.
[3] Such anticipated objections are indicated by expressions such as: *at inferunt; si dicitur; sed dices mihi; forsitan dicis.*

course of the composition of other treatises and settled there and
then were already to hand when Anselm was writing. Yet there
is every indication that he felt the *Proslogion*'s structure could
not be made to accommodate the points which Gaunilo raises.
The literary and conceptual unity it possesses as it stands would
have been entirely disrupted, if Anselm had enlarged the elegantly compressed chapters which contain the argument for the
existence of God so as to meet Gaunilo's questions. In any case,
since he felt that Gaunilo's words were founded on misunderstanding, to introduce them into the treatise would have been
to give the whole glad affirmation of the central chapters a
negative cast, and to take away that sharp contrast with the
note of hungry longing for understanding which Anselm had
taken such care to create in the first chapter of the *Proslogion*.

That is not to say that Anselm intends only to disparage
Gaunilo's comments. He does say that it seems to him that even
a rank beginner in the art of argument should be able to see
that Gaunilo is wrong:

> qui vel parvam scientiam disputandi argumentandique
> attigerunt.[1]

But in view of his generally amicable tone throughout the reply
to the Fool, we cannot suppose that he intends to make Gaunilo
feel uncomfortable. He has, after all, paid him the very considerable compliment of taking his comments seriously and at
some length, and, finally, he has given Gaunilo the doubtful
pleasure of seeing his words added to the end of the *Proslogion*
(if only in order to be refuted).

The overall impression the whole makes upon the reader is a
genial one. Anselm cannot think that any true Christian[2] could
find his faith diminished by the *Proslogion* arguments, even if he
is not appreciably strengthened in it. The strongest argument
he has to offer against Gaunilo's objection that he cannot in
fact think at all of that than which nothing greater can be
thought, is that his very faith makes nonsense of his claim:

> Quod quam falsum sit, fide et conscientia tua pro firmissimo
> utor argumento.[3]

('I use as the strongest argument that that is utterly false, your
own faith and conscience.') In other words, as a Christian,
Gaunilo cannot claim that he is unable to conceive of God.

[1] S 1.136.24–5.   [2] S 1.130.4–5.   [3] S 1.130.15–16.

Anselm had always intended that the *Proslogion*'s arguments should be read in an attitude of faith, and he had gone to some trouble in Chapter 1 to evoke appropriate emotions in his readers, to make sure that each of them could say, as he read, *credo ut intelligam*.[1] His own confidence is not at all shaken by Gaunilo's response, and Gaunilo himself is evidently not a man whose faith is at risk. What has taken place is a stimulating exchange of ideas. Anselm has recorded it for future readers, just in case others take what has been said in a way it was never intended to be taken, as a serious onslaught on the fact of the existence of God.

What we can glean from Anselm's own comments on this appendix to the *Proslogion*, then, suggests that he saw no need to re-work the first chapters of the treatise and disrupt the unity he had achieved there, but that he felt it worthwhile to ensure that Gaunilo's exact words and his own replies were not lost. It is unlikely that he considered the possibility that Gaunilo might inadvertently have encouraged later readers to give so much prominence to the first chapters by focusing attention upon them, that the work would rarely be studied as a whole. Gaunilo concedes that the rest of the piece seems to him magnificently written:

> Cetera libelli illius tam veraciter et tam praeclare sunt magnificeque disserta, tanta denique referta utilitate et pii ac sancti affectus intimo quodam odore fragrantia.[2]

('Other points in the treatise are so truly and excellently and brilliantly handled, and so full of profit and so fragrant with the pervasive scent of devout and holy feeling . . .'.) But this final compliment does little to redress the balance, largely because it is tucked away at the end. Anselm's *Response*, then, meets objections to only a small part of the whole argument of the *Proslogion*. It has not prompted him to re-think more than one small section, but perhaps partly because of Gaunilo's work, that section has become by far the most fully-studied.

ii: *The Matter*

So much for Anselm's attitude to the writing of this appendix; but there is something to be discovered here, too, of his developing attitudes towards some of the ideas which had seemed, at

[1] S 1.100.18.   [2] S 1.129.20–5.

the time of the writing of the *Proslogion*, so finished and contained. The most important of these is the statement that God
is a special case. This is a principle so self-evident in terms of
Anselm's world-picture that it scarcely seemed to him to require statement in the initial formulation of the *Proslogion*
argument. In later works it becomes a frequently-used device
for demonstrating why, although all other men are subject to
Original Sin, Christ was not, why God cannot lie, and so on.
Under Gaunilo's prompting, Anselm states clearly that the
force of his argument for the existence of God lies in the fact
that only God can be spoken of in the way he has proposed:

> Fidens loquor, quia si quis invenerit mihi aut re ipsa aut sola
> cogitatione existens praeter 'quo maius cogitari non possit',
> cui aptare valeat conexionem huius meae argumentationis.[1]

('I say with confidence that if anyone finds for me anything,
whether it exists in reality or only in thought, to which the
sequence of my argumentation can be applied, except for that
than which a greater cannot be thought . . .'). There is nothing
new in Anselm's thought here, but he has been obliged, by the
failure of one of his readers to understand him as he intended,
to state a principle he had thought it sufficient to leave implicit.
He was to fall into the habit of doing so more and more, as he
went on to write works especially designed for the theologically
less well-informed reader.[2]

The notions of beginning and end and the relation of time and
place to our idea of God had been discussed at some length in
the *Monologion*,[3] and rather more briefly in the *Proslogion*.[4]
Anselm comes back to them here, in order to apply them, as he
had not done before, quite explicitly to the proof of the existence
of God.[5] This, too, he had not thought it necessary to state
clearly before, but in doing so here he gives himself material for
further reflection on time and place in the *De Incarnatione Verbi*
and elsewhere.[6]

Anselm's methods, too, take on a character more in keeping
with those of the *De Veritate*, the *De Libertate Arbitrii*, the *De Casu
Diaboli* and the *De Grammatico*, than with the arguments of the

---

[1] S 1.133.6–9, cf. S 1.134.16–17.
[2] See the chapters on the *Cur Deus Homo* for a fuller discussion of this point.
[3] Chapters 18–24.   [4] Chapter 13, S 1.110–11.
[5] S 1.131–2.   [6] S 2.33–4.

Proslogion proper, as he undertakes a defence of his position against Gaunilo. He suggests, for example, rather teasingly, that it is perfectly possible even for a man who knows that he himself exists to think that he does not.[1] This device of putting a paradox before the reader reappears in the *De Veritate*: 'Why is it surprising if the same thing both ought and ought not to be?'[2] It is used in the *De Concordia* of apparent contradictories: *simul ponamus*[3] ('let us put it that both alike exist'). He takes up Gaunilo's point about *genus* and *species* with alacrity.[4] Throughout the *Response* he appeals to technical methods and terms of grammar and dialectic.

Most telling for the support it gives to the view that the *argumentum* of which Anselm speaks at the beginning of the *Proslogion*[5] is intended by him to refer specifically not to the whole argument of Chapters 2–4, but to the self-evident axiom which runs throughout the whole of the *Proslogion*'s sequence of argumentation, is the fact that he tends to speak of *argumentatio* here; he refers to the *conexio*, the stringing together of his argumentation.[6] He is discussing the whole extent of the sequence, not a single principle. Again, it appears that technical exactitude, while by no means absent from the *Proslogion*, is allowed to appear undisguised in the *Response*, as it is in the other works written relatively soon after the completion of the *Proslogion*.

Gaunilo has himself, perhaps inadvertently, encouraged this tendency. He speaks of *voces*, or ordinary words, rather than of the *naturalia verba* to which Anselm must have intended his view of the way we think about God in the *Proslogion* to be referred.[7] Gaunilo's objections are founded upon his experience of ordinary usage: he speaks of thinking *secundum vocem*,[8] according to the word, not *secundum verbum*, in terms which make it plain that he means to refer to Boethian *voces*, conventional words. He goes on to speak of *litterarum sonus vel syllabarum*, 'the sound of the letters or syllables', of *vocis auditae significatio*,[9] 'the meaning of the word when it is heard'. He admits that he cannot apprehend

---

[1] S 1.134.7–8. [2] S 1.186.10. [3] S 2.246.2.
[4] S 1.126.31–127.2 and 137.11–12. [5] S 1.93.5 and 6.
[6] S 1.132.10, 133.8–9, S 1.93.5.
[7] Cf. Chapters 9 and 10 of the *Monologion* with Chapters 2–4 of the *Proslogion*. Anselm explains that we can think in ordinary words that God does not exist, but we cannot do so by direct apprehension (or *naturalia verba*), S 1.103.18–20.
[8] S 1.127.13. [9] S 1.127.15–17.

God directly, as Anselm suggests the reader should try to do, in both the *Monologion* and the *Proslogion*.[1] And yet the kind of apprehension Anselm demands as the very starting-point for his argument involves, *per definitionem*, that image or *verbum* which comes closest to a direct apprension of God within the limitations of the human mind. For Gaunilo, it is the special nature of the conception required which rules the argument out. For Anselm it is exactly that uniqueness which proves his case. Anselm has perhaps found Gaunilo's objections here of no account precisely because his own developed understanding of the nature of language, so fully set out in the *Monologion*, makes this no question at all for him. We do not know whether Gaunilo had read the *Monologion*. In any case, he has chosen to rest his case on a Boethian, rather than an Augustinian view of the roots of language.

This view is borne out by Gaunilo's assertion that there is, to him, something lacking in a conception arrived at by merely hearing a word for something, when that something is not known to the hearer by any other means:

> cum secundum vocem tantum auditam rem prorsus ignotam sibi conatur animus effingere.[2]

('When the mind tries to picture something hitherto unknown to it after hearing only the word for the thing'). Anselm had said something about this problem in the *Monologion*, not least in the passage where he points out that everything of which we have any inner picture has been present to actual experience either through some previous intuitive or sense-perception, or because an idea of it can be made up of the parts of familiar things.[3] Gaunilo is not, however, strictly speaking referring to the Augustinian and Anselmian notion that this very lack of capacity for thinking of something new demonstrates the dependence of the human mind upon the God who made it. Such a view would make the problem he has outlined a factor weighing in favour of the *Proslogion* argument, not against it. The fact that we cannot think of God because he lies at the limit of our understanding, except as the very thought which does lie at the limit of our understanding, is exactly what Anselm wants his readers to accept. If it were possible to understand the word for God fully, God would lie within the grasp of

[1] See p. 73, n. 7.   [2] S 1.128.6–7.   [3] S 1.26.3–22.

created beings, and he would be less than God. That is not perhaps to do full justice to Gaunilo. He is saying some very acute things,[1] and he has had his defenders. What is important for our purposes, however, is that he has parted company from Anselm's teaching in the *Monologion* on a critical point of technical vocabulary. He has consistently spoken of *voces*, ordinary words, without reference to the *naturalia verba* which are so crucial to Anselm's own thinking about the language in which we can talk of God.

The *Responsio*, then, shows us Anselm moving on, rather than going back over old ground in the terms he had used before. Gaunilo has prompted him to do so, and his own work upon whatever parts of the *Tres Tractatus* or the *De Grammatico* he may have already begun, would have encouraged him towards this plainer and more technically straightforward mode of demonstration. Where Anselm looks back to the *Monologion*, he does so as to something so firmly argued as to constitute a finished treatment. The same is true for his view of the *Proslogion*. And yet he is discovering new things to say about topics raised in both.

[1] Gaunilo states his objections very clearly, and makes an important preliminary *divisio*. S 1.125.

4

THE THREE TREATISES

i: *The writing of the* Tres Tractatus *and the* De Grammatico

DURING the decade after the *Proslogion* was finished, Anselm wrote three treatises which he regarded as a group, and the *De Grammatico* which he lists with the others in the Preface to the *De Veritate*, but which, he indicates, is a rather different kind of work.[1] For our purposes, too, the *De Grammatico* is something of an outsider.[2] It is evident that it belongs to a period of Anselm's life where his interest was engaged by some of the technical possibilities of grammar and dialectic, but his intention in writing it was merely to introduce the beginner to the study of dialectic; the other three works, the *De Veritate*, the *De Libertate Arbitrii*, and the *De Casu Diaboli*, have a further purpose. They are intended, Anselm says, to help those who wish to study Holy Scripture.[3] But all three bear the marks of Anselm's interest in the technical skills of the arts of language.

They were written in an order which cannot be determined, and at various times,[4] in response to the direct request of brothers and pupils of Anselm's who had found that the *Monologion* revealed difficulties which they had not perceived before. The impression they give is that they arise out of vigorous discussion. They are far more than academic exercises. Hugh of St. Victor describes a scene which cannot be much different from similar scenes in Anselm's community.

Once when I was sitting with my brothers and they were asking questions and I was answering them, many things had been put forward for discussion. At length our talk came to a point where we all began to sigh, and to wonder greatly at the instability and unquietness of the human heart.[5]

As a result of this discussion, his brothers asked Hugh to write them a book, and he composed the *De Arca Noë*. Unfortunately Eadmer was not at Bec at the time when Anselm was working

[1] S 1.173.2–8.
[2] See D. P. Henry, *A Commentary on the De Grammatico* (Dordrecht 1974) for details of his earlier work.
[3] S 1.173.2.   [4] S 1.173.3.   [5] PL, 176.617–18.

on the three treatises, and his account of their composition tells us nothing about the atmosphere in which they were produced.[1] He does describe Anselm in conversation on a number of occasions during the course of his biography and it is clear that Anselm, like Hugh, was in the habit of talking often and deeply with his monks. Like Hugh, he enjoyed the respect of affectionate pupils, who regarded him as exceptional in his powers of resolving theological difficulties. He met their uncertainties kindly and willingly.

At one level, then, we might say that the three treatises were written because Anselm was asked to write them. But that will not account for his choice of subject-matter among all the topics we must suppose his pupils to have raised; nor will it explain why he wrote only what he did, and why he wrote it during this period. It is usual to regard the *Proslogion* as the work in which Anselm reaches the high point of his philosophical penetration—in the argument or arguments of Chapters 2–4. Yet the *Proslogion* was only his second treatise. He was to go on writing for another thirty years, and we cannot regard those years as a period of declining powers. Despite what he himself seems to have felt to be the completeness of his achievement in the *Proslogion*, there were topics touched on there and in the *Monologion* which raised more questions for him and for others than he could settle in these two works. Ironically enough, the very compositions which had given him satisfaction because, taken together, they demonstrated all the essentials of Christian belief,[2] provided him with a means of approach to further discussions. For the most part—and this is in no way surprising—these treatises refer back to the *Monologion* rather than to the *Proslogion*. If we ask how Anselm was able to write a sequel to such a work as the *Proslogion*, the answer must be that he did not. He wrote, instead, a series of treatises which carry on the work of the *Monologion*, beginning, in the *De Veritate*, with a direct reference to a problem the book has suggested. He sets about explaining matters which he had treated to his own satisfaction in the *Monologion* in terms which it would be easier for beginners to grasp. In the process he discovers new issues of philosophical and theological interest to himself, and he is led on to consider them in their own right. If the treatises smack of

---

[1] VA, p. 28, I, xix.   [2] S 1.93.6–10.

the school textbook in a way that the *Monologion* and the *Proslogion* do not, they are none the less rich in philosophical insights for that.

It is difficult to assess the length of time this process took. We do not know how long a time elapsed between Anselm's completion of the *Monologion* and his pupils' being permitted to read it. The book would not have been entirely new to its first readers in any case. Anselm says at the beginning of the *Monologion* that he has been in the habit of discussing matters raised there with his pupils and brothers.[1] The monks of Bec had evidently been allowed to read it before it was sent to Lanfranc, since it was only the demand for more copies which prompted Anselm's appeal to his old master. The three treatises were probably put together in Anselm's mind over a considerable period, during which the *Monologion* itself, perhaps the *Proslogion* too, and the daily intercourse of the schoolroom, all contributed to the development of their final form. Some of the issues they raise may have been under discussion even before the *Monologion* was written. It seems more likely that some such continuous process as this gave rise to the three treatises, than that Anselm found himself facing the task of finding a subject for a new book after he had finished the *Proslogion* where he felt that he had made so complete a statement of his thought about God. Most probably he already had several points of departure to hand, and perhaps some parts of the three treatises were half-formed in his mind.

When the three treatises and the *De Grammatico* were finished, Anselm wrote a collective Preface setting them all in place. Its chief practical purpose was to instruct future copyists to follow a particular order in writing them out.[2] But the Preface also tells us that Anselm considered that the works possessed some unity. Although, as he says, they are united by no continuity of composition (*quamvis nulla continuatione dictaminis cohaereant*),[3] yet their subject-matter (*materia*)[4] and their identical treatment of the subject-matter in dialogue-form (*similitudo disputationis*),[5] makes it necessary for them to be written and read in a certain order. Apart from a likeness of form and style which makes all three treatises and the *De Grammatico*, too, suitable for teaching

---

[1] S 1.7.1–5.   [2] S 1.174.5–7.   [3] S 1.174.3–5.
[4] S 1.173.4.   [5] S 1.173.4.

purposes, it is the development of a single line of thought running through them which makes them one. This is the kind of
'order' Anselm perceives in the three treatises, and, we may
reasonably infer, the 'order' of his own thinking through of the
problem.

But there is something else to be deduced from the Preface of
much greater importance for the history of Anselm's own
thought. In the main body of the text, as we shall see, he refers
back in detail to the *Monologion*. But in the general Preface, he
says that all three treatises pertain to the study of Holy Scripture
(*pertinentes ad studium sacrae Scripturae*).[1] The exact sense in which
he intends this is never made clear. It is tempting to compare
Otloh of St. Emmeram's strictures on the uses and abuses of
grammatical and dialectical principles in the study of Holy
Scripture, in the Preface to his *Dialogus de Tribus Quaestionibus*.[2]
There, Otloh brings out into the open devices which Anselm
uses without acknowledging his debt to the study of the *artes*
in so many words. Otloh recognizes them for what they are, as
Anselm does only implicitly. The overall purpose of Anselm's
explanations throughout these works is to show the young
student of grammar and dialectic the right way to use his
technical skills. The nearest he comes to a straightforward
statement of his intention occurs in the *De Casu Diaboli*:

Vide ne ullatenus putes, cum in divinis libris legimus aut cum secundum
illos dicimus deum facere malum aut facere non esse, quia negem propter
quod dicitur, aut reprehendam quia ita dicitur. Sed non tantum debemus
inhaerere improprietati verborum veritatem tegenti, quantum inhiare
proprietati veritatis sub multimodo genere locutionum latenti.[3]

'Be sure you do not think when we read in Holy Scripture or when we say
according to Scripture that God makes evil or causes something not to be,
that I would deny what is said, or that I would reproach anyone for saying
so. But we ought not to cling firmly to the impropriety of expression which
disguises the truth, so much as to draw out the propriety of the truth which
lies hidden under so many forms of expression.'

Anselm is arguing that in order to understand Scripture clearly
and accurately, we must examine the ways in which words are
used there; for Anselm and his contemporaries that can only
mean that Scripture is to be subjected to analysis by such
technical means as the study of grammar and dialectic provides. While Otloh is arguing for great caution in the use of

[1] S 1.173.2.   [2] PL, 146.60–1.   [3] S 1.235.8–12.

such devices, Anselm is not advocating too free or careless a use, by any means, but only an informed attitude to the reading of the Bible and the development of an eye for words. He has not found it necessary to separate the study of the Bible from speculative theology in giving this advice.

This concern is indeed the common thread running through these treatises. Their subject-matter has a limited direct application to the study of specific passages of Scripture. Anselm quotes the Bible frequently, but chiefly for purposes of illustration, and not because he has set a passage before his readers for close analysis. The story of the Fall of Satan is not told in the Bible at all. Anselm is encouraging the student to develop habits of study which will stand him in good stead whenever he reads the Bible, to give him a generally applicable technique of analysis. It is in this strictly-defined sense that the treatises pertain to the study of Holy Scripture.

It was not a method Anselm intended to be employed by beginners only. He himself continues to use it throughout his writings, always maintaining a careful balance between the application of a technical principle and the danger of over-interpreting or bending the sense of Scripture to a special purpose. It is possible that he did not fully see the dangers inherent in the method, since he himself possessed so firm a grasp of the immovables in any argument that he was unlikely to be tempted to press a technical issue too far. He seems to have been surprised and even a little affronted, when Roscelin deliberately over-extended his analogy between the Trinity and the man who is *iustus, grammaticus* and *albus*.[1]

This process of development of a sequence of thought begun in the *Monologion* about the origins and functioning of language,[2] has probably, then, been given a certain direction by the particular questions of brother-monks, and by Anselm's own comprehensive grounding in the technicalities of the arts of the *trivium*.[3] But it follows naturally in any case upon the reflections of the *Monologion* about language at large. There, Anselm had remarked upon the fact that there are many languages in use among the races of mankind which differ in

[1] S 1.283.1–6.   [2] Ch. 10, S 1.24 ff.
[3] Beginning perhaps in Italy and certainly consolidated in the years at Bec under Lanfranc's tutelage.

their vocabulary from the great *naturalia verba* or universal images which make up the 'ultimate language' of God.[1] Now he looks more closely at some examples of words in ordinary language, and at the ways in which they function.

ii: *Talking about Truth*

The problems Anselm poses for himself in the three treatises are less grand and all-embracing than those he had dealt with in the *Monologion* and the *Proslogion*. For the moment, he has said all that he wants to say about God himself, but he has not finished discussing the uses of language in theology. A steady concentration upon the functioning of words in these works leads to two things: Anselm's methods of argument begin to develop increasing refinement, especially his definitional method. Nowhere else does he explicitly discuss the use of definition quite as he does in the *De Veritate*.[2] In other words, he sees language as a vehicle of discussion, as well as an object of discussion. Secondly, he examines the technical knowledge of the functioning of language with which his study of grammar and dialectic has provided him, so as to see what further uses it may be put to, beyond those suggested by Boethius. In this way he develops a theory of ordinary language to balance the views put forward in the *Monologion* about *naturalia verba* or universal ideas.

He moves, in pursuit of these objectives, from a consideration of truth (in relation to words and to things and in its essence) to some treatment of 'ought' problems. Then he examines the relation between truth and rightness and righteousness (or justice). This leads, in the *De Libertate Arbitrii*, to a consideration of righteousness in relation to free will, grace, predestination and divine foreknowledge, sin and temptation. The *De Casu Diaboli* works out the implications of these matters for the Fall of Satan and incidentally for the Fall of Adam, and it contains a discussion of the nature of evil. Throughout these discussions Anselm brings technical language and technical principles to bear.

He does so, however, in a manner which shows that his thought in the three treatises reflects only a shift of emphasis,

---

[1] S 1.25.12–13.   [2] S 1.176.21, S 1.191.1–24.

not a thoroughgoing reappraisal of his earlier views about
language. When he discusses the nature of evil, he gives a good
deal of space to the problem Augustine raises in the *De Magistro*:
if every meaningful term (*nomen significativum*) must, by definition, have a meaning, an actual *res* to which it refers, what are
we to say of the word *malum* or of the word *nihil*? If 'nothing'
signifies as it should, it signifies nothing, and so it seems that
there is no *res* to which it refers. If evil, too, is nothing, as
Augustine believes (and Anselm agrees with him), the word
malum, too, must be meaningless, in the sense that we cannot
point to the thing it signifies.[1] When Anselm discusses the
abstract concepts which form his subject-matter in the three
treatises, he does so in ways which indicate his continued
awareness that the nub of the problem of language lies in the
manner in which words are linked with *res*. The idea of *veritas*
is something which can be perceived only directly, by intuition,
in Anselm's view. We label it with a Latin word, a *nomen
significativum* or *vox significativa*, so that we can talk about it. But
however far we refine the language available to us for discussion of truth, our perception of the nature of truth involves
naturalia verba, the God-given 'words' of the mind, which constitute universally recognizable principles. Anselm never
entirely separates his technical treatment of language in these
treatises from these prior considerations. Indirectly, if not
directly, he is still talking about God.

   The notion of 'truth' picks up a number of thoughts which
Anselm had developed so far and no further in the *Monologion*.
The very posing of the problem by the *discipulus* of the *De Veritate*
recalls strikingly the question raised at the beginning of the
Monologion: since there are so many goods, are we to believe
that each has its own goodness, or are they all good because
they share in some common goodness?[2] In the *De Veritate* we
have:

> Quoniam deum veritatem esse credimus, et veritatem in
> multis aliis dicimus esse, vellem scire an ubicumque veritas
> dicitur, deum eam esse fateri debeamus.[3]

('Since we believe that God is truth, and we say that there is
truth in many other things, I should like to know whether we
ought to say that wherever we speak of truth, that truth is

[1] S 1.246–51.   [2] S 1.14.7–9.   [3] S 1.176.4–6.

God.') The difference in the posing of the two problems lies in the fact that in the *De Veritate*, we are directed to think about the special difficulties of 'talking about' the truth, of using words for the truth, rather than about the nature of the abstract notion of truth itself. The distinction is chiefly one of emphasis, since it rapidly becomes clear that Anselm and his pupil are very much interested in the nature of this 'common factor' of truth itself. But that change of emphasis reflects Anselm's new concern with problems of language and expression of a more or less technical kind.

Anselm never forgets the *res* which lies behind the *verbum*. But here he tries to come at an understanding of the *res* by examining closely our conventional usages of the *verbum*, the actual word or *vox significativa*, *veritas*. After quoting the passage from the *Monologion* which has caused him difficulty,[1] the pupil says, 'Therefore I hope to learn a definition of truth from you.'[2] A definition must be framed in words. Besides, definition was one of the standard procedures of elementary dialectic,[3] and in the course of the three treatises, it proves to be a favourite method of Anselm's of resolving problems of meaning. What is more, the pupil makes what may be a brief pun, before he introduces the quotation from the *Monologion* which helps to encourage the reader to think firstly of 'truth of utterance'. 'For you, too, in your *Monologion* demonstrate through the truth of a saying.'[4] Our attention is thus directed from the first towards the particular difficulties we encounter when we try to speak about truth in connection with sayings, or with any kind of verbal expression.

Anselm seems to have chosen truth as his example, from among all the attributes of God considered in the *Monologion*,[5] precisely because the most natural and immediate sense which comes to mind is, as he says, truth of utterance: 'For everyone talks about the truth of meaning but few consider the truth which is in the essence of things.'[6] Anselm never inadvertently

---

[1] S 1.176.8–19.   [2] S 1.176.19–20.

[3] See the work of Marius Victorinus on Definition, which is printed in PL, 64.891–910, among Boethius' treatises, for a convenient introduction to the topics raised in this connection in Anselm's day. See, too, L. M. de Rijk, 'On the Curriculum of the Arts of the Trivium at St. Gall from *c.* 850–*c.* 1000', *Vivarium*, 1 (1963), 35–86; and P. Hadot, *Marius Victorinus* (Paris 1971).

[4] S 1.176.6–7.   [5] S 1.29.30–3.   [6] S 1.188.28–9.

separates truth of utterance from truth of signification, that is, from the question of the meaning of the utterance.[1] He has moved here into a new and larger area of discussion of language-problems. In continuing and expanding what he has said about language in the *Monologion*, he proceeds from a consideration of single words and their relation to single *res*, or things, in order to look at whole statements, propositions, sayings or utterances, from *voces*, *nomina*, *verba*, to *enuntiatio* and *propositio*. The progression was natural enough. It is exactly the move Aristotle makes from speaking of *voces* to discussion of *enuntiationes*.[2] Anselm would have been encouraged by his training in dialectic to follow much the same line of thought, just as he would have been led by the same means to think about the signification, not only of single words, but of whole statements.

Perhaps because even a beginner in dialectical studies would recognize the technical term *enuntiatio*, and understand how we often use truth and falsehood of propositions, Anselm makes the pupil of the dialogue take this as a starting-point for discussions which will both meet his own needs and provide Anselm himself with a congenial line of development of his earlier thoughts about words:

> Quaeramus ergo primum quid sit veritas in enuntiatione, quoniam hanc saepius dicimus veram vel falsam.[3]

('Let us then first ask what is truth in a saying, since we often call a saying true or false.') He immediately tries to connect the *enuntiatio* or statement with the *res* to which it refers. A statement is true, the pupil claims, when what it speaks of exists (*quando est quod enuntiat*). Master and pupil are embroiled at once in a considerable philosophical problem. This is no technical restatement of Boethius' commentary on the *De Interpretatione*. The thing signified, for all that it exists, cannot in itself constitute the truth of the proposition. Nothing is true unless it participates in the truth (*nisi participando veritatem*) but the thing which is spoken of is not itself 'in' the saying:

> res vero enuntiata non est in enuntiatione vera.

So the *res* itself cannot be the truth, nor is truth to be found

---

[1] S 1.178, *passim*.

[2] C. Meiser edits both versions of Boethius' commentaries on the *De Interpretatione* where Aristotle begins with this discussion (Leipzig 1877). Anselm most probably knew of the Aristotelian treatment through his reading of Boethius.

[3] S 1.177.6–7.

within the saying itself (*ipsa oratione*).[1] We may, on the contrary ask 'when' a statement is true,[2] as though it may on occasion not be true, even if it is *sometimes* true. The furthest we may go, it seems, is to say that if there is truth in the *res*, that truth may confer truth in its turn upon the *enuntiatio*; the truth of the *res* may be said to be the cause of the truth of the saying.[3] None of this applies to the *naturalia verba* of the *Monologion*, which refer to eternally existing—and therefore eternally true—ideas in the mind of God.[4] But as soon as we begin to make statements in ordinary language about the ephemeral objects of the created world it becomes necessary to separate 'truth of essence' (*veritas essentiae rerum*)[5] from truth of *enuntiatio*, truth of utterance. Anselm is thus clearing up a difficult point for himself, as well as helping his pupil to define 'truth' itself.

He now confronts the question of signification directly. We might enquire whether the truth lies in the *oratio* or in its meaning, or in the components of its definition:

> Vide ergo an ipsa oratio aut eius significatio aut aliquid eorum quae sunt in definitione enuntiationis, sit quod quaeris.[6]

('See therefore whether the saying itself, or its meaning, or any of the things which are in its definition, is [the truth] you seek.') The pupil concedes that truth cannot lie in any of these, since these are all constant, and we have already agreed that a statement is not necessarily always true.[7] Anselm goes on to develop the notion of signification in particular, and to speak of correct or true signification, common usage, and a variety of other principles of considerable importance in later works.[8] In yet another echo of the *Monologion*, he reminds his readers that all sorts of signs, as well as conventional words, may be used to signify.[9] The ramifications of these discussions would detain us too long here; but perhaps enough has been said to indicate that when Anselm uses the problems posed by truth of *enuntiatio* as a preliminary method of approach to the task of defining truth

---

[1] S 1.177.13–19.   [2] S 1.177.9.   [3] S 1.177.18.
[4] *Monologion*, 9–11, S 1.24–6.   [5] S 1.185.7.   [6] S 1.177.20–1.   [7] S 1.178.1–3.
[8] S 1.178 and S 1.179.10–28. On signification in general, see LA, *passim*.
[9] S 1.180.2–3. There is an interesting reference to *loquela digitorum* which recalls the Pseudo-Bede treatise on counting on the fingers which is printed in PL, 90; Anselm's contemporary, Ralph of Laon, includes in his treatise on the abacus, a section on *loquela digitorum*.

which his pupil has set him, he does so for a double reason. Firstly, he himself is interested, both as a philosopher and as a theologian, in the functioning of words and statements; and secondly, every pupil in the school at Bec would have been familiar with the elements of grammar and dialectic, and so he, too, would feel himself to be on home ground.[1]

Next Anselm extends his investigations into other areas where, he asserts, we commonly say that something is true or false. Some of these usages now ring strangely. He looks at truth of thought (*cogitatio*, *opinio*), truth of will, truth of natural and non-natural actions,[2] and so on. As he goes on, he develops further the ideas on which he has begun to work in connection with truth of *enuntiatio*, partly no doubt so as to give firmness and coherence to his sequence of argumentation, but also because he himself expected the same, or very similar, principles to apply to the analysis of *res* as to *verba*. If all truths participate in Truth itself,[3] it would be absurd to suggest that we may profitably look for quite different kinds of truth in words and in things.

iii: *The Place of the Three Treatises*

The *De Veritate* and its fellows hold a position among Anselm's works which has not always been fully appreciated. So temptingly full are they of technical terms and technical devices that they have become something of a happy hunting ground for those in search of the sources of Anselm's technical skills of argument. The studies of D. P. Henry in particular have made an immense contribution to our understanding of these matters.[4] But perhaps it is time to consider the place of the three treatises and the *De Grammatico* in the overall development of Anselm's thought, and of his interests (with the reservation that in the *De Grammatico* Anselm avoids any direct confrontation of the special difficulties of talking about God). It becomes increasingly clear that when he wrote the *De Veritate*, the *De Libertate*

---

[1] 'Every pupil' in Lanfranc's day perhaps. It is difficult to assess how much teaching of the elements of grammar and dialectic Anselm did on his own account, after Lanfranc had left Bec. He remarks in Letter 20 that he has given up the teaching of elementary grammar: S 3.127.7–9.

[2] *De Veritate*, Chs. 3 ff.   [3] S 1.177.14–16.

[4] For a bibliography of his earlier writings, see his *Commentary on De Grammatico* (Dordrecht 1974).

Arbitrii, the *De Casu Diaboli*, Anselm was still primarily interested in the problem of talking about God. He was looking back to the *Monologion* even as he wrote. But by the time he had finished these treatises, he had, perhaps inadvertently, sown a good many seeds which he was to find growing quietly later when he came to write other works. Most of the later adaptations of principles mooted here occur in works which Anselm almost certainly did not envisage writing at this early date. But when he examined the issues raised in the *Cur Deus Homo* or the *De Concordia*, he discovered that he had already done a considerable amount of the groundwork. These treatises can therefore be reckoned to look both forward and backwards, and to encapsulate much of the most crucial stage of Anselm's development as a thinker, from the time of the early triumph of the *Proslogion* to the period when he was ready to write his mature works. Compared with the theological works which Anselm drew from them, these treatises are, if not dull stuff, at least rather tame. But because they show us how Anselm felt his way to a point where he could continue with his more grandiose schemes, they possess a vital interest.

We might look briefly at three aspects of these treatises: at the evidence that Anselm was looking back to the *Monologion*, and that he was still happily engrossed in talking about God; at the evidence that he was working out procedures and principles which were to be taken up again later; and at the kinds of technicality he found helpful for both these purposes.

Anselm's pupil asks for a definition of truth. But it is the *summa veritas*, God himself, who has prompted the question in Anselm's own mind. In the opening passage quoted from the *Monologion*, we are reminded how Anselm has already proved that the *summa veritas* has no beginning or end.[1] He devotes some space in the *Monologion* to demonstrating how God is without beginning or end, whether we regard him as the *summa natura*, the *summa veritas*, or by the name of any other supreme good.[2] Anselm therefore begins on his discussions in the *De Veritate* with more than an echo of his earlier thinking in his mind: he sets the *summa veritas*, God himself, directly before him as his subject-matter. Whenever the argument permits, he returns to his theme. When he examines the *rerum natura*, the

[1] S 1.176.7.   [2] *Monologion*, Ch. 18, S 1.32–3 ff.

nature of things, the example he chooses is that of Christ himself, who, in his human flesh, must surely have felt the prick of
the nails and had his flesh actually penetrated by them.[1]
According to the nature of things, that is perfectly proper,
Anselm argues, but no one would say that Christ 'ought' to
have been crucified, according to his deserts. Here, Anselm is
merely using an example in which he takes Christ as the centre-
piece. But in doing so, he has fallen into a habit which was to
become more and more entrenched in his thought as time went
on. God is not only the object most congenial to his reflections;
but, philosophically speaking, God always provides the 'special
case', which Anselm so often needs for purposes of demonstration. In this instance Christ alone and most strikingly, embodies
a nature which 'ought' to be subject to wounding and pain,
and a nature which 'ought' to be incapable of suffering, and
upon which no unkindness can ever rightly be inflicted.

Anselm makes use of the special case of God almost at once.
God, he points out, is under no kind of obligation:

Omnia enim illi debent, ipsa vero nulli quicquam debet.[2]
('For all things are under obligation to him, but he himself is
under obligation to nothing.') Yet the whole sequence of argument up to now, from the moment when it was agreed that a
true statement says that what is, is,[3] had tended towards the
view that truth or rightness has to do with what ought to be so.
In God alone, that is, in the Supreme Truth alone, truth consists simply in being, and not in being as being ought to be;
God is the point of reference for 'ought':

nec ulla ratione est quod est, nisi quia est.[4]
('There is no reason why he is, except that he is.') One is reminded, although Anselm does not explicitly make the connection, of the Scriptural statement, 'I am that I am.'[5] When we
talk about God, then, as Anselm has already amply demons-
strated in the *Monologion*, we shall generally find that God is the
exception which not only proves, but explains, the rule. The
chain of obligations, for example, proceeds from its ultimate
cause, the *rectitudo* or *veritas* of God himself, and he alone provides a unifying principle. Anselm finds himself philosophically
obliged—as well as spiritually inclined—to talk about God

[1] S 1.187.33-5.   [2] S 1.190.3-4.   [3] S 1.177.10.
[4] S 1.190.4.   [5] Exodus: 3.14.

because the fact of God alone can 'explain' matters which cannot be resolved, in Anselm's view, by reference to the created world.

He returns, too, to the subject of the natural language, or *naturalia verba* of the *Monologion*. There, he had suggested that certain images or concepts or ideas in the human mind are universally recognizable, and that they constitute a kind of universal language which approaches as closely as it is possible to come to the ideas in the mind of God. But most of the instances discussed there have to do with concrete objects, not with abstract ideas.[1] Now, however, Anselm comes to grips with the common elements in abstract ideas, those *communis animi conceptiones*,[2] which make it possible for all mankind to recognize the notion of truth or that of righteousness. Anselm concedes that the highest form of *iustitia* we can grasp is perceived only by the mind, not by the senses; it is, in fact, a concept:

Et quoniam de rectitudine mente sola perceptibili loquimur, invicem sese definiunt veritas et rectitudo et iustitia.[3]

('And since we are talking about that rightness which is perceptible only to the mind, truth and rightness and righteousness are to be defined in terms of one another.') Truth and rightness and righteousness are closely interrelated concepts precisely because each participates in the *una veritas* which constitutes the truth in all true things.[4] This remains the case even when we move from the concept of *veritas* to the truth which includes *iustitia*:

quoniam de rectitudine mente sola perceptibili loquimur, una res significatur quae genus est iustitiae.[5]

('Since we are speaking of the rightness which only the mind grasps, [we must show that] the same thing is signified; this is the generic term under which righteousness falls.') The organizing principle of this sequence of argument has been provided in the *Monologion*, and it is inseparable from Anselm's idea of God. All goods, of whatever kind, can ultimately be shown to

---

[1] Anselm speaks, in particular, of the picture a craftsman has in his mind before he makes something; that 'something' is clearly envisaged by Anselm as being in no way an abstraction.

[2] Boethius, *De Hebdomadibus*, I, ed. H. Stewart and E. K. Rand, *Theological Tractates* (London/New York 1946), p. 41.

[3] S 1.192.7–8.   [4] S 1.196.27.   [5] S 1.196.29–30.

derive their good qualities from the *summum bonum*, the God who sets a standard of goodness simply by existing. Our best attempt at conceiving of truth is that which comes nearest to God's thought about himself, and the closer it approaches, the more gladly will it be recognized by other people, who themselves possess a grasp of the same concept simply because God created them that way.

This explicit and implicit link between thinking about God and working out a definition of truth reappears in new and varied connections throughout the three treatises. Anselm suggests in the *De Libertate Arbitrii* that although 'the free will of man differs from that of God and the good angels, they should have in common the element in their definition which concerns the word "freedom" '. (*Quamvis differat liberum arbitrium hominum a libero arbitrio dei et angelorum bonorum, definitio tamen huius libertatis in utrisque secundum hoc nomen eadem debet esse.*)[1] In other words, freedom is a good; as in the case of all other goods, the ultimate good must be the common factor in every example of that particular good in the created world. Freedom of the will must be one freedom, even if the will of man in itself differs significantly from the will of God or the will of a good angel. The underlying principle is exactly the same as that which Anselm had employed for talking about goodness itself in the *Monologion* and truth in the *De Veritate*, and for examining greatness in the *Proslogion*.

In the *De Casu Diaboli* we meet a very telling instance of the way in which Anselm normally associates conceiving of an idea with thinking and talking about it, whether in the language of ordinary discourse, or in the language of the *naturalia verba*, the universally recognizable ideas. He points out that it is difficult to see how the Devil could have conceived of the idea of being equal with God, or of being greater than God if, as he has shown in the *Proslogion*, God is that than which nothing greater can be thought:[2]

> Si deus non potest cogitari nisi ita solus, ut nihil illi simile cogitari possit; quomodo potuit diabolus velle quod non potuit cogitare?[3]

('If God cannot be thought of except as the One whom nothing can be imagined to be like, how could Satan will what he could

---

[1] S 1.208.3–5.   [2] S 1.101.8.   [3] S 1.241.31.

not conceive of?') Here, perhaps most notably of all, Anselm associates the ideas which he is working out in the three treatises with principles established in the *Proslogion* and the *Monologion*, in the special area of talking about God. He can be seen to be building upon his earlier work, and to be constructing a considerable edifice upon it at that. It is possible to read the three treatises and the *De Grammatico* without reference to Anselm's earlier works. But to do so is to take them out of their context in the development of Anselm's thoughts about that problem of talking about God which interested him most.

If we look next at the seeds Anselm was sowing to be harvested later, their number and variety defies any attempt at summary. Again, it will be possible to take only a few examples. In the *Cur Deus Homo* Anselm is much preoccupied with *debere*. The explanation he proposes there of the absolute necessity for the world to be redeemed by a God-Man depends on the view that a debt is owed which only man has an obligation to pay. Yet, as Anselm had established in the *De Veritate*, no obligation is binding on God.[1] God could only rightly and properly pay the debt if he was also Man.[2] The echoes here of Chapter 8 of the *De Veritate*, with its discussion of *debere* and *non debere*, *posse* and *non posse*,[3] are clear; the principle of *rectitudo* has also been fully discussed throughout the treatise on truth, and Anselm has shown that whatever God does is, by definition, right. So in paying for the sins of the world in the form of a man, Christ was doing something in every way right and proper. When Anselm came to compose the *Cur Deus Homo* he seems to have fallen back quite naturally upon these earlier modes of explanation, not out of idleness, but because there was a good deal of matter in them still. He had not yet utilized them to the full; he went on to do so in the *Cur Deus Homo*.

Another preliminary task carried out in these three works was of crucial importance in the forming of the *De Concordia*. At the beginning of the *De Libertate Arbitrii* Anselm says, through his pupil:

Quoniam liberum arbitrium videtur repugnare gratiae et praedestinationi et praescientiae dei: ipsa libertas arbitrii quid sit nosse desidero.[4]

('Since free will seems to contradict the existence of grace and

---

[1] S 1.190.3–4. [2] S 2.94–6. [3] S 1.186–8. [4] S 1.207.4–6.

predestination and the foreknowledge of God, I wish to know what that free will is.') When he wrote the *De Concordia* he turned the question round, and, without further preliminary consideration of the nature of free will, he examined the notions of *praescientia, praedestinatio* and *gratia* in turn, setting each against free will for consideration. He could not have done so, had he not long ago settled to his own satisfaction a definition of the nature of free will. The subject-matter of the *De Concordia* is already there, however, in the initial statement of the *De Libertate Arbitrii*, and, again, there can be no doubt that Anselm's later thinking was conditioned and directed by this preliminary exercise.

As early as the *De Veritate* we find statements of the principle that the possession of a rational will is a *sine qua non* for righteousness:

> Ergo quoniam omnis iustitia est rectitudo, nullatenus est iustitia quae servantem se facit laudabilem, nisi in rationalibus.[1]

('Therefore since every righteousness is a rightness, the righteousness which makes him who keeps it praiseworthy is present only in rational beings.') This must be so because only a rational being with free will is to be praised for keeping to the right;[2] a stone deserves no commendation for fulfilling its function as a stone.[3] This principle appears again and again in later works. Just as righteousness lies only in rational wills, so sin is possible only for those with rational wills, as Anselm shows in the *De Conceptu Virginali*.[4] And just as God makes something right merely by doing it, as Anselm has shown in the *De Veritate*, so he cannot sin, because everything he does is *ipso facto* right. The will of every rational creature ought to be subject to the will of God, Anselm points out in the *Cur Deus Homo*:

> Omnis voluntas rationalis creaturae subiecta debet esse voluntati dei.[5]

So when God does his own will, he cannot sin; that will in itself sets the standard for righteousness.

Without labouring the point, we might mention Anselm's use of the notions of necessity, permissive and causative will, power, evil and nothingness, and a dozen other instances of principles

---

[1] S 1.193.4–5.   [2] S 1.193.1–2.   [3] S 1.192.11 ff.
[4] Ch. 3, S 2.142.12–143.21.   [5] Book I, 11, S 2.68.12.

of demonstration and habits of thought which were to be
borrowed and refashioned in the works composed while he was
Archbishop of Canterbury. He himself makes the *discipulus*
remark that no sooner has Anselm chopped down the tree of
one difficulty than fresh problems sprout from its roots:

> Sed nescio quid sit, ut cum me spero iam ad finem quaestionis
> pertingere, tunc magis videam velut de radicibus succisarum
> quaestionum alia pullulantes consurgere.[1]

('I don't know how it is, but when I hope I am coming to the
end of the problem, I see new difficulties sprouting vigorously
forth from the roots of the tree which has been felled!') Anselm's
own experience was perhaps rather different—there is no
reason to think that he is declaring his own feelings of despair
here. He seems to have discovered, not fresh and insoluble difficulties as he resolved each aspect of the problem in hand, but
rather materials which would help him in the resolution of
future difficulties. He never loses control of the argument in the
Tres Tractatus; instead, he confines it carefully within the bounds
he has set, and leaves other matters until later. But the comment which he puts into the mouth of his pupil demonstrates
clearly enough that he saw how closely interconnected were all
the issues which had been raised. He is fond of remarking on the
fact that problems of language and expression and problems of
theology are inextricably related. We have seen how he came to
that conclusion when he wrote the Preface to the *De Veritate*.[2]
He says something very similar early in the *Cur Deus Homo*.[3]
The structure of the *De Concordia* depends upon the same idea.

This very interest in the relationships between ideas and
words brings us to our third aspect of the *Tres Tractatus*—that
of the specific technical devices Anselm uses to bridge the gap
between his thinking in the *Monologion* and the *Proslogion* and
his later theological writings. Wherever it is possible to do so,
Anselm looks for concords—for agreements at every level between apparently disparate principles and methods. In the *De
Concordia* he was to suggest that the best way to demonstrate
that free will could coexist with predestination, grace and the
foreknowledge of God, is to propose the view that both exist,
and see whether any impossibility follows from that, as it
should if the two are *repugnantia*.[4] In the *De Veritate* he sets out

---

[1] S 1.244.11–13.   [2] S 1.173–4.   [3] S 2.49.7–13.   [4] S 2.246.2–7.

to show, in a very similar frame of mind, how the same thing both ought to be and ought not to be.[1] This technique of juxta-position of apparent opposites and contradictories has its technical side; but it also reflects a fundamentally Anselmian habit of mind. Faced with a paradox, he examines its com-ponents closely to see whether he can find some means of allowing both to stand, by making their exact area of reference perfectly clear.

It is possible to list a variety of technical terms: *proprie*, *communis locutio*, to do with Anselm's theory of language; *substantia*, *qualitas*, *actio*, *passio*, *facere*, *pati*, to do with the Ari-stotelian *Categories*; *aequivocatio*, *nomen* and *verbum*, *vox signifi-cativa*, as expressions which lie on the borderland between grammar and dialectic. Anselm is not afraid of employing such terms, because he expects his readers to find them helpful. On the other hand, neither in the *Tres Tractatus* nor in the *De Grammatico* does he simply make the argument a vehicle for the introduction of as many terms as possible. He prefers to demonstrate how technicalities may occasionally be useful as a means of clarifying thinking. Just as the technique of setting apparent contradictories side by side and showing that they are no such things often stands him in good stead, so does the con-verse procedure of demonstrating the existence of several senses in one word. At one point he asks the pupil whether they have looked at all the *sedes veritatis*, a phrase which recalls Cicero[2] and which indicates his determination to leave no sub-division of his subject-matter unexplored. Sometimes he de-liberately steps back from a statement in order to make a state-ment about that statement. He remarks, for example, that when he said in the *Monologion* that truth had no beginning or end, he did not mean to imply that the statement, 'truth has no beginning or end' was in itself without beginning or end.[3] Such an argument is almost breathtaking in the daring with which a simple device is used; it has about it all the marks of a venture into what might in more recent years have been called a meta-language. Listing technical terms will tell us something about

[1] S 1.186.10.
[2] Cicero says in *Topics*, II.7 that Aristotle calls topics *quasi sedes e quibus argu-menta promuntur*.
[3] S 1.190.16–17.

Anselm's methods in these works, then; but it has limited value in showing off the skills of argument he is able to draw upon by bringing together his educational skills and his metaphysical reflections.

Enough has been said, perhaps, to show how many indications of the potential greatness of future arguments there are to be found in these treatises. Had the later theological treatises never been written, perhaps we should have been obliged to conclude that Anselm had stumbled upon some potentially exciting ideas and some fruitful methods of argument. These treatises would have been of interest because they show something of what could be done with the technical resources which Anselm had at his disposal.[1] But the later treatises were written. The continuous development of Anselm's thinking from the point he had reached at the end of the *Proslogion* to the completion of the *De Concordia*, stretches before us. But even if we had had to do without this almost complete conspectus,[2] it would be very evident that Anselm had no difficulty in picking up the threads he had left hanging in the *Monologion* and in going on to develop his ideas. The completeness of the *Proslogion* achievement lies in the special unity of that work in itself. It did not satisfy Anselm's restless spirit of enquiry for long.

iv: *The Value of the Three Treatises*

What Anselm has had to say in these treatises is internally so consistent that it is difficult to fault it in detail, provided we accept his initial assumptions. He has perceived a good many generally recognizable problems of language and meaning, and none of them has proved insurmountable in terms of the system of explanations he is working out. More: often what he says in these treatises serves as a platform on which to build further arguments. If the philosopher's task is to provide a consistent and systematic explanation for the phenomena of mind, Anselm has done it. If the theologian's task is to reconcile such an account with the given principles of Christian faith, so that nothing jars, Anselm has done that too. It might be objected that these simply will not do as working definitions for modern

---

[1] A list of these is provided in JH, pp. 246–53.

[2] Anselm had, according to Eadmer, planned another work, on the Soul, VA, p. 142, I, lxvi.

philosophers and theologians, and again we are brought back to the irreducible minimum of concession we must make to Anselm if his account is to make sense to us. Harmony and consistency were important to him. Behind every one of his arguments is the imperative need to show that there is no discrepancy between doctrinal orthodoxy and the conclusions the reason can draw from its independent reflections. The character of the account Anselm gives is coloured by the terms and methods he had available to him. His expectation that every question must have an answer, and that the right answer for faith, echoes a more timeless attitude of mind.

5

THE *DE INCARNATIONE VERBI*

i: *An Open Letter*

Anselm's letter *On the Incarnation of the Word* was, in its day, the most controversial of his treatises, not because he wanted to make it so, but because it was written in circumstances of controversy. It seems that Roscelin of Compiègne had got hold of some saying of Anselm's in which he had proposed an analogy for the Trinity, and he had used it to demonstrate by formal logical methods that Anselm had propounded a view which made nonsense of the orthodox doctrine. Roscelin was a dialectician of some note and he had a following. His assertions could not be ignored because he was determined to provoke a response, and, as it turned out, he was unwilling to let the matter drop even when he had brought down official disapproval on his own head. Anselm never discussed the issue with him face to face. Their debate was carried on, unsatisfactorily enough, by the written word and by means of reported accounts carried back to Anselm by men who had heard what Roscelin had said. Neither wrote directly to the other; Anselm's *Epistola* is an open letter, in which Roscelin's name is never mentioned.

Were it not for a few letters dating from the end of Anselm's period as Abbot of Bec, the identity of the 'certain clerk' who had been making false accusations would not have been revealed by Anselm himself. Perhaps he had no appetite for a confrontation of the kind experienced by Lanfranc in his dealings with Berengar—a business Anselm must have had at the back of his mind.[1] Certainly he went to some trouble to avoid anything of the kind. Roscelin's sayings probably first came to Anselm's ears in a letter from John, a monk of Bec, who had been perturbed by what he had heard. 'He says', he tells Anselm, 'that

---

[1] On Lanfranc and Berengar, see A. J. Macdonald, *Lanfranc: A Study of His Life, Work and Writing* (Oxford 1926); R. W. Southern, 'Lanfranc of Bec and Berengar of Tours', in *Studies Presented to F. M. Powicke* (Oxford 1948), 27–48; J. de Montclos, *Lanfranc et Bérengar, Spicilegium Sacrum Lovaniense*, 37 (1971); M. T. Gibson, *Lanfranc of Bec* (Oxford 1978).

Archbishop Lanfranc has conceded this view, and that you have agreed to it in debate with him.'[1] Apparently Roscelin had been saying that Lanfranc and Anselm had both agreed that the Father and the Holy Spirit had been incarnate with the Son.[2] Anselm replies, more briefly he says than he would have wished, but chiefly so as to set John's mind at rest about his own views and to confirm that he holds the orthodox doctrine.[3] That was not enough. In Letter 136 we find him writing at greater length to Fulk, Bishop of Beauvais, instructing him to speak for him at the Council of Rheims—and to say something on Lanfranc's behalf, too, since Lanfranc has recently died. He provides Fulk with a detailed account of what he wants him to say.[4] Whether or not Anselm was free to attend the Council of Rheims we do not know, but it may be significant that he made no effort to be present in person. He took no pleasure in controversy, and he had no wish to carry on any campaign of retribution against Roscelin.

The matter continued to be troublesome and disturbing for some years, at a time when Anselm was himself under pressure. Between 1090, when John wrote to him, and 1092–3 when the final version of the *De Incarnatione Verbi* was finished, he had reluctantly accepted the See of Canterbury in Lanfranc's place. Things went badly from the beginning, and Anselm's own misgivings about accepting the post were an additional source of discomfort to him.[5] The continuation of the theological controversy with Roscelin must have been especially unwelcome in the circumstances. All that Eadmer tells us of Anselm's feelings about the *De Incarnatione Verbi* is that Eadmer himself regarded it as a much-needed and valuable work in the circumstances of the time.[6] It was the rumour that Roscelin's recantation at the Council of Soissons had been short-lived which seems to have prompted Anselm to enlarge and polish his first *Epistola* and complete the *De Incarnatione Verbi*, rather than any spontaneous wish on his part to prolong the controversy.[7] No other work of his was put together in this way, and it cannot be said to reflect

---

[1] S 3.270–1, Letter 128, written about 1090. On John's career see VA, p. 106, n. 1.

[2] S 3.271.11–13.   [3] S 3.271–2, Letter 129.   [4] S 3.279–81.

[5] See AB, pp. 122–63 on Anselm's early years as Archbishop, and Letter 148, S 4.3–6, for Anselm's feelings about his appointment.

[6] VA, p. 72.   [7] Cf. AB, p. 80.

the natural development of Anselm's thought in quite the way that the earlier treatises do.

The problem Anselm was trying to solve in the *De Incarnatione Verbi* was not, then, of his own making. In the first draft of the work to be published he tried to restrict himself to rebutting the specific accusations which had been reported to him: 'It is enough for me to reply on behalf of the Archbishop. . . . But for myself I answer . . .'.[1] His tone is therefore defensive. Since this reply did not quiet Roscelin, Anselm adopts another tone in the final version: decisive, assured, allowing for short *discursus* into related questions, but, above all, no longer anxious on his own account to the same extent. The Anselmian analogy on which Roscelin had based his case has gone.[2] Anselm comes to grips with Roscelin's heretical views at once, and wastes no time on explanations of what he himself had really said. Perhaps he had found that his attempts to justify himself made matters worse and created new misunderstandings. Whatever his reasons, Anselm is now purposeful and clear. He is writing a book about the Trinity, not merely a defence of his own orthodoxy.

ii: *Plurality and Trinity*

The *Proslogion* contains only passing reference to the three Persons; we must look to the *Monologion* for the only extended treatment of the problems posed by the doctrine of the Trinity which is to be found in Anselm's early writings. In his references in the *De Incarnatione Verbi* to the earlier treatise, Anselm shows that he was himself conscious that he had last examined these issues in the *Monologion*, where he had been expounding the orthodox view; now he was engaged in the essentially negative task of showing, not what the Trinity is, but what it is not. He attempts to deal, not with Trinity and unity but with plurality; he has to scotch the view that there can be plurality in the Godhead. In order to do so, it is necessary for him to mention a series of erroneous views, which cannot be disproved unless they are first stated. He also found that he was obliged to return to issues he had hoped were fully explained in his earlier works.

---

[1] S 1.282.16, 20.
[2] That is, the material in S 1.282.12–283.6 is not in the final version.

The whole exercise has an untidiness of a kind Anselm always found uncongenial. But under pressure he became more inventive, and the *De Incarnatione Verbi* contains fresh ideas which have, perhaps, a less monumental quality than the thoughts of the *Monologion* and the *Proslogion*, but which indicate something of the multiplicity of Anselm's intellectual resources.

He did not achieve his new insights at once. Even if we leave out of account the earlier version or versions of the work,[1] it is clear from the finished version that Anselm has begun his thinking more or less from the point where he left off in the *Monologion*. There is a short homily on the proper frame of mind for constructive thinking about God, which we shall look at later.[2] Then Anselm proposes the first 'division' (*divisio*) of the question, with a proper regard for dialectical procedure. Roscelin has been saying that if the three Persons are one 'thing' (*res*), and not three separate things, like three angels or three men, and if their power and their will are one, then the Father and the Holy Spirit must have been incarnate with the Son.[3] Augustine's distinction between those attributes of God which belong to all three Persons—his power, his goodness, his blessedness, for example—and those which are proper to individual Persons—Fatherhood, Sonship, and so on—had already been touched on by Anselm in the *Monologion*.[4] Roscelin is deliberately blurring this distinction. He forces Anselm to move away from the contemplation of the common attributes of all three Persons, which had given him so much pleasure and satisfaction in the early works, to examine their individual attributes. As he points out early in his argument, discussing Father and Son,

Those things which are common to them—like omnipotence, eternity—are understood to belong only to their unity, and those things which are proper to them individually—like 'begetter' or 'begetting' to the Father, or 'word' and 'begotten' to the Son—are signified by these two names, that is, those of Father and Son.[5]

He is putting the well-worn distinction to work. He tries to demonstrate to Roscelin and his followers, much as he had tried to show to Gaunilo, that they are using the word 'thing' (*res*) imprecisely, and that a good deal of their confusion arises from

[1] On the evidence as to the number of recensions, see AB, p. 34.
[2] S 2.6.5–10.17.   [3] S 2.10.22–11.1.   [4] Augustine *De Trinitate*, V.x.11.
[5] S 2.11.21–5.

their failure to make just this division.[1] They are, in other words, failing to perceive the relationship between words and things as Anselm himself sees it. Words for common attributes of the Godhead refer to God's unity, and words for individual attributes of the Persons refer to the Persons individually. The *res* itself is, paradoxically, both one and three, and there lies a mystery. But there need be no mystery about the use of terms for the *res*, and no confusion over their specific application. To reason from a misuse of words to a heretical viewpoint is, in Anselm's eyes, simply foolish.

Anselm's mode of reasoning here, like Augustine's, owes much to the Aristotelian *Categories*. Anselm abandons the discussion of the 'theological categories' of substance and relation and number[2] later in the work, for other means of demonstration, but he did not dispose of such means of discussing the paradox of the Trinity for the scholars who came after him. The theologians of the first half of the twelfth century were to remain deeply interested in the principles they entail.[3] But it is not in these first relatively derivative chapters, with their clarification of the commonplaces of contemporary arguments, that the real conceptual novelties of Anselm's arguments against plurality in God occur. Here, his first concern is to show Roscelin, by means he will, as a dialectician, recognize and respect, that he is simply being inconsistent in his statements. Anselm's intention is to ridicule his opponent by making it plain to him that he has made grave dialectical errors; he tries to injure his pride as a dialectician.

If God is one and the same through and through, and the Father, Son, and Holy Spirit are all one Person,[4] a dialectician must accept that what is true of something which is numerically one and the same cannot also be simultaneously untrue:

eadem re non est vera simul affirmatio et eius negatio.[5]

Yet if there is nothing proper to any one Person, there can be no relation in God:

---

[1] S 2.11.15.   [2] S 2.13.17, S 2.21–2 etc.

[3] See, for example, the *indices verborum* to *Petrus Abaelardus Dialectica*, ed. L. M. de Rijk (Assen 1956); *Gilbert of Poitiers: Commentaries on Boethius*, ed. N. M. Häring (Toronto 1966); *Commentaries on Boethius by Thierry of Chartres and his School*, ed. N. M. Häring (Toronto 1971).

[4] S 2.14.10–11.

[5] S 2.15.1.

Quare nec ulla erit ibi relatio, quae nullatenus ibi est nisi secundum hoc, secundum quod alii sunt ab invicem.[1]

It would therefore seem absurd to speak of Father and Son at all. On the other hand—and here Anselm allows for possible misquoting of Roscelin by the reporter[2]—if Roscelin is really saying that there are three Gods, then God's very nature is not simple but composite,[3] and that, too, is absurd, since it is a cardinal Boethian principle that what is simple is greater than what is composite (*simplicia praestare compositis*).[4] We cannot suppose that there is anything greater than God. In short, says Anselm, if he were to try to cover all the absurdities and inconsistencies Roscelin's views imply, he would fill a very large book:

Codex magnus implendus est, si voluero scribere absurditates et impietates quae sequuntur.[5]

And these are the inconsistencies of a purely dialectical kind, whose force Roscelin will be bound to see.

This is the point in the work at which Anselm turns from proofs based on dialectical notions and attempts to discover other means of demonstration which will go beyond the powers of these principles of elementary dialectic. He perceives that he may have been playing into Roscelin's hands. Roscelin may argue that the existence of these inconsistencies is precisely what he has been pointing out:

cum tu ipse mecum probas innumera inde nasci inconvenientia.[6]

('since you yourself, like me, prove that innumerable inconsistencies arise from this.') Anselm is not, in fact, resolving the issue, but further compounding the problems it raises: *non solvis sed magis ligas quaestionem*.[7]

Anselm's mind goes back, as it had done at first, to the work he had done in the *Monologion* and the *Proslogion*. He suggests to Roscelin and his like that they may find there arguments based, not on Scriptural authority, but on reasoning alone, which they will not find it easy to refute, and which put the 'positive' side of the case for orthodoxy:

Sed et si quis legere dignabitur duo parva mea opuscula, *Monologion* scilicet et *Proslogion*, quae ad hoc maxime facta

[1] S 2.16.10–11.   [2] S 2.16.21–17.1.   [3] S 2.17.14.   [4] S 2.17.15–18.
[5] S 2.19.12.   [6] S 2.20.7–8.   [7] S 2.20.6–7.

sunt, ut quod fide tenemus de divina natura et eius personis praeter incarnationem, necessariis rationibus sine scriptura auctoritate probari possit.[1]

('And if anyone will condescend to read my two little books, the *Monologion* and the *Proslogion*, which were written expressly for the purpose of proving by necessary reasons, without the authority of Scripture, what we hold by faith about the divine Nature and its Persons. . . .') Anselm makes it plain in the passage that follows that he wrote these works in no spirit of controversy.[2] He has said nothing which is out of harmony with patristic teachings. He hopes only to help those who are humbly endeavouring to reach a better understanding of these matters of faith:

> ad adiuvandum religiosum studium eorum qui humiliter quaerunt intelligere quod firmissime credunt.[3]

But he clearly acknowledges to himself that these works will have limited powers of convincing those who sneer at the faithful (*derident credentes*).[4] For such men, it seems, he feels that he must go on to deal, not with the positive proof of the truth, but with the refutation of error. He merely says that he does not wish to oblige his readers to seek out a book which may not be easily accessible to them.[5] But perhaps it is not reading too much into his remarks here to assume that his reasons for going on with his present task at such length were rather more forceful. His readers needed, not a convenient alternative to the longer arguments set out in the *Monologion* and the *Proslogion*, but an altogether novel philosophical approach to the 'negative' aspects of the problem.

These consist for the most part in the handling of the question of 'plurality'. Anselm poses for himself a problem nearly as considerable as that which he faced in the *Proslogion* when he set out to prove 'that God truly exists[6] (*quia deus vere est*).[6] Never, in the *Proslogion*, had he confronted the related issue of proving that there are not several Gods, but only one. The whole direction of his thought in the earlier works had been towards showing how the highest Good must necessarily be one, not many.[7] That done, he could turn his attention to the nature of that Good, and later, in the *Proslogion*, to demonstrating its

[1] S 2.20.16–19. [2] S 2.20–1. [3] S 2.21.2–3. [4] S 2.21.2.
[5] S 2.21.5. [6] S 1.93.7. [7] *Monologion*, Chs. 1–4.

existence. Now Roscelin has brought him back to the issue
which had simply never constituted a problem for Anselm himself. His thoughts turn naturally enough to what he has already
shown; he refers at once to the notion of the Highest Good:

> Quod autem unus solus deus sit et non plures, hinc facile
> probatur quia aut deus non est summum bonum, aut sunt
> plura summa bona, aut non sunt plures dii, sed unus solus.[1]

('It is easy to prove that there is one God and not many, for
either God is not the highest Good, or there are several highest
Goods, or else there are indeed not several Gods, but only one.')

It is a principle of Anselm's thinking that the very definition
of God sees him as standing at the top of whatever pillar of
thought the human mind can erect. In the *Monologion* he had
suggested that the way to think about God is to run one's mind
over all the good things of ordinary human experience and to
arrange them in order of 'goodness', so as to see that, whatever
we can conceive of as good, God must lie beyond that conception in the degree and nature of his goodness.[2] In the *Proslogion*
he had stated much more plainly that God is that than which
nothing greater can be thought:

> aliquid quo maius nihil cogitari potest.[3]

Here, he takes up the idea again:

> Deum vero summum bonum esse nullus negat, quia quidquid
> aliquo minus est, nullatenus deus est, et quidquid summum
> bonum non est, minus est aliquo, quia minus est summo bono.[4]

('No one denies that God is the highest Good, for whatever is in
any sense "lesser" is not God, and whatever is not the highest
Good is "less" than the highest Good, and so it is "less" than
something.') This proof, formal and syllogistic as it is, lacks the
grace—and also the inspirational quality—of the great *Proslogion* proof. But it is not altogether inferior to it; nor is it very
different from it in conception. Both rest on the same assumptions, except that here there is no need to make the controversial appeal from thought to reality because the actual
existence of the highest Good is not in question.[5]

Now Anselm moves on to look at the problems posed by the
suggestion that there may be several highest Goods, and thus
several Gods. Several highest Goods would necessarily be equal.

[1] S 2.22.22–4.   [2] S 1.14.5–9.   [3] S 1.101.8.
[4] S 2.22.24–6.   [5] S 1.101.15–16.

None could take precedence of any other, or they would not all be highest Goods (*Si enim plura summa bona sunt, paria sunt*).[1] This, too, was an issue which Anselm had considered in the *Monologion* and the *Proslogion*,[2] where he uses the terms *equalis* and *pariter* in discussing the nature of the Good. In the *De Incarnatione Verbi* he is chiefly concerned to show the absurdity of this—not, in this case, a dialectically-defined absurdity, but an almost aesthetic untidiness and inconsistency which, he feels, offends every man's sense of decency. For much the same reasons, and in much the same way, we cannot conceive of plurality of *substantia* or of *essentia*, or of *natura* in the highest Good.[3]

Anselm's thought here clearly owes nothing to the Boethian *opuscula sacra* which were to cause so much re-thinking of the question of plurality in God during the first half of the twelfth century.[4] He envisages the problem much as he had done a decade earlier when he wrote the *Monologion*. It seems to him a very obvious and perfectly suitable procedure to try to lift Roscelin's problem on to another plane, where formal logic is an aid, but only an incidental one. He is trying to appeal directly to the sense of 'fittingness' which he considered every man to possess, and whose gratification gave him, personally, so much pleasure.

The mode of Anselm's arguments in the chapters which follow often makes use of formal logical techniques—especially that of *divisio*. But the appeal of the points he makes is generally to the reader's sense of appropriateness or *convenientia*. When, for example, he proposes an argument to show that the Son alone was the only Person who could have been incarnate, he suggests that if the Father or the Holy Spirit had been incarnate, there would have been nothing but *inconvenientia* in the event.[5] If the Father had been born to the Virgin, he would have been a 'son', and his 'sonship' would have been inferior to that of the Son himself, since Christ would have had a divine Parent and the Father a human one. That would clearly have been anomalous, because it would have made two Persons of the Trinity un-equal. The same would be true if the Holy Spirit were to be born

---

[1] S 2.22.27–8. [2] S 1.15.7, S 1.117.4. [3] S 2.23.3–4.
[4] Gilbert of Poitiers and Thierry of Chartres ed. cit. contain perhaps the most influential commentaries on these works. Cf. *Theological Tractates*, ed. cit., p. 6.
[5] S 2.25.22.

of the Virgin. In the Father's case, a further anomaly would arise: the Son would be the grandson of the Virgin, although she would have no part of him, and the Father himself would be the grandson of the Virgin's parents.[1] In the face of all these ludicrous possibilities, Anselm asserts that there cannot be even the slightest inconsistency in God:

> Quoniam ergo quamlibet parvum inconveniens in deo est impossibile.[2]

He notes quite explicitly that the test of these absurdities is the sensibility of the human mind:

> et convenientius satis suscipit mens humana.[3]

For Anselm himself, and for those who had come directly under his influence, such a 'test' was perfectly sound—indeed, it was, in the last analysis, the only test available to a man's mind.

But Anselm himself seems to have felt that perhaps he had allowed himself to be carried away along pleasantly familiar lines of thought by the interest of exploring these novel demonstrations. He recalls himself to the task in hand. He had allowed himself to examine an aspect of the problem which had not been raised, as far as he knew, in quite the same way by Roscelin himself: *Dicunt enim quidam*,[4] ('For some say . . .'). Now he acknowledges that he had had no means of access to any of Roscelin's sayings except for those to which he has made direct reply:

> De scriptis illius cui respondeo in hac epistola, nihil potui videre praeter illud quod supra posui.[5]

But he hopes that what he has said has so laid bare the truth of the matter that no one who understands his arguments will be able to deny their force:

> Sed puto sic rei patere veritatem ex iis quae dixi, ut nulli lateat intelligenti nihil quod contra illam dicitur vim veritatis tenere.[6]

This might be regarded as apologetic in this special context. As a rule when Anselm declares himself satisfied with his proofs, he lets them stand and does not attempt to add to them. But we have already seen how, when he feels he has shown the technical logical absurdities of Roscelin's position, it does not seem to him that he had done enough. He goes on to give a

---

[1] S 2.25–6, Ch. 10.   [2] S 2.26.3–4.   [3] S 2.26.12.
[4] S 2.28.15.   [5] S 2.30.7–8.   [6] S 2.30.8–9.

series of demonstrations—albeit of rather different points—
which depend for their force on the ridiculousness of the implications of the erroneous view. Here again he has said he is
satisfied. But one more attempt at proof, of yet another kind, is
to follow. Anselm introduces an extended analogy.

Almost impatiently, he says that if Roscelin denies that what
Anselm tells him is true, on the grounds that there is no counter-
part for it in nature, Roscelin must simply accept that there are
things in God beyond his understanding.[1] Then he relents. 'Let
us see if there is anything in the created world in which may be
found that which he denies to be so in God': (*Videamus tamen
an in rebus creatis . . . inveniri possit aliquatenus hoc quod negat in deo*).[2]
Anselm finds what he is looking for in the Augustinian image of
the watercourse, whose spring is the Father, whose river is the
Son, and whose pool or lake is the Holy Spirit. The water which
flows through all three is the divine nature.[3] In introducing
this extended analogy, Anselm makes use of a mode of reasoning
perfectly familiar to contemporary students of dialectic,[4] but of
rather a different kind from the appeal to the technical terms of
Categories studies, or the appeal to 'fittingness' he has employed
so far. We do not know which, if any, of these modes of demonstration Roscelin found convincing. Their interest, for our purposes, lies in the fact that Anselm has found himself compelled
to use all three in the hope of succeeding with one of them at
least. This is a very different procedure from that of the *Cur
Deus Homo*, where he says that a single solid argument will be
enough to convince any right-minded man.[5] Roscelin had
already shown himself not to be such a person.

But again and again throughout the work Anselm returns to
the happier ground of the *Monologion* and *Proslogion* arguments.
He concludes with an attempt at contemplation of the *summa
natura*,[6] and with further, though briefer, analogies to demonstrate how God's eternity is one, not many, just as his omnipotence is single, not plural.[7] These were all matters with which he
had dealt very amply before, but which he now felt compelled

---

[1] S 2.31.4–6.   [2] S 2.31.10–12.
[3] I have looked more fully at this analogy in 'St. Anselm's Images of Trinity',
Journal of Theological Studies, xxvii (1976), 46–57.
[4] Ibid.   [5] S 2.48 and 51–2.   [6] S 2.33.10.
[7] See my article, 'The Use of Technical Terms of Mathematics in the Writings
of St. Anselm', *Studia Monastica*, 18 (1976), 67–77.

to mention again, simply because the question of God's plurality had been raised as a controversial issue. Earlier he had been able to enjoy the paradox of the Trinity, as something to be wondered at and worshipped. Now he was forced to analyse it, to demonstrate its properties to someone who regarded the paradox not with awe, but with irritation. It must have been an uncomfortable procedure. Anselm clearly had difficulty in finding his way through the task he was required to perform with his customary sureness. For reassurance and inspiration he returned to his earlier explanations; it is not at all surprising that he should have done so. But we owe to the irritant provided by Roscelin some entirely novel thoughts about the difficulties raised by the Incarnation in particular.

iii: *Unity and Trinity: the Anselmian Position*

It is perhaps fair to say that it is not the concept of the unity of God, but the paradox of his Trinity which has caused theologians the greatest difficulty, since Early Christian times. Judaic and Greek influences alike encouraged the view that to regard God as anything but One was a retrograde step, whose natural consequence was a lapse into polytheism. The strongest possible theological and philosophical pressures encouraged the first thinkers to attempt to formulate Christian doctrines in terms which would emphasize the unity of God. The Bible has much to say about the oneness of God, but it does not contain a fully explicated account of the doctrine of the Trinity. It was left to the first biblical scholars to work out the implications of those passages which mention aspects of the relation of Father, Son and Holy Spirit, and to put together a coherent body of doctrine.

Anselm, too, found it philosophically easier to discuss the unity of God. Such references to the Trinity as occur in the *Monologion* and *Proslogion* are not, on the whole, the product of one of Anselm's exercises in going back to first principles. He largely assumes his position of doctrinal orthodoxy and he borrows Augustinian imagery without seriously questioning its helpfulness to the unbeliever or the agnostic. It was only in the writing of the *De Incarnatione* that he tackled systematically the implications of the 'threeness' of God, without relying heavily on the props provided by his reading. He adduces arguments by

reason not by authority, partly because he must meet Roscelin's dialectical objections directly, but also because he wants
to show that if we begin with the minimum of doctrinal assumptions, we shall find that Trinitarian doctrine emerges complete,
by means of reasoning alone. The burden of his argument is
that the doctrine possesses not only the truth recognized by
faith, but also the philosophical elegance reason demands.

Richard of St. Victor held the same view. He argues in his
De Trinitate that necessary arguments must exist to prove that
what-must-necessarily-be is so. If we cannot find them for the
moment, our failure does not suggest that they do not exist.
Every necessary thing must have a necessary reason.[1] We are
again coming close to the point where Anselm's philosophical
position may be said to rest on assumptions which we must
grant him, if we are to agree with him in what he deduces from
them. Again, the problem resolves itself into one of language.
If God creates human language and human reason, so that men
may talk about him and understand something of his nature, it
follows that his Trinity must present no ultimate philosophical
anomaly, and that we can usefully discuss the doctrine
with a view to understanding how the paradox may be
resolved. Again, Anselm's starting-point is one of philosophical
optimism.

That makes him confident. He saw no need to attempt to
demonstrate the truth of the whole of Trinitarian doctrine.
Even if we put together the subject-matter of the *De Incarnatione
Verbi*, the *Cur Deus Homo*, the *De Conceptu Virginali*, and the *De
Processione Spiritus Sancti*, there are aspects given little space: the
Resurrection, for example, or the indwelling of the Holy
Spirit. In the *De Incarnatione Verbi* itself the restricted scope of
the subject-matter is even more apparent. First Anselm demonstrates the fact that God is both one and three, then that the
Father and the Holy Spirit were not incarnate with the Son, as
Roscelin had asserted they must be. Then he shows that Christ
assumed another nature, not another Person, so that there are
no more than three Persons in the Trinity. The book takes much
of Trinitarian doctrine as given, once the first principles of unity
and Trinity are established, and goes on to consider two speci-

---

[1] PL, 196.887–992, Book I, 4.

fic problems in isolation. The first is surprisingly rarely raised by earlier theologians. For Athanasius, for instance, there is no question but that it was proper for the Word alone to redeem mankind.[1] The second was to be a burning issue of the twelfth century, when Boethius' views on the two natures of Christ in the *Contra Eutychen* came under active discussion. It might almost be argued that this problem replaced the difficulties raised during the Eucharistic controversy of the eleventh century as the subject of discussions about how two substances might subsist in a single entity. Both involved currently fashionable dialectical topics. These two problems do not exhaust the list of specific difficulties which have been raised in connection with the doctrine of the Incarnation by any means. But it can be said for Anselm's writings on Trinity and Incarnation that everything he says is consistent with the Creeds, and that he nowhere resorts to any bending of his central beliefs in order to accommodate a special argument. His philosophical position encouraged him to believe that there should be no need to do so.

Even before Roscelin's wayward interpretations of the evidence of his own reason has reached his ears, Anselm was aware of the threat of heresy. In the *De Incarnatione Verbi* itself, he identifies Roscelin's views with the Sabellian heresy, which he would have learned about in Augustine.[2] His confidence is not of the kind which ignores the existence of difficulties in other men's minds, or assumes that the right view will make itself felt unaided. But he was sure that once he had demonstraged the error of the heretics to any open-minded and reasonable man, it would have no further hold upon him. His is not, in the apologetic sense, a defence of orthodox doctrine; it is something much more positive than that: a setting out of the evidence for all to see, so that no one need remain in doubt. It seemed to him necessary to deal only with points where specific doubts had been raised. Anselm's assumption is that everyone's views are fundamentally orthodox, unless he has allowed himself to be led astray; there is something to be gained by helping a man to a fuller understanding of what he believes, but there is no point in refuting objections unless those objec-

[1] I. Athanasius *De Incarnatione*, ed. R. W. Thomson (Oxford 1971), p. 149 ff.
[2] S 1.287.24–37, S 2.15.13–16.2.

tions have actually been raised. Here he displays a confidence in the force of the right view to hold its own in the mind unless the mind is tampered with, which is altogether in keeping with his notion of the way the mind is made.

PART II

THE RECEPTIVE MIND

Anselm had always made allowances for those of his readers who were inadequately trained, or simply inexperienced in the arts of argument. He simplified complex issues and divided his exposition into manageable portions, so that none of his pupils was likely to get lost in the course of the argument. He chose topics which his pupils had raised and which he knew to be of interest and importance for them. But for all his excellent qualities as a teacher, he cannot be said to enter sympathetically into his readers' anxieties in the earlier works in the way he does in the *Cur Deus Homo*. Nor does he propose in his first books any preliminary exercise designed to put his reader into a suitable frame of mind for thinking effectively, as he does in the *De Incarnatione Verbi*. The *Proslogion* is the obvious exception, but there Anselm is describing his own devotional experience rather than attempting to understand the nature of other men's responsiveness to God. The *Cur Deus Homo* and the *De Conceptu Virginali* in particular show Anselm at work, not merely upon his own reflections, but in close encounter with another mind. His regard for Boso, and Boso's power of going some way to meet him in discussion, have encouraged him to consider the limitations and difficulties of his readers in a new light. This is not a sudden change. Anselm had never entirely failed to have regard for the needs of his reader. But it is a change of emphasis.

The novel character of the approach in these treatises takes two forms: Anselm teaches his readers how to prepare their minds, and he attempts to sustain the receptive condition into which proper readiness puts them by giving unremitting attention to the removal of stumbling-blocks. The first he accomplishes most forcefully in the homily at the beginning of the *De Incarnatione Verbi*, though he is saying nothing there which cannot be pieced together from passages in other writings. He has not discovered the principles laid down there for himself only recently; but only in this treatise does he find it necessary to give a coherent account of his views. The second means of approach to meeting his readers' individual needs is most fully in evidence in the *Cur Deus Homo* and the *De Conceptu Virginali*. There, every chapter has the mark of Anselm's efforts to enter into the minds of others, and to understand how things which are clear to him may be obscure to his readers.

This may be seen as a movement away from Anselm's first preoccupation with talking about God. But perhaps he had accomplished the bulk of what he could say for himself out of his private reflections by the time he had written the *Proslogion*. Further developments, as we have seen already in the *Tres Tractatus*, occurred to him at least partly because his pupils asked questions, or because others declared themselves perplexed. A good deal of Anselm's inventiveness in finding topics for discussion was apparently prompted by others, even if the solutions he discovers are probably entirely of his own making. There is, in other words, some evidence that he was becoming more responsive to the power of friends and pupils to breathe life into his thinking, and that, consequently, he himself became more deeply concerned with the workings of other mens' minds. Such a development does not lead him away from talking about God. But it does encourage him to talk in language increasingly well matched to other men's needs. As he attempted to make their minds receptive, his own understanding was enlarged in company with theirs.

6

A LITTLE HOMILY

Anselm's was not one of the great ages of preaching. Guibert of Nogent, his younger contemporary and friend, wrote a short treatise on the right way to preach, but he is more concerned with the moral purpose of the sermon than with its form. The eleventh century produced no St. Bernard, unless we count Anselm himself, and there is nothing which may be compared with the work of twelfth-century preachers such as Stephen Langton and Alan of Lille, whose skills were bred in the schools. Still less is there anything to set beside the achievement of the compilers of the thirteenth-century manuals of the art. In most communities the sermons of Augustine or Gregory were used in preference to new compositions, and the art of homiletic was in abeyance in Anselm's day.[1]

Eadmer tells us that Anselm frequently took advantage at meal times of the licence the Rule allowed him to speak 'briefly' for the 'edification' of his monks.[2] Edifying his conversation may have been, but it cannot often have been brief; there seems little doubt that Anselm interpreted the freedom this dispensation gave him rather largely. Here and elsewhere in his formal addresses to the community he delivered homilies which, unless they took a serial form and were completed over several days, must have taken some time in the telling. Some records of these talks were preserved by Anselm's friends,[3] but as far as we know he himself never attempted to write them down. He did not compose formal written sermons as Bernard did. Such was his reputation as a preacher, however, that a large body of sermons purporting to be his was in circulation during the Middle Ages, and it is only comparatively recently that their lack of authenticity has been demonstrated. So it is that when Dom Wilmart established that the homilies which had borne

---

[1] For a recent survey and bibliography, see J. J. Murphy, *Rhetoric in the Middle Ages* (California 1974).

[2] VA, p. 78, cf. Rule of St. Benedict, xxxviii.

[3] These are edited in the *Memorials* (MA).

Anselm's name for so long are spurious,[1] he left us with only second-hand accounts of Anselm's preaching and table-talk.

Yet on occasion Anselm shows off something of his talents as a preacher, when he falls into a homiletic style in writing by giving advice to his readers directly. When he does so he indicates clearly what part he believes the reader should play in the exercise of reading. Anselm's readers, like the pupils who take part with him in the dialogues, are actively discouraged from adopting an attitude of mere receptiveness. They are to prepare themselves adequately, and to work as hard as they read as the 'pupil' of the dialogue is made to do. An underlying receptiveness is important, but it is not to become passive. If we are to argue that Anselm became increasingly aware of other men's difficulties and limitations, we must allow that he also made increasingly clear-cut demands upon his readers to put intellectual and spiritual effort into their reading.

Occasions on which it was proper and natural for him to preach in writing might be expected to arise more frequently in the writing of letters than in the treatises. The pastoral letters do contain passages of homiletic. Anselm often appears to be forced to say there in writing what he would prefer to put to his correspondents face to face. In many instances it is clear that he wishes he could address his remarks to a larger audience than the single monk or small group of monks to whom the letter is addressed. It is not therefore surprising to find him using passages from an earlier letter again, when he comes to write to another friend whose needs are much the same. He sometimes quotes verbatim from his earlier letter, as though he had gone to some trouble to compose the little homily and felt that he could not improve upon it.

A single brief written homily is to be found in Anselm's introduction to the collection of his Prayers and Meditations. First comes a Prologue in which Anselm describes the frame of mind in which he would like the Prayers to be read. Again, he is anxious to ensure that the reader prepares himself adequately for reading. When he begins, he is to go slowly, and not to try to take in too much at once: they are not to be read in a tur-

---

[1] A. Wilmart, 'Les homélies attribuées à S. Anselme', *Archives d'histoire doctrinale et littéraire du moyen age*, 2 (1927), 5–29.

moil, but quietly, not skimmed in a hurry, but read a little at a time with concentration and solemn meditation:

non sunt legendae in tumultu, sed in quiete, nec cursim et velociter, sed paulatim cum intenta et morosa meditatione.[1] The important point, for our purposes, lies in Anselm's intention that the reader shall use the Prayers as starting-points for his own prayers. They are to inspire him, not only to make careful use of their contents, but also to go on to pray in his own words. They are to be used to inspire a desire to pray: *ad accendendum affectum orandi*, or *ad excitandum affectum orandi*.[2] The purpose of this, as of every other written 'homily' of Anselm's, is to prompt the reader to do something on his own account. Here, he is to pray, either by composing his own prayers in his mind, or perhaps even wordlessly, in 'fear or love of God';[3] Anselm does not say which.

In a remarkably similar way, the homilies of the Letters encourage the reader to become spiritually energetic. The Letter to Odo and Lanzo, Letter 2, contains material used again in exactly the same form in Letters 35 and 51, which were addressed to Herluin, and to Herluin, Gundolf and Maurice together, respectively.[4] Anselm was not Abbot to these monks: he addresses them not as a father, but as a friend. With proper modesty he says to Odo and Lanzo that he would feel it absurd that so lukewarm a zeal as his should attempt to warm their fervour, were it not that he remembers how a cool wind can fan a fire into life.[5] But despite his presumably quite genuine reservations about the propriety of doing so, he does not hesitate to address himself to the task of preaching with *Moneo itaque et precor*,[6] ('and so I advise and pray'). His advice amounts to this: be on your guard at all times; make sure that you progress a little each day; it is much more difficult to recover lost ground than to conquer new territory; even if you cannot

---

[1] S 3.3.4–5. Sister Benedicta Ward provides an assessment of recent studies on these devotional works in her introduction to *The Prayers and Meditations of St. Anselm* (tr.) (London 1973).

[2] S 3.3.7, S 3.4.10, in the prefatory letter to Countess Matilda.

[3] S 3.4.7.

[4] These were monks of Bec taken by Lanfranc to Canterbury and thus separated from Anselm. The list of monks at Bec is given by M. Rule, *The Life and Times of St. Anselm* (London 1883) 2 vols., I, 394–6.

[5] S 3.99.22–5.   [6] S 3.99.31.

achieve as much as you would like, go on striving. Remember that even if you now seem to be among the 'few who are chosen' you cannot be sure how few they are to be at the last, and so you cannot afford to relax your efforts to do better still.[1] This is the substance of the passage repeated in Letter 51.[2] It has exactly the character of a brief sermon.[3] The same might be said for the succeeding passage, where Anselm offers this encouragement: Do not fall into the trap of thinking that the longer you live the remoter death appears. In fact the further you have travelled from the day of your birth, the closer you have come to the day of your death. Be the more careful, then, to try harder and harder as each day passes, and to let no fatigue deter your efforts.[4] Again, the advice is to be found in the later letter,[5] in exactly the same words. These passages, among many, indicate clearly enough that when Anselm adopts his 'preaching' tone, his overriding purpose is to spur others to be spiritually energetic.

In the final recension of the *De Incarnatione Verbi*,[6] for the first and only time in the treatises, Anselm tells his readers how he feels they should go about the task of thinking about God. He explains, not the role of religious emotion, as he does at the beginning of the Prayers, nor the role of good behaviour, as he does in many of his 'letter-sermons', but the part played in the Christian life by the exercise of the intellect. It is easy to see why Roscelin's accusations, and the unpleasantness of the controversy in which Anselm found himself involved, had prompted this methodical thinking-out of Anselm's own viewpoint. Very probably he had felt no need to speak at length before about an attitude of mind which came so naturally to him that he may not have envisaged the possibility that it might present any real difficulty to any right-minded man. Anselm's writings show him to have possessed an exceptionally balanced temperament; neither feeling nor curiosity often ran away with him, and he was always able to test his intellectual insights against the intu-

---

[1] S 3.99.31–100.53.   [2] S 3.165.18–39.

[3] Beryl Smalley gives details of recent publications in this field: 'Oxford University Sermons 1290–3', *Mediaeval Learning and Literature: Essays Presented to R. W. Hunt*, ed. J. Alexander and M. T. Gibson (Oxford 1976), 307–27.

[4] S 3.100.54–70.   [5] Letter 35, S 3.142.6–143.21.

[6] For two views of the number of recensions of this work Anselm composed, see AB, p. 34.

itions of faith, and to give orderliness to his strong emotions by the exercise of rational thought. One of the most revealing aspects of the *De Incarnatione Verbi* is the evidence it provides that Anselm was coming to understand more clearly that other men were not all like himself, either in their gifts, or in their attitudes.

Again, Anselm emphasizes his own inadequacies. He is, he says, merely a *contemptibilis homuncio*.[1] But once he has paid this tribute to nice feeling and convention, he sets to work with vigour. That is not to say, for all the energy of his expressions of reproach against those who abuse the powers of their intellects, that he attacks the miscreants viciously. He goes to some trouble to make it plain that he feels no rancour against the trouble-maker Roscelin himself. 'If he who has put this afore-said proposition about has come round to the truth, with God's help, let him not think that I write this letter against him, for he is no longer what he was':

> Sed si ille qui praefatam protulit sententiam, deo corrigente ad veritatem rediit, nullatenus putet me in hac epistola contra se loqui, quoniam iam non est quod fuit.[2]

He had in fact felt at first that there was nothing to be gained from polishing his first draft of the work if, as he had heard, Roscelin had recanted.[3] But he now perceives that if Roscelin still maintains his position, and if he is saying something which constitutes a genuine stumbling-block to others, there is every reason to finish the task he has begun. *Sentio plures in eadem laborare quaestione*[4] ('I know that many struggle with the same problem'), he says. There is every indication that when Anselm composed his prefatory homily on the proper use of the intellect in thinking about God, he meant neither to make a personal attack on anyone, nor to be contentious, but only to advise those who had been led astray, principally by the 'heretical dia-lecticians',[5] how best to set about using their God-given reason for its proper purpose. Just as he had felt that it might avoid difficulty if he had Gaunilo's objections and his own reply attached to future copies of the *Proslogion*, because he knew that some readers were troubled by it, so here he intends first of all to protect the easily-led.

---

[1] S 2.5.7.   [2] S 2.5.22–4.   [3] S 2.4.9–12.
[4] S 2.6.2.   [5] S 2.9.21–2.

Nevertheless, Anselm envisages many of his readers as engaging in some activity, as active philosophers, not as passive absorbers of what he is about to tell them. When he wrote the Prologue to the Prayers and Meditations, he instructed his readers to pray for themselves; here he teaches them how to think. Nowhere else in his treatises does Anselm attempt anything like this quite so openly, although it might reasonably be argued that he is teaching his readers to think in every sentence. But in general, his audience in the dialogues, and the friends to whose asking of questions he credits the inspiration of many of his works, play the part of humble enquirers. They are rarely seen to take any initiative so forceful that it causes Anselm to change the direction of his argument.[1] In the *De Incarnatione Verbi*, Anselm is writing for men who have already tried their hand at philosophizing, and who need some guidance in the handling of theological problems if they are not to go seriously astray.

The little homily is full of unusually colourful imagery, designed to capture the imagination in a way most uncharacteristic of Anselm's writing in the majority of his treatises: tossing of horns, moving of stones, climbing of ladders, the blowing away of impostors on the wind; all these are introduced partly to impress readers accustomed to evocative writing,[2] and partly because Anselm himself feels what he has to say strongly. He uses vigorous expressions: *audent; nefanda temeritate; praesumere.*[3] His intention is to strike some reaction from his readers, to win the respect of unsympathetic strangers for his point of view, as well as that loving acceptance he had come to expect in his own friends and pupils. He wants them all to remember what he has said when they next attempt to solve a theological problem; it is the more necessary for him to do so because they will, when they make the attempt, be to some extent on their own. Just as Anselm had tried to guide those who would be using his prayers alone, in private meditation,[4] and to help those who were trying to live the monastic life well away from daily contact

---

[1] The possible exception is Boso, who seems to have been a real help to Anselm in working out the arguments of the *Cur Deus Homo*.

[2] In the first version of the work, Anselm speaks of the *colores rhetorici* as to a readership which will appreciate the reference: S 1.282.26–7.

[3] S 2.6.6.

[4] Benedicta Ward, op. cit., pp. 35–43 looks at private prayer.

with him, so he attempts here to expound a view of the right
use of the intellect to those whose thinking he cannot guide
personally. There is something of the anxiety of the teacher
here, frustrated because he cannot watch over the development
of all his pupils as he would wish. That anxiety is clear enough
in Anselm's letters to Maurice, for whose spiritual welfare he was
concerned long after he had left Bec for Canterbury on Lanfranc's summons, and for whose intellectual development he
shows an equal and continuing care.[1] The would-be *dialectici* of
the schools were not of course Anselm's personal responsibility.
Nevertheless he wishes to see them guided aright.

The advice he gives is sensible enough. Firstly, he suggests
that man is given reason, not so that he can question the tenets
of Christian faith, but rather so that he may hold his faith more
strongly when he has understood it fully. His aim should be, not
to ask *quomodo . . . non sit*, how it may not be so, but to try to see
quomodo sit, how it may be so.[2] By this means, reason may come
to support faith. If a man tries to use his reason to upset the
facts of faith, that is like trying to roll a great stone with his
'horns' like a silly animal; it is more likely that the stone will
tear out the horns than that the horns will move the stone.[3] In
this graphic way, Anselm shows how important it is to preserve
a sane recognition of the relative powers of the human intellect
and those of God. A second danger suggests itself. A man may
believe that he understands everything when he has really
attained only to an understanding of some small part. Then he
may try to tackle the deepest questions of faith before he is
ready:

altissimas de fide quaestiones assurgere.[4]

Without the necessary spiritual wings he may try to leap at the
heights; climbing upwards is really, says Anselm, a matter of
painstakingly ascending a ladder.[5] The first rung of that ladder
is faith, and unless we tread upon it we cannot ascend to understanding. To try to leap at the truth only produces a variety of
errors (*multimodi errores*).[6] Thus Anselm provides his readers
with two simple principles: firstly, they should look for reasons

---

[1] Among the letters to Maurice, Letter 64 in particular shows Anselm's concern
for Maurice's continuing education.
[2] S 2.6.10–7.2.   [3] S 2.7.5–6.   [4] S 2.7.7–10.
[5] S 2.7.11.   [6] S 2.8.1.

to accept their faith, not for reasons to question it; secondly they should be patient, content to progress little by little in their understanding.

Then he goes on to say something rather more difficult to grasp, which demands something closer to a specifically monastic attitude on the part of his readers. They are to approach the task of reasoning only after they have first made spiritual preparations. The mode of understanding which they will find most fruitful is one in which belief and understanding are linked together by an inner experience. Here we are on the ground of homiletic indeed. A series of preparations must be made. First, the heart must be cleansed (*mundandum est cor*),[1] and it must be cleansed by faith. The heart, it should be emphasized, is the seat of thought in Scripture, and Anselm himself uses it in that sense in the *Proslogion*.[2] Then the eyes of the mind must be illuminated or given light to see,[3] by keeping God's commandments. Then humble obedience will produce that simplicity of mind to which Anselm particularly speaks in the *Cur Deus Homo*,[4] through holy living.[5] There can be no doubt that such step-by-step procedures would have a direct appeal to those trained in monastic observances, but even the secular cleric could be expected, in some sense, to 'recognize' them, and it would become a common method in the sermons of the later twelfth century to employ some such device to assist the listener to climb up step by step to some higher spiritual experience.[6] The difficulty for Anselm's readers lies not so much in following this comparatively straightforward procedure, as in understanding the theory of knowledge he now puts forward.

Belief and understanding are united, he says, by experience:

Nam qui non crediderit, non experietur; et qui expertus non fuerit, non cognoscet.[7]

('For he who will not believe will not experience, and he who has not experienced cannot know.') So much greater and better is this kind of knowledge than that gained merely by hearing about something, as a direct knowledge of any object is better than merely hearing a description of it:

[1] S 2.8.7–8.   [2] S 1.103.18.   [3] S 2.8.8–9.
[4] S 2.48.5–12.   [5] S 2.8.11–9.1.
[6] Alan of Lille begins his *Ars Praedicandi*, printed in PL, 210, with a reference to the climbing of just such a ladder.
[7] S 2.9.5–6.

Quantum enim rei auditum superant experientia, tantum vincit audientis cognitionem experientis scientia.[1]

This could be interpreted in various ways for what it tells us of Anselm's theory of knowledge; but it must be agreed that he sets his readers a hard test of their 'knowledge'. Those who have obtained it derivatively and who hold it only superficially cannot but feel the force of his argument. He has tried to show them how worthless any other mode of understanding is, so as to create in them a sense of dissatisfaction with their purely dialectical speculations, and a hunger for something better.

He ends with two further points, which make the total number of ideas to be grasped not unmanageable. (Anselm has been careful not to try to say too much in this little homily). He suggests that knowledge apparently gained can be lost, if it has not been arrived at in a proper manner, and, more importantly, that it may simply be wrong—not knowledge at all, but a series of mistakes.[2] In this way he destroys yet again whatever remaining confidence his readers may have in the power of dialectic used without faith. Then he makes the rhetorically cogent—if philosophically debatable—point that those who abandon themselves to the things of the flesh will find that their thinking, too, cannot rise above the level of bodily things to the abstract. It will remain entangled in bodily images (*in imaginationibus corporalibus obvoluta*).[3] Here, too, Anselm is deliberately hitting at the points of special pride in the minds of such men as Roscelin. Their very claims to special powers are shown to be empty. He has given his readers a positive line to follow; but he has not neglected to demolish any alternatives they may wish to suggest.

The end of the sermon is clearly marked. 'I have said this', says Anselm, 'in case anyone should presume to discuss the highest questions of faith before it is appropriate.'[4] 'And now we must come to the reason why we began':

Iam veniendum est ad id propter quod incepimus.[5]

The beginning had been equally clearly marked:

Sed priusquam de quaestione disseram, aliquid praemittam . . .[6]

[1] S 2.9.7–8.   [2] S 2.9.16–19.   [3] S 2.10.2–3.
[4] S 2.10.14–15.   [5] S 2.10.16–17.   [6] S 2.6.5.

('But before I deal with the question, let me say something first . . .').

The little homily is therefore quite separate, and can be read without reference to the rest of the *De Incarnatione Verbi*. Anselm had deliberately given it that 'separateness' in the final version of the text. Much of the material in the homily occurs in the *prior recensio*,[1] but there it does not take the form of a distinct homiletic composition. Instead, Anselm speaks in the first person, as though he himself has been thinking about his own attitude to the part the intellect should play, and perhaps doing so for the first time in a systematic manner:

Si potero intelligere, gratias agam; si non potero non inmittam cornua ad ventilandum.[2]

He is not, then, offering advice to others in quite the same way as he does in the later version; and when he polishes the homily there and gives it its final form, he does not preach to others what he has not already tested upon himself. This, like the instructions which begin the collection of Prayers and Meditations, and like the imparting of the knowledge Anselm has got by experience in the living of the monastic life, in the Letters, shows Anselm giving advice from experience.

What is new in all this is the evidence it offers that Anselm was beginning to extend his sympathetic understanding more and more widely. He enters into the minds of others no longer quite confident that he will find them much like his own. He becomes concerned over the differences of approach he discovers. He learns to adapt himself to the limitations of understanding he finds in many of his pupils. The *Tres Tractatus* show that he had never been blind to the need to organize his explanations carefully, and to go slowly enough for the least able to follow him easily. But now he begins to allow not only for the slow, but also for the misguided and the deliberately perverse. His own confidence in the reasonableness of the universe is never shaken; he never concedes that it may be impossible to provide an explanation which will fail to satisfy the sensible and right-minded man. But he is less sure than he was of the goodwill of his readers, and he goes further to meet their difficulties in the *Cur Deus Homo* and the *De Conceptu Virginali* than he had ever done before. The alteration in Anselm's attitude seems to

---

[1] S 1.283.24–285.19.   [2] S 1.283.24–5, cf. S 2.7.3–4.

have been visible to those who knew him. Eadmer notes in two consecutive chapters of the *Vita Anselmi* that at the time of the writing of the *Cur Deus Homo*, Anselm was *Christianae fidei amore permotus*, and especially anxious to make himself 'all things to all men'.[1]

[1] VA, p. 107, II, xxx, xxxi.

7

GOD MADE MAN

i: *The Writing of the* Cur Deus Homo, *the* De Conceptu Virginali, *and the* Meditation on Human Redemption

WHEN Anselm became first Prior and then Abbot of Bec he found his time taken up with business affairs to a far greater extent than he would have wished; such, at least, is his frequent complaint. When he was made Archbishop of Canterbury, such burdens and responsibilities and calls upon his time were much increased; in addition, he had to contend with the unpleasantness of conflict with the King, since conscience would not allow him to withdraw from the position he had felt obliged to take up at first. Not least among his troubles was his own apparently quite violent initial reaction of distaste for the task which he believed was being forced upon him. It is difficult to find any indication that Anselm took the slightest pleasure in these new responsibilities, although with time his distress subsided naturally into disinclination and he seems eventually to have fashioned for himself a way of life in which he could sometimes recapture an atmosphere of monastic quiet. He carried out his duties conscientiously enough, as he saw them. It must be conceded that much of the evidence we have from his own hand belongs to the period when he had been newly appointed, or when the conflict with the King was particularly pressing. We hear from Anselm himself, in other words, only when he is severely upset. Eadmer describes many episodes of domestic pleasure, quiet travelling, enjoyable visits to English communities. Nevertheless, when Anselm became Archbishop, great changes came about in his life and most of them were not to his liking.

It is striking, therefore, that it was during the first years after he became Archbishop that Anselm wrote the *Cur Deus Homo*, which he finished in 1098. Soon afterwards he composed the *De Conceptu Virginali* and the *Meditation on Human Redemption*, which Eadmer brackets together, saying that he wrote them at about the same time.[1] Both works contain what might be described as the afterthoughts of the *Cur Deus Homo*: the *Meditation* is a devotional piece, in which Anselm has tried to distil out the essence of the *Cur Deus Homo* for contemplation. The *De Conceptu Virginali* carries on a portion of the argument of the *Cur Deus Homo*, and it allows Anselm to develop views at which he had merely hinted there. All three have to do with Anselm's thinking about the work of Christ. They form a group whose coherence suggests that Anselm may have been glad of a long-term, large-scale project to turn to when he had a period of respite from business.

The task of working so much material into two books of argument and one of prayer took time. As early as 1092, when Anselm encountered his old friend Gilbert Crispin at Westminster, he may have been beginning to reflect upon his subject.[2] He certainly made a beginning on the writing of the *Cur Deus Homo* in England, and he finished it during his first exile from England. Eadmer describes his pleasure when he found a remote mountain top in Capua where he could go into comparative retirement and work in peace.[3] Since Eadmer makes a special point of the fact that it was unusual for Anselm to pause in his work when he was composing a treatise,[4] we may suppose that he was steadily working on the *Cur Deus Homo* throughout the years up to 1098, whenever he had the opportunity. Even then he felt that he had been rushed into finishing it, by impatient friends who wanted to make copies.[5] The addition of the other two works has something of the character of a postscript, but the fact that he wrote them at all suggests that Anselm may have come to rely upon the *Cur Deus Homo* as a source of comfort and refreshment which he was reluctant to give up so as to see it finished and published.

ii: *Trinity, Incarnation and Redemption: the Posing of Problems*

Anselm, like other scholars of his day, saw the problems raised by the Trinity in particular and perhaps limited terms.

[1] VA, p. 122, II, xliv.   [2] AB, pp. 205–6.   [3] VA, p. 107, S 2.42.7–8.
[4] VA, p. 140, in a reference to the *De Concordia*.
[5] S 2.42.5–6. On the existence of a shortened version of the *Cur Deus Homo*, once thought to have been one of the earlier drafts stolen by Anselm's friends for copying, see JH, pp. 14–16.

He concentrated his efforts on the attempt to demonstrate how, despite the apparent mathematical impossibility of the matter, it was possible for one God to be three. Further difficulties of this kind presented themselves: how was one Person of the Trinity made Man without the other two being personally involved in the process? How can there be two modes of derivation in God, the Son's begetting by the Father and the Holy Spirit's Procession from the Father and the Son? Even if we can differentiate between the two processes, how can it be that neither mode of derivation is inferior to the other? How can that which is derived from something else not be in some sense secondary to it or dependent upon it? Is the Person of the Son perpetually begotten of the Father, or did his begetting take place once and for all? By the same token, what are we to say of the Procession of the Holy Spirit? A number of these issues present difficulties chiefly because it is natural to try to visualize the relationships between the Persons of the Trinity in finite terms, to do with time and place. Anselm had been at pains to point out in the *Monologion* and the *Proslogion* that God is limitless and eternal and time and place have no part in him. But this is to talk about God in terms which make sense only in connection with time and place, and those terms are helpful only in discussions of the Incarnation. This is rather more than a matter of natural human limitation. It has to do with the habits of thought bred in Anselm and his contemporaries by their training in the secular arts. Grammatical theory and dialectical principles alike encouraged educated men to think in terms of the building-blocks of language, words joined together into sayings, propositions, statements. Given these habits of mind, it is difficult to see how Anselm and his contemporaries could attempt to see the Godhead as anything but three entities held in some formal relationship to one another such as that which obtains between created substances, and yet somehow constituting one entity. Augustine, heir to a similar tradition, which similarly reinforced a natural limitation of human understanding, had come up against exactly the same difficulty. What Anselm tried to do when he discussed the Trinity was to resolve these grammatically and dialectically conceived anomalies, in the belief that if he could do so he would be helping the understanding to grasp the idea of the Trinity more

directly. It almost seems as though he saw these principles of
the secular arts as stumbling-blocks, rather than as the aids to
understanding they had once been intended to be. He found the
problems already well defined for him along these lines, and he
did not try to re-define the questions themselves. It is clear that
he thought there would be no questions to answer if only the
existing misunderstandings could be got out of the way.

Among the devices which have been suggested in recent
years, some have to do with psychological notions of identity,
personality, and consciousness within the Trinity. These explanations entirely circumvent a number of the difficulties
which had so much force for Anselm. They do not answer the
questions he was asking, however, and it is doubtful whether he
would have been satisfied while those questions continued to
nag at him. But they do provide a point of entry to the solution
of the problem of the Trinity which goes beyond anything
Anselm could attempt. When he shows himself so skilled in
understanding the workings of other men's minds, he does not
show himself a theoretical psychologist, but only a man of
developed insight and natural sympathy.

There are parallels for the 'psychological approach' among
the analogies of Anselm's day. Augustine's trinity in the mind
of man (memory, will, and understanding), and the alternative
'trinity', *mens, notitia, amor*, are obvious examples. But these have
no bearing upon the problem of the identity of the Persons
which lies at the heart of Trinitarian theology. Augustine never
suggests that the memory, the will, and the understanding have
distinct identities, as the Persons of the Godhead must in some
sense possess separate consciousness as well as shared consciousness. Nor does he examine the nature of the 'I' or *mens*
which unites memory, will, and understanding in one personality. He has merely suggested a helpful analogy with a necessarily limited scope of application.

Most of the other analogies which were current in Anselm's
day were designed to meet the conventional 'structural'
problems of metaphysics rather than psychological ones. The
image of sun, light and heat, for example, or that of tree, root
and branch, river, pool and spring, or the slightly different
Boethian example of sword, blade and point, all have the
characteristic of trying to demonstrate how one entity may be

more than one, and yet still one, by means of grammatical or logical devices. These are mostly analogies involving objects in the natural world, the relationship of whose parts to one another can readily be perceived by the senses. They serve usefully as analogies because the words we employ in speaking of them are sometimes ambivalent. 'Sun', for example, includes in its reference the light and heat of the sun; 'tree' includes branch and root; 'sword', blade and point; 'river', spring and pool. Such accounts of the Trinity depend for their force on peculiarities of usage, and on observable aspects of the natural world. These were the kinds of analogy Anselm handled most readily.[1]

The doctrine of the Trinity, then, may raise metaphysical problems of one kind for patristic and mediaeval writers, and of another kind for writers of later centuries. But in either case its acceptability rests upon philosophical considerations which lie largely outside the scope of experimental science. In the last analysis, we cannot lay hold upon the idea of the Trinity by experimental observation; we must work by analogy. All those questions of time and place, substance and relation, which must be got out of the way if we are to understand anything of the nature of the Trinity, present a very different picture, however, when we look at the problem of the Incarnation. There we have to account for God's being physically limited by time and space and the laws which govern substance and relation in the natural world. Experimental science cannot be set aside. J. I. Packer has pointed out that it is at the points where Christ's life on earth appears to contradict scientific laws that many people find stumbling-blocks.[2] Virgin Birth, miracles, Resurrection from the dead are not easily acceptable to minds conditioned by a non-specialist knowledge of modern biology, physics, or chemistry.

Two things must be said here. Firstly, just as Anselm found that many of the objections put forward by the dialecticians of his days were founded on an inadequate knowledge of dialectic, and that dialectic itself would frequently serve to refute them, so it might be argued that it is not beyond the scope of modern science to admit the possibility of parthenogenesis, events

[1] On these analogies, see my article, 'St. Anselm's Images of Trinity', *Journal of Theological Studies*, xxvii (1976), 46–57.
[2] *Knowing God*, pp. 45–6.

which appear to infringe natural laws, resuscitation after some of the criteria of death have been satisfied. Theologians are faced with the task of defending the literal truth of the Gospel accounts not against a science which might accommodate it, but against a general public attitude which will not, because it lays claim to a general scientific authority for what has come to seem a common-sense attitude. There are marked parallels with Anselm's own position.

Secondly, just as in Anselm's day, a man's conception of what was 'reasonable' was conditioned by his education and training, so his notion of what was 'scientifically possible' was formed by the culture of his time. The science of Anselm's day accommodated itself to such anomalies in the natural order relatively easily. Anselm himself remarks in the *De Conceptu Virginali* that there are various ways in which something may happen, amongst them the miraculous way.[1] He therefore finds it unnecessary to attempt to give an account of miracles, the Virgin Birth, the Resurrection, as scientific oddities. He concentrates his attention rather on the bearing of the Virgin Birth upon the question of the absence of Original Sin in Christ.

Anselm's contemporary readers and his modern ones might, however, agree, in finding a common stumbling-block in the notion of God's becoming Man, although their areas of uncertainty might differ. Because of the ways in which he saw the issue, there is much that Anselm leaves out of account. His attention is focused on the reasons for the Incarnation, rather than on the mode of Redemption. He finds no difficulty in understanding how Christ's death could wipe out the sin of the whole human race. Nor does he pause to examine at length any aspect of Christ's work except his coming and his atoning death. His central interest lies in a single question—the issue he sets before him for contemplation in the *Meditation*—why did Christ redeem the world? The question resolves itself at once into several subsidiary questions. Why did no one else do so? Could anyone else have done so? Why did God trouble to redeem fallen man rather than create a new race of good men, or simply forgive mankind? Why could God not have left things as they were? Why did God not redeem the fallen angels?

[1] *De Conceptu Virginali*, 11.

Could he have done so? Did the Devil have a God-given right to harass mankind, as scholars in Anselm's day were arguing that he did?[1] Was God under any obligation to redeem mankind? Did the Father force the Son to become incarnate? If the Son became incarnate of his own free will, why did he dispose his will to do so? It will readily be seen that Anselm could give only one answer to a number of these questions, if he was to preserve an orthodox position, although some of them allowed more than one possible answer within the bounds of that limitation. In general, however, he begins the *Cur Deus Homo* with the answers to his questions firmly before him, and the task which he has to carry out is to demonstrate by reasoning that his answers are sound.

The *De Conceptu Virginali* deals with a further series of questions which arise out of Anselm's discussions of the nature of sin in the *Cur Deus Homo*. It rapidly becomes clear that answers to the *Cur Deus Homo* questions must involve the development of a full explanation of the role and nature of sin, or it will be impossible to understand in how desperate a position fallen man stood; how the Son discarnate had no affinity with sinful man; how the Son Incarnate was fully Man, although unique among men in being without sin; how nevertheless, because he was Man he could offer himself as a sacrifice for the sin of man, and the sacrifice would not be inappropriate; how it follows from this that the Redeemer must be both God (so that he was sinless) and Man (so that he owed the debt of man to God for sin). A good deal of the *Cur Deus Homo* is, as a result, concerned with sin.

In the *De Conceptu Virginali* Anselm tries to answer the question: How was it possible for Christ to be born of a human mother without deriving from her the taint of Original Sin?[2] He had given some account of the matter in the *Cur Deus Homo*, but now he provides an alternative argument. He suggests that every child that is born has a built-in necessity-to-sin when he reaches the age at which his rational will comes into operation. But that necessity of sinning consists in three things: every man has an obligation to make recompense for the sin of Adam; yet

[1] See AB, pp. 357–61.
[2] See AB, p. 296 on the tendency of later critics to associate Anselm with arguments for the Immaculate Conception, despite his own clear arguments against it.

no man has the power to do so, so every man sins by failing to do so; the soul in a corrupt body cannot understand righteousness fully, and so it cannot preserve righteousness. Because the soul of Christ is divine, he has power to make recompense and he understands and preserves righteousness. The first constitutes no problem, if Christ has both the will and the power freely to make the recompense which is owed.[1]

This sequence of demonstration itself gives rise to further questions, particularly those concerning the nature of Original Sin, which pass somewhat beyond the immediate issue of the work of Christ. Anselm is trying to show how it was possible for Christ to fulfil the conditions which it was necessary for him to fulfil if Redemption was to follow the course he believes it did. The aspects of Atonement, Redemption, hamartiology, soteriology and so on which Anselm examines are, then, intimately interconnected within his scheme of argument; one question demands consideration of another. Certainly, many of Anselm's questions were in other scholars' minds, but in the Sentence literature of contemporary schools they were generally being considered in isolation.[2] Anselm's achievement is to demonstrate their connections with one another, to construct from a series of related topics a single consistent account which would meet every problem which had been raised. Anselm of Laon and the theologians of his school took such questions as, 'Why did God become Man?'; 'Are the actual sins of the fathers the original sins of the children?'; 'What is sin?' one at a time.[3] Anselm found it impossible to separate them.

iii: *The Solidity of the Argument*

An insistent theme of the *Cur Deus Homo* is the *soliditas*[4] of what is being established about the redemption of the world. Anselm thought that what he had to say was unshakeable, firstly because his conclusions, the conclusions of doctrinal orthodoxy, were true, and secondly because if he had succeeded in carrying out his stated intentions, his readers would recognize

---

[1] *De Conceptu Virginali*, 8, S 2.149–50.

[2] AB, pp. 84–5 discusses the occurrence of these questions in the debates of contemporary schools.

[3] O. Lottin, *Psychologie et morale aux xiie et xiiie siècles* v (Gembloux 1959), contains editions of surviving Sentences.

[4] S 2.51.19, 52.3, 104.13–14, for example.

that truth for themselves. The experience of recognition is an important feature of Anselm's own thought. He believed that it constituted grounds for absolute certainty. It is a special case of self-evidence, where some groundwork has had to be carried out first, but where, ultimately, acceptance comes by direct intuitive perception of an axiomatic truth.

At a more pedestrian level, Anselm expected his words to have the *soliditas* of mature exposition, because he presented a plain setting-out of a series of arguments which had been thoroughly tested on his friends and pupils over a number of years. In the process, he had arrived at lucidity. The firmness of Anselm's conclusions makes itself felt because of the clarity, even the obviousness, the arguments possess for Anselm himself, and which he thought they would possess for others. He has tried to say nothing which will not be comprehensible to every one of his readers. Comprehensibility is a prerequisite if the arguments are to help them towards recognition.

The *Proslogion* is shot through with the light of Anselm's excitement at his discovery of the ontological argument. He breaks off his exposition frequently to address himself to God in prayer. The *Cur Deus Homo* has nothing of this febrile quality. We cannot imagine that Anselm sat down to write it white-hot with inspiration. Indeed we know that he did not.[1] Yet the tightness of argument of the *Cur Deus Homo* was something at which Anselm had always aimed in everything he wrote. There is no reason why the leaping powers of mind which give their peculiar quality to the *Proslogion* insights, should have been in any way constrained by the demands of exactness of argument. Where Anselm sets out his arguments in the *Proslogion* he does it with his usual neatness and economy. The difference lies in this: in the *Proslogion* Anselm's purpose is to share his illumination with his readers, while in the *Cur Deus Homo* he wants them to experience his own calmer certainties. The *soliditas* of its plain reasonableness is entirely in keeping with this intention.

Anselm had lately learned, in writing the *De Incarnatione Verbi*,[2] to present as tightly-knit a defensive front to his de-

---

[1] He describes in his Preface how he worked patiently on the text over a period of time, S 2.42. See, too, R. W. Southern's account of the writing of the *Cur Deus Homo* in AB, p. 77.

[2] Finished *c.* 1092–3.

tractors as he could. He knew well enough that what he saw as
unassailable certainties in constructing his arguments were not
always as plain to others as to himself. He writes in a letter to
Abbot Rainald that he is afraid there are those who will read
the *Monologion* with an eye to its faults, and look for signs of
unorthodoxy in it.[1] He is as genuinely concerned in case others
are led astray, as he is for his own reputation.[2] Even though he
received Gaunilo's challenge with good humour—'You have
reproached me with goodwill, not with ill-will,' he says[3]—he
learned here, too, that no argument was safe from attack. He
displays concern even in minor matters where he feels a misunderstanding has been created by his failure to make himself
clear.[4] His anxiety is correspondingly greater when it is put to
him that he may be seriously misleading his readers. He concedes to Lanfranc that some of the things he has said in the
Monologion 'could have been better put'.[5] The cumulative effect
of these experiences in the reception of his earlier works must
have encouraged him to give a good deal of attention to the
task of leaving no gap at all in the chain of his reasoning in the
Cur Deus Homo.[6] When he makes the bold claim that his arguments there are solid, he does not do so lightly.

It may be, too, that the subject-matter of the *Cur Deus Homo*
accounts in some measure for its solid, earth-bound, quality.
R. W. Southern has pointed out that in the *Cur Deus Homo*
Anselm treats of the 'historical fact' of the Incarnation, and not
of the 'metaphysical reality' with which he generally prefers to
concern himself. This assumes that the line between metaphysics
and history is to be drawn somewhere in the area between
matters which have to do strictly with the Trinity as a whole,
and matters involving Christ's coming to earth as a man at
some specific time in the past. Ritschl would, it seems, want to

[1] Letter 83, S 3.207.3–208.11.

[2] S 3.208.21–5.

[3] S 1.139.11–12. We can, I think, rule out the possibility that Anselm himself
perceived and framed Gaunilo's objection and then answered it in his own *persona*,
by the style of Gaunilo's reply—and also because it would have been most uncharacteristic of Anselm to do so.

[4] See, for instance, Letters 12–13 to Rodulfus, over a misunderstanding to do
with the lending of some books, S 3.115–19.

[5] Letter 77, to Lanfranc, S 3.200.30–2.

[6] Boso refers to it as a *contextio*, S 2.130.2; with this might be compared the *con-
catenatione contextum argumentorum* of the *Monologion*, S 1.93.5.

draw the line elsewhere, so that almost every aspect of these central topics of theology would fall within the field of history:

not only the dogma of the two natures, but the whole metaphysical background of ecclesiastical Christology is thus got rid of . . . and replaced by an historical view of the subject. . . . Metaphysical attributes of the deity cannot be ascribed to him for the simple reason that they are altogether outside the religious method of cognition, which is concerned only with judgements of value.[1]

Anselm himself, it might be argued, tries hard to deal metaphysically with even the historical aspects of the Incarnation; he would certainly want to draw the line much closer to the opposite end of the theological spectrum. It is by no means certain that he can have envisaged the Incarnation as a historical fact in the sense that it happened at some determinable point in the sequence of past events. He had no means of acquiring a 'sense of history' of that kind. But he was forced to look at something which came about at a specific point in the past, rather than at the eternal verities of the nature of God and the perpetual relation between the Persons of the Trinity. This alone might be expected to tie his speculations more firmly to the ground. It gives him, at any rate, several points of reference in matters of common human experience, and this may have encouraged him to feel that he had made out a case which would meet his readers' understanding at a straightforward everyday level of thought.

A third factor would have discouraged Anselm from allowing the leaven of devotional fervour to alter the texture of the work. He has chosen to attempt to prove the necessity for the Incarnation, *remoto Christo*, without having recourse to any 'given fact' about Christ himself, or the events described in Scripture.[2] The phrase implies not only, as J. McIntyre has put it, that Christ is the 'excluded premise' of the *Cur Deus Homo*,[3] but also perhaps that his very presence is in some measure excluded from the dialogue. Christ is very much present to Anselm in the Meditation which was written as a companion work to the *Cur Deus*

[1] AB, p. 82, and cf. O. Pfleiderer, *The Development of Theology in Germany* (London 1923), pp. 189–90.
[2] S 2.42.11–12.
[3] J. McIntyre, *St. Anselm and his Critics: a Reinterpretation of the Cur Deus Homo* (Edinburgh 1954), p. 53.

Homo—the *Meditation of Human Redemption.*[1] But whereas in the
Proslogion, Anselm's dialogue (of which we hear only one side)
is with God himself, in the *Cur Deus Homo* Anselm talks to Boso
because, under the terms he has imposed upon himself, he cannot talk to Christ as he thinks his arguments through.

These are shifts of emphasis, not indications of fundamental
changes in Anselm's outlook. He has not lost the joy of his faith,
as parts of the *Meditation on Human Redemption* show; nor has he
lost his sense of the presence of God. His caution in putting his
arguments together has not made him tedious. But the overall
impression of *soliditas* after which he was consciously seeking in
the *Cur Deus Homo* nevertheless implies that it was written with
a more serious pleasure than the sometimes frenetic joy with
which he composed the *Proslogion*.

iv: *Simplicity and Enjoyment*

Studies of the *Cur Deus Homo* have tended to concentrate upon
certain aspects which have seemed to possess special relevance
for modern critics. It has, for example, been customary to consider the balance between the respective roles of faith and
reason in the *Cur Deus Homo* almost to the exclusion of other
aspects of the work.[2] But perhaps this is a question which presents itself to Anselm's modern readers in a guise which Anselm
himself would scarcely have recognized. M. Charlesworth finds
in it the reason for much 'ambiguity in Anselm's position',[3] and
sees him as 'groping his way confusedly' towards a clearer
statement of his position.[4] But the mark of the work, for Anselm
himself, seems to have been the very clarity and simplicity with
which his arguments were to convince everyone who read it. He
certainly felt no confusion in his own mind; in fact he was
rather pleased with the way in which he felt he had cleared up
obscurities. Of course the queries raised by Anselm's modern
critics, both of the *Cur Deus Homo* and of the *Proslogion* argument,
have to do with real philosophical and theological problems,
and it may well be that Anselm's accounts will not satisfy

---

[1] VA, II.xliv and AB, p. 36.
[2] McIntyre devotes a substantial proportion of his study to a discussion of the
credo ut intelligam question. See, too, M. Charlesworth, *St. Anselm's* Proslogion
(Oxford 1965), pp. 30–40.
[3] Charlesworth, p. 34.   [4] Ibid., p. 38.

criteria of distinction developed in later centuries. But if we pursue such lines of criticism too far, we shall lose sight of Anselm's own intentions. It is perhaps in the long run more illuminating to try to understand the assumptions which led Anselm himself to believe that he was being perfectly clear and consistent in his account of the Incarnation. Faith and reason for Anselm were always mutually supportive, and he can hardly be expected to have thought about them separately with the intention of distinguishing two internally consistent and independent modes of thinking about God. When he says that he intends to prove by reason alone, he means that proof to be slotted into the scheme of faith as soon as it is devised.

There is one further point at which Anselm's modern critics have tended to emphasize one side of what he says to the exclusion of another. He lived in an age which was to produce a series of dialogues between Christians and Jews, and sometimes with philosophers, too. His old friend, Gilbert Crispin, is the author of one of these.[1] When Anselm claims that he hopes to deal with the objections of unbelievers, the *objectiones infidelium*,[2] it is natural enough to assume that his intention is to convince unbelievers, as well as to strengthen the faith of Christians by showing them reasons for their beliefs. But early in the *Cur Deus Homo* he makes it plain that he has another division of his audience or readership in mind, too. He says that he wants not only the educated, the *litterati*, but also the uneducated, the *illiterati*, to find pleasure in his explanations.[3] This is a sentiment he had expressed in earlier works. In the *Monologion*, for example, he says that he had written as clearly as he could, using commonly-recognized arguments and simple means of demonstration:

plano stilo et vulgaribus argumentis simplicique disputatione.[4] He wanted even those of slower wits[5] to understand him. His

---

[1] See J. Armitage Robinson, *Gilbert Crispin Abbot of Westminster* (Cambridge 1911). Gilbert's *Disputatio Christiani cum Gentile de Fide Christi* is edited by C. C. J. Webb in *Mediaeval and Renaissance Studies*, III (1954), pp. 55–78, and his *Disputatio Iudei et Christiani* by B. Blumenkranz (Antwerp 1956). Cf. Peter Abelard's *Dialogus inter Philosophum, Judaeum et Christianum*, ed. R. Thomas (Stuttgart 1966). See, too, AB, pp. 88–91.

[2] S 2.42.10–11 and Chs. 3–4, pp. 50–2.

[3] S 2.48.5–6.   [4] S 1.7.9–11.

[5] S 2.48.12.

conclusions are to have *soliditas* not only for those of advanced educational attainments, but also for everyone else who will give his mind to what he has to say. With this end in view, Anselm tries throughout his writings to be clear and simple, but nowhere does he do so as obviously and as consciously as in the *Cur Deus Homo*. He wrote the book for Boso, as well as with his aid, as the beginning of the *De Conceptu Virginali* shows. Yet Boso is not its 'onlie begetter': 'You encouraged me to write it more even than the others, and I took you for my partner in the dialogue.'[1] Maurice was perhaps the chief inspiration of the *De Casu Diaboli*.[2] But even where Anselm wrote for a single friend, he also wrote for all his other friends and pupils,[3] and he never allowed the fact that not all his readers were of Boso's intellectual stature to slip to the back of his mind. He tried to make himself so clear that everyone would be able to share his own realization of how clear and simple and certain were the truths of the Christian faith.

Karl Barth remarks that 'Anselm's theology is simple. That of the plain secret of his "proving".'[4] There is, however, more to Anselm's simplicity than the mere use of technically simple modes of discussion, important though these are. He displays a simplicity of conception and exposition hard won through many years of discussion and private thought, which had been systematically directed towards making things plain. Anselm does not set about the task in the spirit of a Hugh of St. Victor, by reducing complex matters to their component elements in order that his pupils may get their learning out of an encyclopaedia.[5] He looks instead for a means of expressing the intrinsic simplicity of theological truths which time and thought have made plain to him. Anselm wants, in the words of T. S. Eliot,

[1] S 2.139.5–7.
[2] S 3.225.17–21.
[3] The Prayers to the Virgin, for example, were written for Gundolf and 'someone' else, but they were circulated far more widely than that. See Letter 28, S 3.135–6.
[4] K. Barth, *Anselm: Fides Quaerens Intellectum* (Zurich 1958), English tr., I. W. Robertson (1960), p. 68.
[5] It would not be fair to suggest that Hugh regarded his *Didascalicon*, ed. C. Buttimer (Washington 1939), as his most important work. But it is clear from this and his *Opera Propaedeutica*, ed. R. Baron (Notre Dame 1966), that he was greatly concerned to provide simple versions of difficult arts for the beginner, rather than to simplify profundities for every man's understanding.

to save his pupils a lengthy journey, at the end of which they will 'arrive' back where they 'started':

And know the place for the first time.[1]

Anselm himself has attained a recognition of the simple truths which were always implicit in his theological beliefs, and he tries in all his works, but especially in the *Cur Deus Homo*, to show them to others.

This is a very different matter from the 'simplifying' of Hugh of St. Victor. It is the simplicity and 'obviousness' which is the mark of greatness in original thought. The apparent simplicity of much of what Anselm has to say masks an underlying complexity, and it has been arrived at as a result of processing and comparing a great deal of information and a variety of principles. Some of that groundwork is evident in the *Cur Deus Homo* in the early chapters where Boso lists the views of previous writers.[2] It is also apparent in the degree of emancipation from his sources which Anselm displays in almost never quoting except from Scripture. What had been perhaps a weakness in the *Monologion* had now become one of the principal strengths of Anselm's thought. Once stated, Anselm's insights have the quality of appealing directly and immediately to the understanding of any interested reader, whether or not he possesses the specialist knowledge to follow the processes by which the new thought has been arrived at. Anselm never expects his readers to know his authorities, or to be able to furnish authorities of their own to support his conclusions. If he did so, he would be making his arguments less than clear in their own right. All this is generally true of at least the major thoughts of St. Anselm—and of a good many of the minor ones, too. R. W. Southern has suggested that Anselm's ideas are capable of giving an 'intense pleasure' to the 'amateur'.[3] They do so today if they are received as Anselm intended them to be received, without carping over what may be anachronistic technicalities, and in a spirit of *simplicitas*.

Anselm's intention was exactly this. By the standards of modern philosophers, theologians and logicians, every one of

[1] T. S. Eliot, The Four Quartets, *Little Gidding*, *V*, The Complete Poems and Plays (London 1969), p. 197.

[2] Book I.3–8.

[3] R. W. Southern, *Mediaeval Humanism* (Oxford 1970), p. 15.

Anselm's readers was an 'amateur'. Neither Anselm himself nor
any of his contemporaries could have followed many of the
analyses which have since been made of his work, without first
being given an introduction to the modes of reasoning and
symbols, whose first principles, as well as their finer points,
would in some instances have been unfamiliar to him. That
reflects not merely changes in terminology and the use of
ordinary language and technical language and methods of
notation, but a fundamental difference between Anselm's
intentions and those of a number of later thinkers. The change
of direction was to come very soon; it is already under way in
Abelard's day. It was still possible for Anselm to believe that his
proofs lost nothing in forcefulness for being clear, simple and
technically uncomplicated. McIntyre's description of Anselm's
thought as being characterized by a 'vastness and grandeur'[1]
does not altogether allow for the way in which its apparently
bold effects rest on an underlying simplicity of conception. It
seems that Anselm's thinking transcends technicalities, rather
than ignores them, in a way which no later writer would have
dared to do.

When he remarks on the way in which others sneer at the
simple-mindedness of Christian believers, at *simplicitatem nos-
tram*,[2] Anselm is saddened that they are missing a God-given
pleasure. Unbelievers deride, even believers worry over doctrinal problems (*et fideles multi in corde versare*).[3] But there is no
need for them to shut themselves off from the pleasure of understanding how clear and simple it all is (*omnibus intelligibilis . . . et
rationis pulchritudinem amabilis*).[4] He could not have written so
fifty years later, because the great accretion of technical expertise, especially in the field of the *artes*, would have presented him
with far greater problems in making himself clear to 'amateurs'
without blurring technically important distinctions. The technical knowledge Anselm possessed has all been integrated into
his scheme of reasoning; he is never guilty of woolly argument.
But the task of integration and of working through the detail to
a simple overall picture would have been vastly greater half a
century later, and perhaps even Anselm could not have
achieved it.

His simplifications do not always take the form of great

[1] Op. cit., p. 2.   [2] S 2.50.24, 51.4.   [3] S 2.48.2.   [4] S 2.48.8-9.

generalizations; indeed they rarely do so. Their most obvious characteristic is that they make each component part of an argument clear and simple, so that the reader may follow Anselm stage by stage to a fuller understanding. Anselm is not given to providing short cuts, except perhaps in the *Proslogion*, where the stages of the arguments are highly condensed so as to bring the reader rapidly and unimpeded to a perception of the deceptively simple profundity of the ontological argument. Lucidity of the quiet and orderly kind which is much more typical of Anselm's other treatises is inseparable from a positive pleasure in understanding. This pleasure Anselm sees as a natural concomitant of the satisfaction of the God-given urge to 'know God'. Karl Barth's view of the note of pleasure in the *Cur Deus Homo* and the *Proslogion* has been rendered as if it amounts to no more than 'a genial inclination to please'.[1] But Anselm clearly intends something more. He says at the very beginning of the *Cur Deus Homo* that those who have asked him to write down for them the explanations of the Incarnation he has proposed to them in answer to their questions on many occasions, have assured him that his replies have both pleased and satisfied them:

Dicunt enim eas sibi placere et arbitrantur satisfacere.[2]

They have felt pleasure because their reasons have been satisfied; they have 'judged' themselves satisfied (*arbitrantur*). They have asked to have the explanations in writing so that they may further enjoy the pleasures of understanding and contemplating these matters of belief:

ut eorum quae credunt intellectu et contemplatione delectentur.[3]

Pleasure is of course a sensation, and the reason cannot experience sensation, but the satisfaction of the demands of the reason[4] can give rise to pleasure, and that is the pleasure which Anselm seems to have in mind here. Certainly no one, in Anselm's experience, can be expected to derive pleasure from being in a state of muddle-headedness, whereas even those who had found the whole question difficult and almost intractable (*in quaerendo valde . . . difficilis*),[5] are filled with delight when it is explained to them:

---

[1] Op. cit., p. 15. [2] S 2.47.7–8. [3] S 2.47.9.
[4] S 2.48.16: *rectus ordo exigit*. [5] S 2.48.7.

in solvendo tamen omnibus est intelligibilis et propter utili-
tatem et rationis pulchritudinem amabilis.[1]

('Its solution is understandable to everyone and lovely in its
profitableness and the beauty of its reasonableness'.)

Anselm's special concern for those of less pronounced intellectual gifts is well in evidence here. Many, he says, find
question and answer the easiest way to learn, especially those
who are naturally slow to grasp new ideas:

multis et maxime tardioribus ingeniis magis patent et ideo
plus placent.

('To many, and especially those who are less able, such arguments are clearer and therefore more pleasing'.[2] It would be
difficult to find a plainer statement of the association in Anselm's
mind between clarity of exposition and the pleasure of the
reader. It must be regarded as even more important a first
principle of his thought if he so obviously wants every kind of
man to share in the pleasure.

It is, in comparison with the more rarefied transports of joy
in the *Proslogion* and some of the devotional writings, a gentle
and altogether reasonable pleasure. Just as some men are
naturally less highly gifted in their capacity for intense religious
emotion than Anselm himself, so some are, he knew, less quick
of mind than he. But both as an emotional and as an intellectual
experience, he felt this quiet pleasure in understanding something clearly to be well within every man's grasp.

v: *Presenting the Argument Simply*

Anselm habitually used analogies in his preaching and table-
talk because he found that everyone could learn from verbal
pictures, even if they could not all benefit from abstract argument.[3] In the *Cur Deus Homo* Anselm compares the solidity of
the arguments of faith with the evanescence of the arguments of
unbelievers by comparing the first with a picture painted on a
durable ground and the second with a picture painted on air.[4]
He uses the image twice.[5] Everyone can understand and enjoy
a picture. But only the right explanation—the picture painted

---

[1] S 2.48.8–9. [2] S 2.48.12–13.
[3] The surviving accounts of Anselm's sayings are edited by R. W. Southern and
F. S. Schmitt in MA.
[4] S 2.51–2. [5] Loc. cit. and S 2.104.113–28.

on *aliquid solidum*—will give lasting enjoyment and enduring illumination. And every man can share in the experience.

In such ways the gentler intellectual enjoyment of the *Cur Deus Homo* is matched by a more restrained use of the stylistic devices which help to heighten the joyous excitement of the *Proslogion*. There, the style of the devotional passages contrasts strongly with that of the passages of exposition and argument. One is clearly a 'fine style', full of antithesis and parallelism, patterned with rhymes and near-rhymes, and the other is a perfectly plain style, in which every consideration of mannered elegance has been sacrificed to the demands of philosophical clarity.[1] By the time he wrote the *Cur Deus Homo*, Anselm had learned to pitch his style somewhere between the two, when it suited his purposes. This is not a matter of his development as a writer; he can still write in the style of the earlier devotional works when it pleases him, as he does in the *Meditation on Human Redemption*:

Anima Christiana, anima de gravi morte resuscitata, anima de misera servitute sanguine dei redempta et liberata.[2]

Here the interplay of sounds and cadences is quite deliberately contrived; no reader could miss it, or fail to be stirred by it: *excita mentem tuam*,[3] 'stir up your mind', says Anselm here, as he had said that the first chapter of the *Proslogion* was an *excitatio mentis ad contemplandum deum*,[4] 'a stirring-up of the mind to the contemplation of God'. There can be do doubt that such stylistic contrasts were deliberately made; there can be little doubt that, in the *Cur Deus Homo*, too, Anselm employs a modified range of stylistic techniques, not so as to stir up men's minds to joyous excitement, but in order to add to their intellectual satisfaction an aesthetic enjoyment of a rather quieter kind. Such sentences as these are common enough throughout the work to give even the more concentrated passages of argument a certain gracefulness of presentation:

Idem namque ipse sibi est honor incorruptibilis et nullo modo mutabilis.[5]

---

[1] The doctrine of the three styles would probably have been familiar to Anselm through the *Rhetorica ad Herennium*, IV.8.11, as well as through the example set by Augustine and others in varying style to suit different purposes.

[2] S 3.84.3–4. [3] S 3.84.4.

[4] S 1.97.3. [5] S 2.72.30–1.

Here, *mutabilis* is made to fall in such a juxtaposition to *incorruptibilis* that the two words are thrown into relief. A similar deliberate patterning occurs in:

Non ergo decet deum hominem peccantem sine satisfactione ad restaurationem angelorum assumere perditorum, quoniam veritas non patitur eum levari ad aequalitatem beatorum.[1]

Perditorum matches *beatorum*, and a number of internal features of the sentence seem to be devised in such a way that words with syntactically similar endings will catch the ear and thus the attention. Such instances might be expected to occur by accident, because of the peculiar structure of the Latin language—especially in its eleventh-century form. But they are far too frequent in the *Cur Deus Homo* for there to be any question of their being unintentional. Anselm is trying to woo his readers into enjoyment not only by presenting them with satisfying arguments, but also by pleasing them with elegant writing.

He says quite openly early in the work that he is aware of the need to express *tam decora materia*,[2] 'such beautiful subject-matter', in an appropriate style:

Unde timeo, ne, quemadmodum ego soleo indignari pravis pictoribus, cum ipsum dominum informi figura pingi video, ita mihi contingat, si tam decoram materiam incompto et contemptibili dictamine exarare presumo.[3]

('Therefore I fear lest, just as I am disturbed when I see the Lord portrayed crudely, in an ugly picture, so I may cause offence if I presume to treat of such beautiful subject-matter without art and in a style which does not do it justice.') In reply, Boso reassures Anselm that so long as he is willing for anyone who can perform the task better than he to attempt to do so in the future, it is enough for him to do his best. But he, too, speaks of writing 'more beautifully' (*pulchrius*).[4] The idea is far from new in Anselm's day that a fine style should be used for the highest subject-matter.[5] Anselm is merely adopting a generally understood view of the matter. But he has more to say about his own view of the theory of fine writing in the *Cur Deus Homo* than anywhere else in his treatises. And if is in the *Cur Deus Homo* that he achieves his most finely tuned adaptation of

[1] S 2.84.22–4. [2] S 2.49.21. [3] S 2.49.19–22. [4] S 2.49.24.
[5] See n. 57. The principle is discussed further by Augustine in Book IV of the *De Doctrina Christiana*.

his stylistic skills to the need to make the subject-matter itself a
source of quiet enjoyment for his readers.

One of Anselm's most striking phrases in the *Cur Deus Homo*
is the *rationis pulchritudo*,[1] 'the beauty of reasonableness' of
Chapter 1. Its implications run as a thread through the whole
work. Anselm emphasizes, for example, that the will of God
never operates in a manner out of keeping with reason:

   voluntas dei numquam est irrationabilis.[2]

The sheer reasonableness and orderliness of the working of the
universe is beautiful and pleasurable to man's mind. The man
who does God's will, helps to preserve the order and beauty of
the universe:

   in rerum universitate ordinem suum et eiusdem universitatis
   pulchritudinem, quantum in ipsa est, servat.[3]

He who disobeys God's will muddies that beauty (*decoloret*).[4]
In one of the prayers to the saints Anselm mentions 'the most
beautiful order', the *ordo pulcherrimus*.[5] This orderliness of the
universe is a source of pleasure only because the reason is designed to perceive it and to be satisfied by it. Anselm remarks at
the beginning of Book II of the *Cur Deus Homo* that God has
made man's rational nature in such a way that it can dis-
criminate between good and evil. But man can not only recognize the good; he has a built-in tendence to love it when he sees
it, and therefore to choose it in preference to evil. Otherwise,
says Anselm, God would have made man reasonable in vain:

   Alioquin frustra facta esset rationalis.[6]

The whole purpose of giving man reason is to enable him to
enjoy the perception of rightness and orderliness, with real
pleasure, not merely with cool, detached, discrimination. This
principle in its turn explains away the apparent presumptuous-
ness of attempting to discuss such 'high matters', the *altiora* of
which Anselm speaks with reverence in his first chapter.[7] The
truth, says Anselm, is there for all to see; if he has failed at any
point, it is because his own understanding has not been able to
grasp the full truth.[8] Man's sinfulness clouds the vision he
would otherwise have of a beautiful and orderly universe, in
which everything is susceptible of reasoned explanation. The

[1] S 2.42.8–9.   [2] S 2.59.11.   [3] S 2.73.4–6.   [4] S 2.73.6–9.
[5] *Oratio* 4, to St. Nicholas, S 3.59.119.   [6] S 2.97.5–7.   [7] S 2.48.25.
[8] S 2.48.25–49.2.

use of the reason in enquiring about God is therefore perfectly proper—indeed it is God's intention that it should be so used. What ignorance makes difficult, knowledge makes easy, says Anselm:

nam earum ignorantia quaedam facit difficilia, quae per earum notitia fiunt facilia.[1]

Reason, rightly used, thus clarifies and simplifies. What is left obscure is infuriating, frustrating; if God meant that to be a normal state of affairs, then he made man's reason in vain.[2]

The means of clarification Anselm uses in the *Cur Deus Homo* are, then, broadly twofold. He tries to make his words both clear and pleasing to his readers by writing well, and in an appropriate style. He tries to make the sense clear by employing means of demonstration appropriate to every man's God-given understanding. Anselm's own place in this scheme of making things clear is something of which he is very conscious. He promises in Chapter 1 that he will reveal whatever God reveals to him:

tamen de illa curabo quod deus mihi dignabitur aperire, petentibus ostendere.[3]

He sees himself as something of a 'middle-man', whose task is to find a form of words which will enable everyone to share his own understanding. It would be misleading to place too much emphasis on the distinction between *aperire* and *ostendere* in this passage. In the passage which follows, Boso asks Anselm to reveal or 'open up' the matter for him (*a te peto mihi aperiri*),[4] so we cannot conclude that this process of revealing is God's alone. Elsewhere, Boso says that Anselm has 'shown him' grounds for his sure beliefs:

sed ut ostendas mihi certitudinis meae rationem.[5]

Anselm himself is able both to 'open up' (*aperire*) and to 'show' (*ostendere*) what God has revealed to him, and the terms seem to be, if not interchangeable, at least both appropriate to the description of Anselm's own part in the work.

The end result of the process of opening up or showing is always the same; the openness and clarity is in itself a source of pleasure; 'they are clearer and so they give more pleasure' (*magis patent et ideo plus placent*).[6] There is not, in any case, always a very clear distinction between the way in which a man may grasp the truth directly because God has made it obvious to him, and the ways in which he may achieve understanding through the medium of another man's explanations. Boso comments on the processes by which God has helped himself and Anselm to reach their conclusions. 'It often happens', he says, 'that God makes clear what was previously hidden, when we talk over a question':

> et reminisci quia saepe contingit in colloquendo de aliqua quaestione, ut deus aperiat quod prius latebat.[1]

Some effort on the part of the man who wants to understand is evidently required here. 'It seems neglectful to me, if, after we have been made secure in our faith, we do not strive to understand what we believe':

> ita negligentia mihi videtur, si postquam confirmati sumus in fide, non studemus quod credimus intelligere.[2]

What a man has learned is not to be hugged selfishly to himself. If he freely imparts what has freely been given him, he will receive still fuller understanding:

> si ea quae gratis accepisti libenter impertiris, altiora quae nondum attigisti mereberis accipere.[3]

This is not merely a matter of giving thanks for revelation by an act of generosity to others; there is here a process of divine revelation and instruction, through conversation.

Boso must often have found this happening in his own mind while he was talking to Anselm, but there is no reason to suppose that Anselm did not sometimes learn from Boso, too. It is easy to assume that Anselm's greater intellectual stature made him always the giver: but he would surely sometimes have been helped to see something more clearly by a pupil's remark. A complex pattern of interaction helped Anselm himself to greater understanding, and to greater pleasure in that understanding. In Anselm's view, the direct inspiration of God himself, his own efforts, and the help of others, all play an important part in revealing and demonstrating the truth. Not least among these influences was the attempt to frame a recently attained grasp of difficult matters so clearly, and in such an orderly manner, that others would be able to grasp them, too. That is the exercise he performs in the *Cur Deus Homo*, and there can be little doubt that

[1] S 2.49.3–4.   [2] S 2.48.17–18.   [3] S 2.49.5–6.

he saw it as an integral part of the process of understanding itself.

vi: *The nature of the Appeal to Reason*

One of the starting-points of this study was the view that a certain patchiness of interest has led to over-interpretation of some aspects of Anselm's writings and comparative neglect of others. What J. McIntyre noted over twenty years ago about the interest shown in Anselm's 'systematic account of the Atonement' and the *Proslogion* argument, almost to the exclusion of his views on the Trinity, the attributes of God, the Procession of the Holy Spirit, free will, and predestination,[1] still holds substantially true. Anselm's theological ideas have still not been studied as a whole to the extent which the internal consistency and interdependence of his ideas would seem to demand. On the other hand, enough has been said about Anselm's theology by way of detailed analysis, to obscure the force of the impression he himself wanted it to make on his readers. We have seen that he meant to present an immediately acceptable case, simply and clearly argued, which would make the truths of orthodox doctrine obvious to everyone (*omnibus intelligibilis*).[2] That was not, as Anselm conceived it, an arrogant claim. It is a fundamental and often-repeated principle of his thought that everything we can know about God is acceptable to reason.[3] Reason is implanted in man precisely so that he can accept such common-sense arguments about God with pleasurable recognition of their rightness and fittingness (*convenientia*).[4] The point which is often missed here is that this is all that Anselm intended to do. He made no attempt to present a detailed treatment of all the ramifications of problems which he well knew to have been the subject of extended analysis in

---

[1] J. McIntyre, op. cit., p. 2. I am grateful to the editor of *Studia Theologica* for permission to base this and the following sections of Ch. 7 on my article 'The Cur Deus Homo: The Nature of St. Anselm's Appeal to Reason', *Studia Theologica* 31 (1977), 33–50.

[2] S 2.48.8.

[3] S 2.48.8–9, and cf. the opening of the *Cur Deus Homo*, II, S 2.97, on the reasons why God made man a rational being.

[4] *Convenientia* and *decentia* occur often enough in the *Cur Deus Homo* for it to seem likely that 'fittingness' was an important consideration in Anselm's mind throughout the writing of the work.

patristic times, or among his contemporaries.[1] Instead he gives
one solution for each problem, or part of a problem, and that a
solution which even a philosophical amateur can easily follow
and find pleasing. Nowhere does he do this with so conspicuously conscious an intention as in the *Cur Deus Homo*.

It is often especially noticeable in the *Cur Deus Homo* that
Anselm is not trying to 'prove' his case in a strictly dialectical
sense. Many of his arguments are acceptable because they are
illuminating or helpful, rather in the way that an analogy may
be enlightening, without necessarily demonstrating anything
finally. Anselm's own technical notion of 'proof' certainly en-
compassed both these meanings, and it also embraced other
senses. He speaks of *probatio* and *probare* in a range of contexts
which includes formal proof by syllogism, proof by means of
adducing authorities, proof by analogy,[2] just as Lanfranc before him was able to use 'proof' of dialectical arguments and of
proof by authority,[3] and Abelard after him was able to say that,
in his view, syllogisms gave the firmest proof, but not the only
possible kind of proof.[4] Abelard, living in an age when dialectical formality was growing apace, was still able to say in his
theological works that some analogy or Scriptural text has made
something plain: *quid autem apertius ad documentum Trinitatis,*[5] . . .
In eodem quique libro apertissime.[6] There is no reason to suppose
that Anselm did not expect his readers to find a point proven
just because it had been made plain to them in terms they found
agreeable. This view goes some way towards explaining Anselm's use of feudally-derived notions as grounds of proof in the
Cur Deus Homo.[7] It is not that Anselm could not have advanced
alternative explanations for God's redemption of the world in
person, rather than through a newly-created sinless man,[8] or
for the question of the Devil's 'rights' over man.[9] Augustine

---

[1] F. S. Schmitt has noted in his footnotes some of the patristic sources Anselm
may have had in mind here.

[2] Schmitt lists some, but not all, of Anselm's uses of *probatio* and *probare*, in his
indices verborum, S 6.289.

[3] PL, 150, 131, 157, 363 *et al.*

[4] *Petrus Abaelardus Dialectica*, ed. L. M. de Rijk (Assen 1956), p. 466, 19–20.

[5] *Theologia Christiana*, ed. M. Buytaert, CCCM, xii, 433.955.

[6] Ibid., p. 438, 1093.

[7] R. W. Southern has remarked on these in AB, pp. 93–102.

[8] S 2.52.14–24.   [1] S 2.55–9.

alone would have provided him with ample choice.[1] But the
'feudal' context of the discussions seems to have been usual in
contemporary schools,[2] and Anselm wanted to employ analogies
which all his readers would find sympathetic to the direction of
their own thinking. A single analogy is, as a rule, enough for
Anselm—or else a single argument of another kind. He does not
give several reasons, as Augustine does. Here again, we can only
conclude that the economy of the demonstration is deliberate;
it preserves the tone of simplicity and easy acceptability which
Anselm strives to maintain throughout the *Cur Deus Homo*. If a
single reason was acceptable, there was really no need to labour
the point, and to do so might well cause confusion.

Only the educated could be expected to possess the skill and
the trained concentration which would make it possible for
them to follow prolonged sequences of technically exact
analysis. Since Anselm is writing for the *illiterati* as well as for
the *litterati*,[3] he keeps each portion of the argument as brief as
possible. He never expects his readers to keep in mind more
than three possibilities at once, or at most, four. All but one of
these are promptly eliminated so that Anselm can take his
reader on to the next 'cross-roads' along the path of his argument. For example, in Chapter 8 of Book II of the *Cur Deus
Homo*, Anselm asks how and whence God assumed human
nature.[4] He puts it that whoever makes satisfaction for another's
offence must either be the same as the sinner (*idem sit qui
peccator*), or of the same race (*aut eiusdem generis*).[5] Thus only
Adam and Eve, or a child of their race, could carry out the
task. And Adam and Eve will not, so we are left with the alternative possibility, that one of their race may do so. Then
Anselm poses another set of alternatives. Could Christ have
assumed human nature best through a man and a woman, like
other men, or through neither, or through a man alone, or
through a woman alone?[6] Anselm considers—and this is surely
an appeal to what he feels to be a commonly acceptable instinct rather than to any logically demonstrable grounds—that
it is altogether cleaner and neater for Christ to have been born
of one sex alone than as a result of any mingling of the two (*de*

---

[1] Parallels with Augustine's *De Trinitate* will be discussed in more detail later.
[2] AB, pp. 93–102. [3] S 2.48.5–6. [4] S 2.102.26.
[5] S 2.103.2. [6] S 2.103.20–6.

commixtione utriusque). [1] It is, he says, *mundius et honestius* for it to be so. [2] Left with the alternatives of man or woman, Anselm feels it *convenientius*, [3] more fitting, that the woman should be chosen. Here again, Anselm appears to assume that his readers will agree with him out of a general sense that it is more appropriate that it should be a woman who is the human parent of Christ. He gives no explicit reason for making this choice between four alternatives; the *quattuor modis*, [4] by which God could have chosen the parentage of his Son. Finally, he asks whether, given that God's choice rests on a woman alone, that woman should be a virgin or not. Here, clearly, there is no need for discussion (*non est opus disputare*). [5] There can be no grounds for preferring a non-virgin.

In this chapter (which is of rather more than the usual length) Anselm has brought together briefly a whole series of arguments by elimination, in such a way that any reader who is prepared to accept the grounds on which he eliminates the discarded possibilities will readily be brought to see that it was proper that Christ should be born of a virgin. Anselm makes no attempt to elaborate his reasons for discarding alternatives. Some of them are slight enough if they are to be seen as having the force of logical necessity. But none of them are unacceptable to the sense of fittingness Anselm expects his readers to possess. All he asks is that they should recognize that what he says is reasonable and be satisfied. Even the *illiterati* can do that.

Anselm's tone is generally one of quiet confidence in setting out these demonstrations. He himself so thoroughly knew and understood the unquestioned assumptions upon which he builds that he never seems to be thinking aloud, or to be finding his way among incompletely mastered principles. To be fair, Augustine had done some of his thinking aloud for him, in his own less elegantly contrived demonstrations and discussions. But Anselm's own certainty of touch was no mean achievement, especially since he sustains the same level of lucid simplicity throughout the work, and never appears to be still wrestling with a point whose exposition is not yet quite clear to him.

Many of Anselm's contemporaries, and writers of the next generation, too, chose to go on struggling with first principles.

[1] S 2.103.28–30.   [2] S 2.103.28–9.   [3] S 2.104.7.
[4] S 2.104.3.   [5] S 2.104.9.

Roscelin was still questioning the roots of the doctrine of the Trinity in putting forward—apparently as a serious challenge —the contention that the Trinity might be like three angels.[1] Anselm himself evidently had to proffer suggestions to his own students which would meet objections at this level; such were the circumstances in which he put forward his unfortunate analogy between the Trinity and the way in which we say that one man is: *iustus, albus, grammaticus*.[2] But this was not the way in which he liked to go about things. He preferred to show the acceptability of the correct *data* of faith by demonstrating their appeal to open-minded reasonableness; he could only do so if both his *litterati* and his *illitterati* were prepared to be open to conviction. In some measure that applies to his modern readers, too. The gentle reasonableness of Anselm's arguments in the *Cur Deus Homo* is designed to satisfy just such sensible men, and not to overthrow the objections of the unreasonably combative.

The sheer conceptual difficulties presented by the doctrine of the Trinity in particular, and of the Atonement and other doctrinal fundamentals, too, are very considerable. In Anselm's day and immediately afterwards, scholars fell back upon the very mediaeval resource of providing standard definitions and stock phrases, which would enable anyone to give an account of his faith without necessarily possessing any very clear idea of what his definitions meant. R. W. Southern remarks on this characteristic of the *Elucidarium* of Honorius Augustodunensis, and cites one instance which illustrates the method very well:

D. What is free will?

M. It is the liberty of choosing good or evil.[3]

Innumerable other examples, less facile, but still depending upon the definitions of thinkers who had been readier to go back to first principles, may be found in the commentaries on the Boethian *opuscula sacra* of the mid-twelfth century.[4] Honorius, like Gilbert of Poitiers and Thierry of Chartres, cannot be

---

[1] *De Incarnatione Verbi prior recensio*, S 1.282.4–8.

[2] S 1.282.12–15, 283.2–6.

[3] AB, pp. 213–14. *Elucidarium*, II.7, ed. Y. Lefèvre, 'L'Elucidarium et les lucidaires', *Bibliothèque des écoles françaises d'Athènes et de Rome*, 80 (1954).

[4] For example, the commentaries of Gilbert of Poitiers, ed. N. M. Häring (Toronto 1966) and of Thierry of Chartres and his school, ed. N. M. Häring (Toronto 1971).

supposed to have been incapable of understanding the definitions he used; but these scholars were content to borrow, to
take an easy way out of many of the difficulties in which they
found themselves. Among their readers and pupils those of less
acute mind than Boso were perhaps likely sometimes to use
stock phrases rather as though they were repeating a cate-
chism, without any real understanding. This is exactly the
kind of avoidance of real understanding which Anselm is so
anxious to prevent in his own readers. He wants them to feel
the reasonableness of his explanations, to grasp his meaning,
and so to understand what they believe as fully as their abilities
permit. Never are they to be content with a mere form of words.

For those able to read the Fathers for themselves with some
profit, Augustine in particular provided a very different means
of finding out about puzzling doctrines. He can never be accused
of being easily satisfied, or of supplying a single facile definition
in the hope of resolving a profound problem. But his tendency
is to go to the opposite extreme, to explore a problem reflec-
tively at such length that the direction of his thought is sometimes obscured. He apologizes in Chapter 3 of Book I of the *De
Trinitate* in case he has not made himself clear to all his readers,
but he claims that, even if he could perhaps have expressed
himself better, his arguments and his doctrine are perfectly
sound, and any obscurity or doubt which remains is likely to be
due to the shortcomings of the reader's own understanding.
Anselm does not allow himself the luxury of this excuse. He sets
out quite deliberately to make himself clear to everyone, whatever the limitations of his understanding.[1] Anselm's freshness of
approach is so marked precisely because he has emancipated
himself from both extremes of method, and pitched his arguments at a level which had never been attempted before. That
is, he tried to provide universally acceptable arguments which
neither glossed over essential details, nor over-elaborated essential principles. His degree of success in so enterprising a scheme
is remarkable in itself.

To take only a few of the questions Augustine raises in the *De
Trinitate* alone is to be made aware at once that Anselm owes
him a considerable debt. Augustine has, again and again, been

---

[1] It is tempting to speculate about the private view of Augustine's treatment
which Anselm had formed by the time he wrote the *Cur Deus Homo*.

instrumental in putting questions into Anselm's own mind, or at least in encouraging him to think hard about issues he may have found in other patristic writings. Augustine asks, for example, how Christ was sent into the world at the Incarnation, although he was in the world already;[1] how Christ's 'single' death (of body) may compensate for our 'double' death (of body and soul) through sin;[2] why we must believe that Christ's death was voluntary;[3] why Christ was the best possible 'victim' for sacrifice;[4] why the Incarnation was not only a good and suitable means of redeeming the world, but the only possible one;[5] why it was necessary for Christ to be born of a virgin and to be a son of Adam.[6] These points are raised at various stages in the *De Trinitate*; they do not form a consolidated body of discussion of the Incarnation. Anselm does not draw equally heavily upon them all. But it is noticeable that when he does consider one of Augustine's questions in his own, more closely integrated, discussions in the *Cur Deus Homo*, he does not offer Augustine's solutions, but solutions of his own. Augustine's part has been to help Anselm to perceive the most useful direction for his questioning, not to supply him with ready-made answers.

For example, in Chapter 5 of Book I of the *Cur Deus Homo*, Anselm looks at the question of why no victim but God in person could have redeemed mankind.[7] Augustine proposes a series of reasons: such a sacrifice must be the best possible sacrifice, made to the one true God, by a holy priest; and the sacrifice must be the gift of the people for whose sins it is to atone. Christ fulfils all those criteria, as no other victim could do.[8] Anselm suggests a single, cogent reason, which has nothing to do with these thoughts of Augustine's. He points out that if a man saves another's life, that man is rightly considered thenceforth to be his servant:

> quaecumque alia persona hominem a morte aeterna redimeret, eius servus idem homo recte iudicaretur.[9]

The exact bond Anselm has in mind here is evidently in inspiration a feudal one; but it seemed to him an appeal to a

---

[1] *De Trinitate*, II.5.8–9.
[2] *De Trinitate*, IV.3–4.
[3] *De Trinitate*, IV.13.16.
[4] *De Trinitate*, IV.14.19.
[5] *De Trinitate*, XIII.10.
[6] *De Trinitate*, XIII.17–18.
[7] S 2.52.14–24.
[8] *De Trinitate*, IV.14.19.
[9] S 2.52.19–20.

natural sense of justice that it should be so—especially when the 'saving' involves not merely bodily death, but eternal death. He has cut through the complex of explanations Augustine gives and discarded them, in favour of a single reason whose force would have been felt at once by any of his contemporaries, and which he himself believed to be of a universally compelling nature. It is, moreover, as Augustine's reasons are not, a form of argument by analogy. We are to conclude that what would hold true in any human context will also hold true if it is applied to divine affairs. Here, quite conspicuously, Anselm is applying his special method of 'appealing to reason'. He intends it simply to 'seem reasonable' that this parallel will hold.

In Chapter 6, Anselm considers why God could not have redeemed the world by any other means. Here, too, Augustine had provided a question and some thoughts upon it as a starting-point.[1] Anselm uses only the starting-point of the question itself. He presents various objections which he knows to have been made. If we say that God could not redeem the world by power alone, we are saying that he is weak; if we say that he could, but would not, we seem to be saying that he is not wise, since he has chosen a more difficult way of doing what could be easily achieved.[2] Anselm does not attempt to resolve these and a series of other related objections in this single chapter. Instead, he leaves his readers with two thoughts in their minds:

> Omnia enim haec quae obtenditis, in eius voluntate consistunt.[3]

('All these points you put have to do with his will'.) And secondly, God's reason for choosing this method of salvation has to do with his love for mankind.[4] A single analogy will not suffice here, but Anselm has placed essential principles in his readers' minds, so that when he returns to them later he will be able to develop them without further preliminaries.[5] His originality of conception here and elsewhere lies, then, not so much in the formulating of the parts of the enquiry, as in his refusal to be side-tracked by existing explanations where a single principle will make things clear.

The preliminary handling of arguments to be fully developed

---

[1] *De Trinitate*, XIII.10–17.   [2] S 2.53–4.   [3] S 2.54.5–6.
[4] S 2.55.2–3.   [5] For example, S 2.68, S 2.89, S 2.107.

later is a feature of the *Cur Deus Homo* which makes it unique among Anselm's works. The account Boso is made to give of the objections of unbelievers is like a mime before a play. Anselm sketches with a verbal gesture the outline of a response to each: we insult God when we say that he was born of a woman, suffered hunger, thirst, weariness, blows, and crucifixion among thieves.[1] No, replies Anselm; the further God has condescended, the greater his mercy appears.[2] Just as death came into the world through man's disobedience, so it is fitting that life should be restored to it through God's obedience as a man.[3] Just as sin took its origin from a woman (*initium habet*), so it is proper that the author of salvation should be born of a woman.[4] Just as the fruit of a tree did the original damage, so death on a tree will repair that damage.[5] These arguments are intended to appeal because they seem 'fitting' (*convenienter*),[6] and because they demonstrate the beauty of this mode of salvation:

> inenarrabilem quandam nostrae redemptionis hoc modo
> procuratae pulchritudinem ostendunt.[7]

('They show the inexpressible beauty of this means of carrying out redemption.') These arguments are meant to appeal to the spiritual 'aesthetic sense' which Anselm believed to reside in every man, as a part of his capacity for appreciating the force of reason. They rest upon a general pattern of complementariness and balance, and again, they are intended to convince because they are agreeable, not primarily because they will stand up to rigorous dialectical analysis. Admittedly, Anselm is here deliberately confining himself to such clear and simple elements as he feels will attract his readers to finish the book. But he tries throughout the *Cur Deus Homo* to depart no further than he must from arguments which have this kind of direct appeal to every man's sense of 'rightness'.

The 'unbelievers'—not surprisingly—reply that such arguments are like pictures and have no compelling necessity:

> Omnia haec pulchra et quasi quaedam picturae suscipienda
> sunt.[8]

('All these reasons are beautiful and are to be accepted as if they were pictures') says Boso on behalf of the unbelievers, who,

---

[1] S 2.50.24–8.   [2] S 2.50.30.   [3] S 2.51.5–7.   [4] S 2.51.7–9.
[5] S 2.51.9–10.   [6] S 2.51.3.   [7] S 2.51.11–12.   [8] S 2.51.16.

he thinks, will not be satisfied until they are shown the solid
ground on which these thoughts rest. There can be no doubt at
this point that Anselm was aware of the differences between
images and analogies and hard syllogistic proof. But he does not
defend what he has said by acknowledging that any part of it
could have been made more immediately compelling by the
use of formal logic. Instead, he proposes another line of explanation which is much more in keeping with his determination that the texture of the whole treatise is to remain clear and
bright and pleasing to every reader. He points out that pictures
painted on clouds or on water might indeed be expected to be
unconvincing, because of their evanescence. But pictures
painted on solid ground are clearly visible and everyone can
enjoy and understand them. If he can show the solid ground of
reasonableness on which his analogies and contrasts rest, the
veritatis soliditas rationabilis, they will seem more than 'pretty
pictures' (*pulchrae picturae*). It will be seen that they represent
the truth.[1] Anselm is here, as it turns out, making a statement
about the nature of the 'necessary arguments' and 'necessary
reasons' which have caused so much controversy in modern
studies of the *Cur Deus Homo*.[2] 'Does it not seem a sufficiently
necessary reason', he says (*Nonne satis necessaria ratio videtur*)[3]
why God did as we say he did, that he wanted to save the human
race which was so precious a part of his creation? (*tam scilicet
pretiosum opus eius*).[4] The ultimate force of a necessary reason
lies not in the formal exactness of its structure, but in its compelling appeal to the minds of reasonable men. It is, in some
sense, a self-evident truth which all men immediately recognize,
just as they 'recognize' the meaning of a picture painted on the
solid ground of what all men understand to be true. To say that
Anselm's analogies and images are like pictures is not, then, in
Anselm's own view, to imply that they had any less force of
conviction than logically watertight demonstrations would have.

vii: *The Making of the Appeal*

The very structure and style of the work is designed to rein-
force the impression such agreeable arguments are intended to

---

[1] S 2.52.3.
[2] M. J. Charlesworth, *St. Anselm's Proslogion* (Oxford 1965), 31–8.
[3] S 2.52.7.   [4] S 2.52.7.

make. After the introductory explanations of how Anselm hopes what he is about to say will please all his readers, and the preliminary survey of just those problems which would have been lodged in the enquirer's mind by the debates he would have heard in the schools of the day,[1] Anselm sets to work on a larger scale to settle each issue in turn. He knew well enough the probable concentration-span of his readers because he had talked over many of these problems with his own pupils.[2] He had instructed that his Prayers and Meditations should be divided into paragraphs so that readers could begin where they liked, and not always at the beginning. It was not possible for him to make the same recommendation when he composed a treatise, whose sequence of treatment is all-important. But he was able to divide the arguments into self-contained units with clear headings. These he instructed future copyists to place at the beginning of the work as *capitula*.[3] This was no literary innovation, but it was something Anselm felt it worth while to emphasize.

While each chapter deals with a topic or part of a topic in its own right, Anselm does not always give himself the 'last word'. Boso is often the last to speak. The chapters do not therefore give the impression that they are nothing but a string of beads of monotonously uniform size and colour. The division between Books I and II falls where it does, Anselm claims, partly to prevent his readers from becoming bored:

Sed ne fastidium haec volenti legere nimis longa continuatione generetur, a dictis dicenda alio exordio distinguamus.[4]

('But in case the would-be reader is wearied by my going on too long, let us make a fresh beginning to separate what has been said from what is to follow.') Anselm's concern for the ready comprehension of every one of his readers extends, then, beyond taking care over the presentation of each part of the argument, to a concern for the effectiveness of the whole work in making them appreciate the simplicity and beauty of the truths he wants them to see.

The style in which the work is couched is, as we have seen, an integral part of the process by which Anselm does this. He remarks at the very beginning that he is anxious not to presume to

---

[1] AB, pp. 82–8.
[2] S 2.47.6–7.
[3] S 2.43.4.
[4] S 2.96.19–20.

treat of such fine subject-matter in a style carelessly contrived or unsuitably bald in its plainness:

> si tam decoram materiam incompto et contemptibili dictamine exarare praesumo.[1]

There is nothing unexpected in this; Anselm had always shown, even in his earliest writings, an ability to separate the style suitable for devotional material from the style appropriate for expressing sequences of plain argument.[2] There can be no doubt that he does so consciously, following a deliberate policy. But the *Cur Deus Homo* has a quality of subdued stylistic patterning which is unlike anything to be found in the earlier works. It is not new for Anselm to restrict himself to comparatively simple and familiar works in preference to the vocabulary of the classical Latin poets. Nor is he doing anything he has not done before in making his style the vehicle of his argument; the use of those figures of thought which are also figures of diction (antithesis and parallelism in particular) is very evident in the devotional writings. Even in his earliest writings, Anselm uses occasional changes of pace and texture to lighten what he has to say, and to keep the reader's interest. What is quite new in the *Cur Deus Homo* is the way in which stylistic devices hitherto used to overwhelm the reader's objections, and to carry him along on a tide of emotional fervour, are here used to help him take his time, and consider the case which is being put to him quietly and rationally. These devices help him, too, to derive pleasure from his understanding, since, as Anselm says, a lovely and reasonable principle may easily appear in less than its full glory, if it is clumsily expressed.[3]

Thus Anselm does not employ antithesis and parallelism throughout his arguments in the *Cur Deus Homo*. Often his case is put in words as unadorned as those of the *De Grammatico*. But here and there, to mark an important point, he contrives an especially elegant sentence:

> sicut non levigat peccatum, ita non excusat non redentem debitum.[4] In quo tractu vel impulsu nulla intelligitur violentiae necessitas, sed acceptae bonae voluntatis spontanea et amata tenacitas.[5]

A number of similar examples of antithesis and contrasts and

---

[1] S 2.49.21–2. [2] Cf. *Rhetorica ad Herennium*, IV.8.11.
[3] S 2.49.17–22. [4] S 2.92.11–12. [5] S 2.65.6–7.

parallels whose force is brought out by the contrivance of a pattern of sounds, are apparent throughout the work. They are never obtrusive; they merely give a moment's pleasure and assist the understanding, as they are intended to do.

In a not dissimilar way, Anselm makes sure that his arguments themselves are varied in type. Within the framework of question and answer he has chosen because it is easiest for most people to follow,[1] Anselm employs whatever technique of analysis appears most convenient. The framework of dialogue is itself something of a literary device; it is certainly not essential to the mode of demonstration as it is in the *De Veritate* and the other treatises *pertinentes ad studium sacrae scripturae*.[2] There, the unnamed *discipulus* is present chiefly to assent to the master's views, and to offer himself as a sounding-board on which the master may try out his arguments. Boso is a much more active partner in the dialogue, and he often takes the argument a little further on his own account. There is no clear line of demarcation between Anselm as progenitor and initiator of each development in the argument, and Boso as his humble pupil. Anselm's readers are to learn easily from this mode of argument not merely by putting themselves in the pupil's place and letting themselves be led to the right conclusions, but also because the device gives life and interest to the whole by, as it were, 'dramatizing' it.

The scheme gives Anselm considerable freedom to vary his modes of demonstration. Sometimes he sets up a row of alternative possibilities and eliminates all but one, as we have already seen him do. This seems a method in direct opposition to the device of arguing *remoto Christo*,[3] as if Christ had never been, as Anselm proposes to do at the beginning. There, one negative axiom is proposed; here, all the possibilities are marshalled, and then reduced to a single, positive conclusion. Anselm also uses definitions,[4] or axioms,[5] either stated or implied, which he believes to constitute acceptable starting-points for further discussion. Again, we have already looked at examples of his use

---

[1] S 2.48.11–12.   [2] S 1.173.2.   [3] S 2.42.12.

[4] For example, in considering 'What is sin'? S 2.68–9, cf. McIntyre, *op. cit.*, pp. 68–76.

[5] On Anselm's use of axioms, see R. Roques, *Pourquoi Dieu s'est fait homme* (Paris 1961), pp. 83–5.

of this technique in the way he arrives at the statement that Christ must have been born of a virgin. Syllogisms are not a favoured method in the *Cur Deus Homo*, though Anselm does refer to the standard definition of man by the *philosophi* in terms which suggests that he expects his readers to recognize its content,[1] and therefore perhaps to know of its usages in elementary dialectic.

There is a notable reference to the *quasi* principle which Anselm employs in the *De Casu Diaboli* and in the philosophical fragments as well as here, in saying that he proposes to argue his case *quasi nihil sciatur de Christo* ('as if nothing were known about Christ'). The method involves attempting to argue 'as if' something were so, in order to see whether the process will lead to conclusions at variance with the assumption that it is really so. In the *De Casu Diaboli* Anselm tries to get round the problem of evil by suggesting that although it is nothing, we may learn something by discussing it 'as if it were something'.[2]

The method of argument by analogy is perhaps commonest of all in the *Cur Deus Homo*. These analogies do not always take the form of the great developed schemes of the 'pearl' image, in which Anselm compares man with a pearl which has been knocked out of God's hand into the mud of sin by the Devil, and which God will pick up and wipe clean before he stores it safely in the treasury of his heaven.[3] Some of his analogies are subtler and altogether slighter stuff, involving no more than an implied assumption that his readers will perceive a parallel between a principle they know to hold in earthly matters, and a principle Anselm wants them to accept as binding in heaven too. In Chapter 22 of Book I, for example, Anselm describes newly-created man as being set between God and Satan with the task of standing firm against the Devil's blandishments; the purpose of the exercise is for man to defend the honour of God, who is his rightful lord.[4] At no point does Anselm say—as he so often did in his talks to the community[5]—that God is *like* a

---

[1] S 2.109.16–18: *idcirco mortale ponitur in hominis definitione a philosophis*; cf. PL, 64.103, in Boethius' *Commentary on Porphyry*.

[2] S 2.42.11–14, cf. S 1.251.10, MA, p. 337.6.

[3] I have discussed this image more fully in 'St. Anselm's Analogies', *Vivarium*, xiv (1976), 81–93.

[4] S 2.90.9–25.

[5] MA, pp. 56, 64, 66, 70.

great lord and the Devil *like* his enemy. He simply assumes that the rules with which every reader will be familiar will seem to everyone to fit the case of God, man and Satan, as well as they do the feudal code of obligation. He avoids any locally peculiar or obscure area of feudal usage in his metaphor, in favour of the most commonly-recognized and generally applicable feudal practices. The variety of modes of demonstration employed in the *Cur Deus Homo* is, then, very considerable. But nowhere does Anselm allow himself to become too technical for his general reader.

The risk of the general reader's losing interest because he finds the argument altogether too close-knit and uniform in texture is also very much present to Anselm's mind. It underlies his conscious use of means of providing variety and interest. It prompts him to make excuses if he thinks there is any risk of his becoming tedious. It makes him careful to carry his reader's interest over from one section of the argument to another. When Anselm says *Adhuc addam aliquid*, Boso replies: *Tamdiu dic, donec me taedeat audire*,[1] ('Go on talking until I am weary of listening.') Anselm has made him speak for the reader; the reader is encouraged to believe that he himself is not yet wearied. Again, Anselm warns that there is more to come (*Expecta adhuc parum*).[2] Boso asks eagerly, 'What more have you to tell me?' (*Quid habes amplius?*) Once more he has taken the protestation out of the reader's mouth at a point where he might be beginning to lose interest. The subject-matter becomes more difficult to follow. Again, Boso speaks for the reader's willingness to try to keep up with Anselm: *Quamvis me in angustias quasdam ducas, desidero tamen multum ut, sicut incepisti, progrediaris*,[3] ('Even if you are leading me into a difficult area, I very much want you to go on with what you have begun.') Boso's own curiosity is intended to sustain that of the reader and to discourage him from giving up when things become difficult.

Small, sympathetic encouragements are offered obliquely to the flagging reader again and again—usually through Boso, who speaks for the reader as Anselm cannot do, since he is the author of the 'difficulties'. 'That is a very solemn thought' (*Nimis est gravis haec sententia*).[4] 'If I did not have faith to console me, this alone would make me despair' (*Nisi fides me consolaretur*,

---

[1] S 2.74.10–11.   [2] S 2.92.4–5.   [3] S 2.88.9–10.   [4] S 2.89.32.

hoc solum me cogeret desperare.)[1] Here Anselm is again being open about the fact that difficulties exist in treating of such subject-matter. He never pretends that understanding will easily be attained.[2] But he always attempts to inspire confidence, by trying to show that he, as master and teacher, is in command of his subject-matter; the reader may therefore trust him in following him to the end so as to see how things will turn out. *Ad quid vis tendere*,[3] 'What are you driving at?', says Boso, in the middle of a long passage of explanation which might be expected to weary even the most patient reader, if it were not interrupted by some direct appeal to his presence.

Where the argument is going smoothly, Boso interjects a note of positive pleasure and understanding from time to time: *Hoc nihil clarius;*[4] *Et hoc apertum;*[5] *Aperte video quia non possum;*[6] *Secundum placitum cordis mei loqueris.*[7] The tone of Boso's interruptions and contributions is by no means always apologetic to the reader, but whatever he says, he says, in some measure, on the reader's behalf.

Sometimes we are merely led firmly from one portion of the argument to another, in such a way as to link the self-contained units of the *capitula*. *Restat nunc quaerere*,[8] 'it remains to consider'; *Nunc quoque quaerendum*,[9] 'now we must also ask'; *Nunc autem restat indagare*,[10] 'now it remains to investigate'. Such tags introduce fresh aspects of the topic, or the next line of departure. Several times the reader is promised that Anselm will be brief: *Breviter mihi de his satisfecisti;*[11] *Breviter tamen hic tange.*[12] Everywhere the reader is presented with purposefulness, a sense of direction, and the assurance that the pace will be neither too rapid for him, nor tediously slow.

The nature of the very real friendship between Anselm and Boso shows through, too. Boso is far from being a cypher who stands in for the *discipulus* of the earlier writings. Anselm makes his apologies for one of the rare digressions of the *Cur Deus Homo* in a passage which has the tone of a relaxed, friendly conversation. Anselm has stated that God intends to replace the fallen angels from among men. Boso requires a reason for the

---

[1] S 2.90.6. [2] Cf. Anselm's *difficilis* of S 2.48.7. [3] S 2.90.16.
[4] S 2.94.4. [5] S 2.94.6. [6] S 2.88.28. [7] S 2.104.12.
[8] S 2.102.26. [9] S 2.105.3. [10] S 2.109.4. [11] S 2.98.26.
[12] S 2.105.10.

statement.[1] Anselm thus makes Boso's request a justification for digression; Boso was, in any case, speaking for the interests of a younger generation of scholars, since it seems that the topic was one much discussed at Laon[2] at this time and immediately afterwards. It may well be that Anselm thought a number of his readers would be disappointed if he did not give some account of his views here. That he did consider the piece a digression is clear enough from the repetition of the statement several chapters later, in much the same terms.[3] as a preliminary to the next stage of the main argument. The presence of the digression is in itself testimony to Anselm's concern to meet the needs of a live audience of readers.

The digression is introduced by a little joke. 'You are leading me astray,' says Anselm. 'We did not propose to deal with anything but the Incarnation of God alone, and you are slipping in other questions':

> Fallis me. Non enim proposuimus tractare nisi de sola incarnatione dei, et tu mihi interseris alias quaestiones.[4]

Boso replies, in one of these rejoinders which reveal him as very much a person in his own right in the dialogue: 'Don't be angry! God loves a cheerful giver! If the giver gives more than he promises, he proves himself a cheerful giver indeed! Give me what I ask, then, with a good grace!'

> Ne irascaris, 'hilarem datorem diligit deus'. Nam nemo magis probat se hilariter dare quod promittit, quam qui plus dat quam promittit. Dic ergo libenter quod quaero.[5]

Anselm, we must suppose, did give in with a good grace and acknowledged himself vanquished by just such a 'reasonable argument' as he has himself been using. The overall purpose of all these literary devices can only have been to make the reader feel that he is really present at the discussion, to bring it alive for him and to show him that his difficulties are being carefully considered.

Matching the subtlety of this system of essentially literary devices of involving the reader and carrying him along, is an equally carefully thought-out process of stringing the argument

---

[1] S 2.74.12–14.
[2] The surviving sentences of the School of Laon are collected in O. Lottin, *Psychologie et morale aux xii et xiii siècles*, v (Gembloux 1959).
[3] Compare S 2.74.12–13 with S 2.84.6–7.   [4] S 2.74.15–16.
[5] S 2.74.17–18.

together. We begin with an exact statement of the problem in hand:

> qua scilicet ratione vel necessitate deus homo factus sit, et morte sua, sicut credimus et confitemur, mundo vitam reddiderit, cum hoc aut per aliam personam, sive angelicam sive humanam, aut sola voluntate facere potuerit.[1]

('For what reason, or under what necessity God was made man, and restored life to the world through his own death, as we believe and trust, when he could have done so through another person, angelic or human, or through the exercise of his will alone.')

Then Anselm explains to his readers what frame of mind he would like them to adopt as they read. If he says anything which a greater authority does not confirm, even though it seems to be attested by reason:

> si quid dixero quod maior non confirmet auctoritas— quamvis illud ratione probare videar,[2]

it is to be accepted, not as a certainty, but as something which seems to Anselm, for the moment, to be the case. Anselm wants his readers to be open-minded about his 'proofs', but never to be open-minded about the objects of those proofs, which are already matters of certainty through faith. It is only within the framework of such beliefs that the reasonableness of Anselm's arguments will be apparent.[3]

We have already looked at some of the considerable bulk of preliminaries, warnings, checks, and balances with which Anselm prefaces even the account of the objections and responses (which are in themselves a form of introduction to the main course of the argument). We might add here a mention of the note of regret with which he says that there really will not be space to consider in full the notions of *potestas*, *necessitas*, *voluntas*, which would, ideally, form the basis for later discussion.[4] Not only, we are made aware, has an immense amount of detailed problem-solving, carried out on various occasions, gone into the construction of the *Cur Deus Homo*, but still more has had to be omitted in order to make the sequence of the argument and its subdivisions clear to every reader. We can only presume that among the 'many' with whom Anselm has

---

[1] S 2.48.2–5. [2] S 2.50.8. [3] S 2.50.8–12. [4] S 2.49.9.

discussed the topics of the *Cur Deus Homo*,[1] some raised issues
which have simply had to be left out. As a teacher and as a
thinker, Anselm had, it seems, always realized that problems
were best clarified by omitting side-issues. It is this, in part,
which singles out even his earliest works from the majority of
those of his contemporaries. In his first chapters, then, Anselm
marks out the ground very carefully, so as to clear the way for
his chain of reasoning in the main part of his argument. And he
tells his readers exactly what he is doing. Boso later reminds his
readers that they have been following a chain of reasoning:
ipsa tamen rationis contextum.[2]

viii: *A Book for Everyone*

It seems clear, then, that Anselm's appeal to reason in the
Cur Deus Homo has little to do with the question of the relationship between faith and reason which has so often preoccupied
modern scholars. The ultimate appeal of Anselm's multi-
farious arguments is to the man who is prepared to be open-
minded in a quite specific sense. He is to be willing to let his
God-given faculty of reason operate as God intended it to do
upon the understanding of theological puzzles. A man who
hears with faith what Anselm has to say will see that it is
reasonable. An unbeliever who is prepared to listen without
condemning the principles of belief on which Anselm builds,
will also find his reason convinced. In both instances, Anselm's
ultimate intention is to 'appeal' to the rational faculty implanted in man by a reasonable God. Every man can recognize
'rightness', and that is all that Anselm asks him to do. This is
certainly the only sense in which he can have hoped that his
case would appear convincing to so wide-ranging an intended
readership. He is far too explicit about his purposes and the
way in which he hopes to achieve them, far too experienced in
the business of explaining theological issues to simple men and
to young philosophers alike, for there to have been any confusion in his mind as to the limitations and strengths of the
method. To object that he makes a greater claim for the powers
of rigorous reasoning than it will stand, is both to misunder-
stand Anselm's own awareness of what he was trying to do, and

[1] S 2.47.5–6.   [2] S 2.130.1–2.

to underestimate the degree of his insight into the workings of other men's minds.

The commendatory letter to Urban II does not reveal, as the Preface to the book does, how mixed were Anselm's feelings in finishing the work. There, he stands back from the whole, and sees it as an exercise in refuting error and confirming the faith of believers, who may 'delight' in the rightness of their belief.[1] But in the Preface proper, Anselm complains that his search for perfect lucidity was interrupted by the impatience of his friends to see the work finished. Perhaps they were simply trying to persuade him to complete it in case—as they must have begun to suspect—he would never feel sufficiently satisfied to let them read it. They took away parts of the work and began to copy them before the whole was ready (*antequam perfectum et exquisitum esset, primas partes eius me nesciente sibi transcribebant.*)[2] Rather than let the work circulate in parts, Anselm felt obliged to complete it quickly.

The direction of his projected revisions seems fairly clear. If he had been left in peace a little longer, he would have lengthened rather than shortened it (*inseruissem et addidissem.*)[3] In so doing, he would presumably have been adding to the system of checks and balances already present in the work, not recasting the whole substantially. Anselm saw his line of thought so clearly marked out for him that there is no evidence in any of his works that he re-shuffled the order of exposition extensively while he was writing it. In an age of digressive arguments and rambling literary structure this was most unusual; by contrast, Anselm's vigorous grasp of an organizing principle stands out even more sharply.[4] For our purposes, what emerges most clearly from this introductory *apologia* is an impression of Anselm's own need to write in conditions of peace and at leisure

[1] S 2.39.6.
[2] S 2.42.2–3. There is no way of knowing how long Anselm's other works took to write. He may have grown slower and become even more of a perfectionist with the passage of time.
[3] S 2.42.5.
[4] In S 2.42.8–9 he mentions the *materia*, the subject-matter of the treatise. The term is a common one in the *Accessus* tradition, which taught masters and pupils to ask, among other things, what the work was 'about' before they began to study it. Anselm may have something of the same sense in mind. On the *Accessus* see R. B. C. Huygens, *Accessus ad Auctores* (Leiden 1970).

(*in quiete et congruo spatio*).[1] Even if he found it helpful to develop
his ideas in live discussion with friends and pupils, he evidently
found that he could present them lucidly only if he had time
and peace to write. The pleasure he himself quite obviously
derived from the actual process of writing was perhaps a
solitary pleasure.

Anselm always places great emphasis in the devotional
writings on the need for opportunities of quiet withdrawal. In
the *Proslogion* he invites his readers not only to enter into the
chamber of the mind (*intra in cubiculum mentis tuae*)[2] so as to
withdraw into contemplation, but also to break off their in-
volvement with their daily concerns (*fuge paululum occupationes
tuas*).[3] *Occupationes* may refer to 'preoccupations' rather than to
actual tasks, but in either case, Anselm is urging his readers to
put practical worries out of their minds. The *Meditation on
Human Redemption* contains no such explicit advice to withdraw
into contemplation, but its burden throughout is the encouragement it gives the reader to fix his mind quietly on the *virtus . . .
salvationis*,[4] the 'strength of his salvation', and to think through
its implications. Preparation, whether for contemplation or for
hard rational thinking, is an essential preliminary, for Anselm
himself and for his pupils.

Boso points out that the very *rectus ordo* whose perception is to
give such pleasure, demands that we first believe, before we presume to discuss matters of faith:

Sicut rectus ordo exigit ut profunda Christianae fidei prius
credamus, quam ea praesumamus ratione discutere.[5]

A conscious reviewing of what we believe precedes the attempt
to make it plain to the reason. But merely to believe, however
firmly, is not in itself satisfaction enough. It leaves the mind
hungry. In Anselm's letter to Urban, he says that he has written
the *Cur Deus Homo* in the hope of feeding those who have faith,
but whose hearts hunger even after certainty has been vouch-
safed to them:

et ad pascendum eos qui iam corde fide mundato eiusdem
fide ratione, quam post eius certitudinem debemus esurire,
delectantur.[6]

The *Meditation on Human Redemption* opens and closes with

[1] S 2.42.5–6. [2] S 1.97.7. [3] S 1.97.4.
[4] S 3.84.6. [5] S 2.48.16–17. [6] S 2.39.4–5.

striking images of hunger unsatisfied, which are familiar enough
in Anselm's devotional writings, but which, in this context
have a very direct bearing upon his attitude to the writing o
the *Cur Deus Homo*.[1] Withdrawal into contemplation, the re
viewing of the articles of faith, are exercises of spiritual value i
themselves; but for Anselm, they are completed only when the
issue in the further exercise of the reason upon the subject
matter of belief. Anselm's own periods of withdrawal were, a
he shows clearly enough, necessary to him not only as times fo
meditation, but also as times for thinking. They were periods o
productivity, in which his pleasure and the clarity of his under
standing were both heightened.

Something of this kind certainly seems to have happened i
the case of the writing of the *Meditation on Human Redemption*
There Anselm achieves a further simplification of his argu
ments in the *Cur Deus Homo*, distilling out of them a still mor
refined and lucid summary of the main principles.[2] He offer
his readers a conveniently brief review of important sections o
the work in the context of a meditation, so that they can mov
from a state of quiet withdrawal into a consideration of thei
beliefs, and then into reflection upon the rational ground o
their beliefs. The whole sequence is compressed into two o
three thousand words, without ever appearing to rush matters
In the fullest Anselmian sense, order is preserved.

The clarity with which Anselm has come to see the issue
involved in the Incarnation and the Redemption in the *Cur Deu
Homo*, is reflected in the *Meditation on Human Redemption* in
series of images of light and darkness. Anselm says that he wa
in darkness, but that God has illuminated him (*In tenebris eran
. . . illuxisti mihi*).[3] He also notes how that illumination ha
taught him to see and delight in things which before wer
hidden from him by the darkness, so that they appeared othe
than they are (*absconditum; celatum; occultum*).[4] Now the *corpu
veritatis*, the 'body of the truth', shines more clearly (*plu*

[1] S 3.84.8–12, S 3.91.208, S 1.98.20–4. This is an aspect brought out clearly i
Sister Benedicta Ward's Introduction to her translation of the *Prayers and Medit
tions of St. Anselm* (London 1973), p. 44.
[2] S 2, S 3 should be compared for footnote cross-references between the tw
works, cf. AB, p. 36.
[3] S 3.90.171 and 179.
[4] S 3.84.21–2.

niteat).[1] The *liberatio*[2] of the Redemption and the *captio*[3] from which it releases us, also have to do with emerging from darkness into the light of understanding. The writing of the *Meditatio* enabled Anselm to employ several of the images of light of which he is so fond;[4] he has been prompted to do so by the realization in the *Cur Deus Homo* that the complex of notions of clarity, lucidity, and pleasure in understanding which have directed its writing are closely related to the 'spiritual vision' of the Prayers and Meditations.

The *Cur Deus Homo* is in every way a work of Anselm's maturity. It has an air of calmness and certainty bred of years of quiet reflection, in the course of which Anselm never found anything to be at variance with the conclusions he had always had in view from the beginning—those of orthodox Christian doctrine. Perhaps the stresses of Anselm's ordinary life during the years when the work was written had heightened his longing for periods of calm when he could return with relief to matters which interested him more than the pressing daily business of being an Archbishop. That would go some way towards explaining why his joy in the reasonableness of the universe seems here a quieter emotion than the excitement which had possessed him when he wrote the *Proslogion*. It was only while he was able to live a relatively peaceful life at Bec that he seems to have needed the contrast of violent and passionate feeling, expressed in the Prayers and Meditations in particular. Held secure, as it seemed, in his monastic peace, Anselm whipped himself into frenzies of self-castigation or threw himself with joy into affirmations of love. Torn from his beloved Bec and cast into the vortex of affairs, he sought a pool of silence in which he could enjoy a gentler pleasure in his faith. In both sets of circumstances, there is a clear contrast between the outward circumstances of Anselm's life and the kind of vision of God he found most helpful to himself, and thought to be most helpful to others.

---

[1] S 2.52.5.   [2] S 2.52.14.   [3] S 2.53.6.
[4] This is more common than any other type of image in Anselm's writing.

8

THE *DE CONCEPTU VIRGINALI*

i: *The writing of an appendix to the* Cur Deus Homo

THE completion of the *Cur Deus Homo* had not left Anselm with the nagging sense of an insight not quite grasped which had made the *Proslogion* argument such a torment to him in its coming and such a delight to him when he had found it and set it out for his friends and pupils to see.[1] So it was that when Anselm wrote the *De Conceptu Virginali* as a sequel to the *Cur Deus Homo*, he did not do so in quite the spirit in which he composed the *Proslogion* to complement the *Monologion*. But when he had finished writing the *Cur Deus Homo*, Anselm saw that there were loose ends to be stitched into the fabric of the argument. Various aspects of the questions he had dealt with had had to be left out of account, or covered only very briefly.[2] He was never so troubled by these omissions that he attempted to treat them all, although he may have been working on one set of problems in the *Philosophical Fragments*.[3] The *De Conceptu Virginali* represents his only thoroughgoing effort to settle an issue which had been left temptingly unresolved in the *Cur Deus Homo*, where he had made a half-promise to deal with it later in another work.[4]

A recurrent problem for Anselm himself, and one which makes itself felt many times in his writings, was that of deciding what to include and what to omit. This is especially pressing where he sees that an issue has larger philosophical and theological ramifications. (And such possibilities of development can rarely have been hidden from him.) Nowhere are difficulties of this kind more evident or more frequently mentioned by Anselm himself than in the *Cur Deus Homo*. He himself was able to list a considerable number of *objectiones infidelium* which he knew to be under discussion in the schools of the day,[5] at the beginning

---

[1] S 1.93.20–1.   [2] e.g. S 2.49.7–13.
[3] AB, p. 117. The fragments have been most recently edited in MA, pp. 334–51.
[4] S 2.126.15–16.
[5] See the Sentences edited by O. Lottin, *Psychologie et Morale aux xiie et xiiie siècles*, v (Gembloux 1959). On Original Sin and the *Cur Deus Homo* issue alone, see pp. 29, 38, 39, 41, 42, 44, 46, 50, 87, 95, 112, 184–5, 187 *et al.*

of the *Cur Deus Homo*;[1] some of these, at least, were probably being discussed in the schools of northern France. Such questions, put to him from, as it were, 'outside', would have added extra problems of organization and subordination to the difficulties already raised by Anselm's own independent perception of the existence of a variety of related issues. Whenever he touches upon a difficulty which does not lie in what he perceives to be the main stream of his argument, Anselm has had to make the decision to leave it out, or to deal with it in passing. The subject of the *De Conceptu Virginali* has proved too cumbersome to be included in the sequence of the *Cur Deus Homo*. That it developed additional ramifications of its own when Anselm came to write about it is in no way surprising.

The problem was partly a structural one. Anselm had permitted one digression of some length in the *Cur Deus Homo*— that which deals with the angels, whose numbers are to be made up (in Anselm's view) from the elect among men.[2] We have seen how he and Boso make something of a joke of the fact that this is a digression. Boso teases Anselm into explaining his assertion in detail by telling him that, since 'God loves a cheerful giver', he will prove himself more than generous by giving Boso a fuller account of the matter than he had promised.[3] When the digression ends three chapters later, Boso says: *Nunc redi ad id unde digressi sumus*,[4] ('Now go back to the point where we began to digress'), and Anselm restates his former proposition before continuing.[5] It might be argued that he could have used some similar device so as to work in the treatment of Original Sin which forms the substance of the subject-matter in the *De Conceptu Virginali*. But to do so would have meant making the *Cur Deus Homo* very much longer. This would have been no digression of a few chapters, but a very considerable addition to the overall length of the work. The finished *De Conceptu Virginali* is more than a third of the length of the *Cur Deus Homo*.

But there is a more substantial objection of a theoretical kind. In the *De Conceptu Virginali*, Anselm goes about the task of giving compelling reasons for the Atonement from a rather different viewpoint. He looks, not at the reason why only a God-Man could redeem the human race, but at the question of how such

[1] S 2.50–61.   [2] S 2.74.12–13.   [3] S 2.74.15–19.   [4] S 2.84.3.
[5] S 2.84.6.

a being could be free from the taint of Original Sin, which made every other member of the human race incapable of justifying himself in the sight of God, let alone of atoning for the sins of his fellows. It is noticeable that while the *De Conceptu Virginali* is full of references to *peccatum originale*, in the *Cur Deus Homo* Anselm prefers to speak of the *initium* or *principium* of sin.[1] There, he is concerned with the nature of sin, rather than with the mode of its transmission, and with Christ's claim to be descended from the stock responsible for the debt caused by its sin, rather than with the question of his own freedom from that universal sinfulness. He goes to some trouble to explain why Christ is sinless, but his account turns on the question of obedience to God's will, rather than on the way in which Christ may be reckoned to be without Original Sin. The emphases of the two works are therefore very different. The order and sequence of the treatment in the *Cur Deus Homo* would not allow Anselm to handle the subject-matter of the *De Conceptu Virginali* except by introducing something rather like a sub-plot. Such a procedure could only have entangled in obscurities a line of argument Anselm was particularly anxious to keep clear in the *Cur Deus Homo*.[2]

Yet the *De Conceptu Virginali* does not stand alone. The reader is repeatedly referred, not only to the *Cur Deus Homo*, but also to the *De Veritate* and the *De Casu Diaboli*, for treatments of topics of great importance for the understanding of the argument. The early definition of *iustitia* which Anselm had hammered out so painstakingly in the 'three treatises pertaining to the study of Holy Scripture', for example, contains elements crucial to the direction of his reasoning here. Unless his reader is prepared to accept that will plays a vital role in righteousness, Anselm can take him no further.[3] If the *De Conceptu Virginali* is to be read independently, a good deal must be taken on trust. Anselm becomes noticeably anxious at moments where he has to ask his readers either to refer back to one of his previous writings, or to accept that he has settled the issue there, to make it clear that he has in fact left no point undefended:

> sufficienter me puto ostendisse in eo tractatu quem feci *De Casu Diaboli*; sed de iustitia plenius in illo quem edidi *De Veritate*.[4]

[1] S 2.51.8, S 2.104.18.   [2] S 2.48.6–9.   [3] S 2.142–3   [4] S 2.147.4–5.

('I think I have made that plain enough in the treatise I wrote "On the Fall of Satan"; but I have dealt with "righteousness" more fully in my book "On Truth".') The whole complex of cross-references shows Anselm for once not engaged in the pursuit of the almost linear consequences of the development of his thinking from one topic to another, but in a most uncharacteristic position. He is working on a parallel argument, and he is not certain where to 'place' what he has to say.

Anselm's awareness of the danger of repeating himself is frequently in conflict with his desire to make himself absolutely clear—especially on technical matters. The meticulous care he takes at every stage either to explain a point afresh, or to refer the reader to an explanation which is available elsewhere, is matched by a similar care in explaining the relationship between two arguments whose purposes would seem to overlap. He does this most obviously in the *De Conceptu Virginali*, where he feels it necessary to show how his argument resembles that of the *Cur Deus Homo*, and how it differs from it. This is especially important since he goes on in the rest of the *De Conceptu Virginali* to other matters which have a bearing on the subject-matter of the second treatise only. But it is a peculiarity of the work that detailed adjustments of this kind are felt to be necessary; Anselm seems to have been acutely conscious that he was engaged in a *discursus* from the main line of his thought. In Chapter 19 he shows precisely where the two arguments meet, and precisely where they differ:

> Quomodo ista ratio et altera alibi data concordent et differant.[1]

('How that reason, and the other I have given elsewhere agree, and how they differ'). Anselm goes on to say—again using the term *ratio* interestingly, to refer to the whole sequence of argumentation in each case:

> Quae duae rationes intellectui meo videntur ad quaestionem unaquaeque per se sufficere.[2]

('These two reasons seem to my understanding to constitute independently quite adequate answers to the question.') Each sequence on its own gives an adequate proof. Anselm does not want his readers to try to conflate the two, or to take fragments of one and try to insert them into the other. He himself has

[1] S 2.159.27.   [2] S 2.159.28–9.

avoided the temptation to do so in writing the *De Conceptu Virginali* as a quite separate work. He intends each sequence of argument to stand independently.

This, however, raises a question of philosophical method to which Anselm had evidently given some thought. He had re-marked in the *Cur Deus Homo* that if several proofs are provided, and one is found solidly convincing, there is no need to worry about the inadequacies of the others:

> verumtamen, si vel una de omnibus quas posui inexpugna-bili veritate roboratur, sufficere debet. Sive namque uno sive pluribus argumentis veritas inexpugnabiliter monstretur, aequaliter ab omni dubitatione defenditur.[1]

('Indeed, if only one of all the arguments I have proposed is supported by indisputable truth, that should be enough. For whether the truth is demonstrated beyond dispute by one argu-ment or by many, it is equally defended against all doubt.') Anselm neither states nor implies here that he thinks there is no value in trying to supply more than one argument. Economy of demonstration demands no more, but there is nothing to be lost in making the attempt. In the *De Conceptu Virginali* he says quite explicitly that there can be no objection to providing another argument:

> nihil enim prohibet eiusdem rei rationes plures esse, quarum unaquaeque sola potest sufficere.[2]

('Nothing forbids there being several reasons for the same thing, of which one alone is sufficient.') That 'one' Anselm considers he has already given in the *Cur Deus Homo*; but it is with this sentence that he concludes his opening plea in justification of the writing of the *De Conceptu Virginali*, in which he proposes to offer another independent and equally convincing argument.

Anselm must have had the intention of doing so quite firmly in mind even while he was writing the *Cur Deus Homo*; there would otherwise be no reason, but a mere literary affectation, behind the passage where he half-promises to write a second treatise. This exchange between Anselm and Boso need not have been allowed to stand. Anselm points out that there is an alternative proof which involves looking at the nature of Original Sin, and at the way in which that sin was passed on to the human race:

---

[1] S 2.94.18–23.   [2] S 2.139.14–15.

Verum quoniam et ista mihi videtur posse sufficere, et si aliam nunc inquirere vellem, necesse esset investigare quid sit originale peccatum et quomodo a primis parentibus in universum genus humanum praeter illum de quo agimus hominem diffundatur, et incidere in quasdam alias quaestiones quae suum postulant tractatum.[1]

('Truly, that seems to me to suffice; besides, if I wanted to look at anything else at this point, it would be necessary to ask what is original sin, and how it was passed on from our first parents to every member of the human race except to him whom we are discussing; and we should have to tackle certain other questions which demand to be dealt with in this connection.')

Boso tries to make him promise there and then that he will deal with this question later if he can:

Ut vis; sed eo pacto ut tu aliquando auxiliante deo illam aliam rationem, quam nunc inquirere vitas, quasi debitum exsolvas.[2]

('As you wish, but on the understanding that you promise to explain that other reason, at some other time, God willing, since you are now avoiding the discussion of it.') Anselm says that he will try to do so when occasion present itself. Boso is, after all, not the *discipulus* of the early dialogues, and he is treated throughout the *Cur Deus Homo* as a real person. There is no reason to suppose that when Anselm complains at the beginning of the *De Conceptu Virginali* that he has been prodded into finishing his task by Boso, he is merely employing a literary convention.[3] On the other hand, Anselm did not always allow Boso to bully him gently into giving way. Boso had his own way over the digression about the angels, but he did not press the point earlier on in the *Cur Deus Homo*, when Anselm said that there was really no space to consider the problems posed by will, power and necessity, at any length.[4] We can only suppose that Anselm has tailored the conversation deliberately, in the finished dialogue, so as to whet the reader's appetite for the second treatise. His strictures about the use of additional 'solid arguments' then fall into place. Anselm has been careful in both treatises to justify the writing of two distinct works which cover, in part, the same theme; in the *Cur Deus Homo* he has paved the way for the writing of the *De Conceptu Virginali* argument, and he has taken the trouble to justify it as methodologically acceptable. But again, it seems that he has felt the need to do

---

[1] S 2.126.8–13.   [2] S 2.126.15–16.   [3] S 2.139.8–9.   [4] S 2.49.7–16.

so only because he finds himself in the curious position of writing one treatise almost alongside another, rather than leaving one subject behind and moving on to another.

Yet the *De Conceptu Virginali* argument, in so far as it deals with subject-matter related to the *Cur Deus Homo*, can only be regarded as something of an appendix to the earlier work. The work as a whole lacks the stature of the *Cur Deus Homo*, and its weight, and this is at least partly because it looks only tangentially at the question of the Atonement. It is concerned first and foremost with the mechanics of the transmission of Original Sin. The most signal difference between the two works, from a compositional point of view, is the fact that, although Boso makes an appearance at the beginning, where Anselm addresses the work to him[1] and credits him with inspiring its completion,[2] he does not take part in a dialogue with Anselm throughout. Perhaps this really was a topic they had not discussed together, and which Anselm had worked on alone. Anselm says that he has felt it unfair to 'hide' from Boso (*dilectioni tuae abscondo*) what he thinks about the problem (*de hoc quod sentio*).[3] That certainly suggests that there had been no collaboration in the composition of the *De Conceptu Virginali*. It also indicates that Anselm may indeed have seen the work as an appendix, an unwieldy block of material which would—apart from its conceptual awkwardness—have made a leaden lump of monologue if he had attempted to insert it into the *Cur Deus Homo* itself.

What is beyond dispute is that Anselm had provided a 'hook' in the *Cur Deus Homo* on to which he hoped one day to hang this second argument. The second argument is indeed secondary, and also subordinate to the first. It deserves a place, but not within the main body of the work. In this respect it contrasts strongly with the *Proslogion* argument which was also not integrated into its parent work, the *Monologion*, but in this case because it stands above and beyond the *Monologion*'s 'chain' of arguments.[4] Nothing had been said in the course of the *Cur Deus Homo* which had lifted Anselm's understanding of the issues involved on to an entirely different plane. The *De Conceptu Virginali* is written to convey ideas of much the same general level as those in the *Cur Deus Homo*. There was nothing to prevent Anselm's writing the two works simultaneously, had he been in the habit of working on two treatises at once, as it seems fairly certain he was not. And he evidently had at least a sketch for the *De Conceptu Virginali* in his mind when he made his provisional promise to Boso.

There were, then, no objections, theoretical or practical, in Anselm's view, to the attempt to supply two *rationes*. Both, Anselm claims, can do the things which he has been at such pains to show that the arguments of the *Cur Deus Homo* can do:

> sed ambae simul animo vim rationis et decorem actionis quaerenti copiose satisfacere,[1]

('Both alike [seem to me] to satisfy the enquiring mind completely in the force of their reasoning and the appropriateness of the events they describe.') Throughout the *Cur Deus Homo* this same two-fold emphasis is to be found, upon cogency of reason and the use of 'necessary reasons',[2] and, on the other hand, upon 'beauty' and 'fittingness'.[3] Anselm does not labour the point in the *De Conceptu Virginali*. If his reader comes to it as an appendix to the *Cur Deus Homo* the peculiar nature of Anselm's appeals to his reason there will be fresh in his mind. Both forms of conviction will seem equally cogent. Anselm notes that the two *rationes* arrive at the same result (*quamvis ad idem tendant*).[4] The twofold force of argument is therefore common to both *rationes*.

The difference, as Anselm sees it, lies not in the presentation of the two arguments, but in their differences of subject-matter. In the *De Conceptu Virginali* Anselm shows that because of the mode of Christ's conception, he would necessarily be righteous, even if the Virgin herself was tainted with Original Sin (*etiam de peccatricis virginis substantia*).[5] In the *Cur Deus Homo* he explains, we see how, that even if the whole being of the Virgin, were sinful, Christ would still be righteous (*etiam si in tota virginis essentia peccatum esset*).[6] In the first case, the argument turns on the fact that sin is present only in the will, and Christ's will cannot err. In the second case, we are shown how the Virgin's inborn sin could be purged by faith, so that she was fit to bear Christ.[7] The argument of the *De Conceptu Virginali* does not, as

---

[1] S 2.159.29–160.1. [2] S 2.48.2, S 2.50.8, for example.
[3] S 2.48.9, S 2.49.21–5, S 2.69.6 *et al.* [4] S 2. 160.2.
[5] S 2.160.2–3. [6] S 2.160.5–6.
[7] Cf. S 2.124.24–6. JH, pp. 202–4 gives a brief account of some of the differences between the two arguments.

Anselm points out, raise a question which was central to the *Cur Deus Homo*: whether Christ had to die, the problem of the *necessitas mortis*.[1] Because will is seen to be essential to sin from the first in the *De Conceptu Virginali*,[2] it is not necessary to show that Christ died of his own free will,[3] as it is in the *Cur Deus Homo*. The operation of his will defines the very nature of sin, and so he cannot have submitted himself to death under any coercion occasioned by sin.

It might be objected here that if the *De Conceptu Virginali* raises fewer difficulties—and avoids such major ones, too—Anselm would have been wiser to select this line of argument for use in the *Cur Deus Homo* itself. But this purpose here is to review as many as possible of the difficulties inherent in the doctrine of the Atonement, so as to settle specific queries on every possible point in the minds of his readers. To propose an argument which circumvents some of those difficulties by simply not raising them would not have served his purposes at all. The problem of necessity is a central preoccupation of the *Cur Deus Homo*, and it was in a chapter especially closely concerned with the difficulty of suggesting that God is bound by any necessity that the *De Conceptu Virginali* argument had been adumbrated.[4]

In any case, these two 'summaries' of the *rationes* in Chapter 19 of the *De Conceptu Virginali* do not by any means cover the whole of each work. They deal only with those parts where their subject-matter is close. We are not, in other words, given two alternative theories of the Atonement, in the *Cur Deus Homo* and in the *De Conceptu Virginali*, but merely two alternative views of one crucial sequence within the argument. Anselm's own account of the 'differences' between the two *rationes* shows that the second work cannot be regarded as a sequel to the first, matching it point by point.

Nevertheless, there are several points of contact between the two works which make it plain that Anselm's summary does not tell us everything he has done in writing the *De Conceptu Virginali*. In chapter 6, for example, he looks back to the point in the *Cur Deus Homo* where he explains that although sin is *nihil*, God does not punish a man for nothing, *ut in praefato libro dixi*.[5] The chapter where this occurs constitutes a brief digression.

---

[1] S 2.160.7–8. [2] S 2.160.3–4. [3] S 2.61.4, *Cur Deus Homo*, I.9.
[4] *Cur Deus Homo*, II.17. [5] S 2.147.14.

Anselm acknowledges as much quite openly. He has found that when people hear that sin is nothing, they frequently ask why, in that case, God punishes man for sin,—for surely no one ought to be punished for nothing:

> Si peccatum nihil est, cur punit deus hominem pro peccato, cum pro nihilo nemo puniri debeat?[1]

Although, as Anselm says, this is the question of a simple man (he may even mean to imply that it is a crude or stupid question), it must be answered, because it causes real difficulty:

> Quibus quamvis humilis sit quaestio, tamen quia quod quaerunt ignorant, aliquid breviter respondendum est.[2]

As Anselm employs the term *humilis* here, it seems to indicate the kind of question asked by those who are unsophisticated in the art of reasoning. But whatever prompts the question, he feels that he ought to try to meet any genuinely-felt difficulty. He is continuing, in other words, to pursue a policy which he had laid down early in the *Cur Deus Homo*. There he had promised to provide explanations for those of limited educational attainments (*non solum litterati sed etiam illiterati*),[3] and for those of slower understanding (*tardioribus ingeniis*).[4] This is one of the few instances in the *De Conceptu Virginali* where Anselm shows beyond question that he is trying to pitch the work at rather the same level as the *Cur Deus Homo*, and for substantially the same readership. (In this respect the addressing of the work to Boso is something of a fiction, for Boso clearly had no need of such concessions.) Only occasionally does a note of impatience creep into Anselm's tone as he pauses to allow the slower reader to catch up. In Chapter 14 of the *De Conceptu Virginali*, for example, he says that if there is any reader who has not grasped the point in hand (*si mens alicuius non capit quod . . . dixi*),[5] he is unwilling to labour it, but he will give a brief account for those who are prepared to concentrate hard for a few moments:

> non hic laboro . . . ut quod non potest capere capiat, sed peto ut quod breviter dicam attendat.[6]

This is not the Anselm who wants his arguments in the *Cur Deus*

---

[1] S 2.147.8–10.
[2] S 2.147.10–11. *Humilis* is of course frequently used of the plainest of the three styles recognized since classical times.
[3] S 2.48.5–6.   [4] S 2.48.12.   [5] S 2.156.4.
[6] S 2.156.10–11.

Homo to be intelligible to everyone (*omnibus intelligibilis*).[1] But neither is it typical of the spirit in which he wrote the *De Conceptu Virginali*. It merely shows, by contrast, how commonly both works strive to meet the needs of every kind of reader.

The formulation of the *nihil* problem in the *De Conceptu Virginali* is of interest for another reason. Elsewhere in his works Anselm had spoken of evil as a *nihil*, in accordance with Augustine's teaching.[2] But here he calls, not evil, but 'sin' nothing. The connection is not far to seek, since to commit a sin a man must 'do wrong' or 'do evil'; and in the preceding chapter Anselm had explicitly linked 'evil, sin, and injustice' (*malum, peccatum, iniustitia*).[3] But the question in very much this form was being raised at Laon, and it may be that young scholars had put it to Anselm among the questions which had played a part in the shaping of the *Cur Deus Homo* itself. Among the Laon Sentences are instances where 'evil' itself is said to be 'nothing' (*sciendum quod nihil malum est*),[4] and cases where 'sin' is said to be 'nothing':

Dicunt quidam peccatum nullum prorsus esse essentiam.
Alii autem dicunt peccatum aliquid esse.[5]

This two-fold usage is echoed in Anselm's *Quod malum, quod est peccatum sive iniustitia, nihil sit*,[6] with the addition of the very Anselmian notion of 'injustice' or 'unrighteousness' in this connection. Among the readers Anselm must have envisaged for the work were those who had heard and perhaps half-understood such teachings at Laon or elsewhere.

The explanation Anselm gives in this chapter must, he feels, at all costs be brief, because the introduction of the topic constitutes a digression. The account he gives relies heavily on a line of explanation followed in the *Cur Deus Homo*.[7] Anselm avoids any attempt to explain philosophically how sin, though 'nothing', is to be regarded as a 'something'. There is no experimenting with a *quasi-aliquid* here.[8] In Chapter 5 Anselm had given a full enough account of the ways in which we recognize evil from its effect on its context.[9] The desires and deeds of an unrighteous will considered in themselves are 'something' (*per*

---

[1] S 2.48.8.
[2] e.g. *De Magistro*, CCSL, 29. 159 (II.3) and chapter following.
[3] S 2.146.2.   [4] Lottin, p. 221 (227).   [5] Lottin, p. 222 (278).
[6] S 2.146.2.   [7] S 2.69–72.
[8] *De Casu Diaboli*, S 1.248–51, cf. MA, p. 337.6.   [9] S 2.146–7.

se considerati aliquid sunt),[1] but the element of unrighteousness, evil, or sin, which gives them their character, is in itself, 'nothing', *quia iniustitia nullam habet essentiam*.[2] Similarly, it is because of the effect of sin in disturbing the world-order that God rightly exacts punishment.[3] For a fuller exposition of this explanation, Anselm refers his readers to the *Cur Deus Homo*. He has been concerned chiefly to get a stumbling-block out of the way as quickly as possible, and because of the circumstances in which the *De Conceptu Virginali* was composed, it is natural to do so by leaning upon explanations already given in the *Cur Deus Homo*. It is also very understandable that in a digression designed to satisfy those who are likely to find special difficulties in understanding his arguments, he refrains from complicating matters further for his less well-educated readers, as he might have done if he had looked at the philosophical implications of the problem at length.

In Chapter 17 he mentions his 'often-cited work', the *saepe-fatum opusculum*, again,[4] and again he does so in order to refer his readers to his earlier and fuller treatment of the reason why it was necessary for God to be incarnated. Once more, this appears to have been an issue raised by students and scholars of Anselm's acquaintance. In Anselm's day and in Anselm's hands, the conventional *Forsitan dicit aliquis*[5] is not necessarily merely a convention. It often indicates that Anselm is about to deal with a difficulty which has actually been put to him. The question in this case is as follows:

Si purus homo qui deus non esset potuit fieri de Adam sine omni peccati contagione, sicut dicis: cur necesse fuit deum incarnari, cum aut per unum talem qui esset sine omni peccato posset peccatores deus redimere, aut tot quot necessarii erant ad perficiendam supernam civitatem homines simili miraculo facere?[6]

('If a mere man, who was not God, could have been made from Adam without any contagion of sin, as you say, why was it necessary for God to be incarnated, since God could redeem sinners through one who was thus without any sin, or by a similar miracle make as many men as were needed to complete the Heavenly City?')

---

[1] S 2.146.21-2.   [2] S 2.146.20.

[3] S 2.147.15-17. Anselm has here no developed ethical principle, but a notion of cause and effect far ahead of his time; he envisaged effects whose causes we can detect only from the presence of the effects themselves.

[4] S 2.158.15.   [5] S 2.158.9.   [6] S 2.158.9-13.

To this, again, Anselm proposes to reply briefly (*ad quod breviter respondeo*),[1] and in order to avoid a long digression, he again falls back on the account given in the *Cur Deus Homo*.[2] At no point, then, does Anselm cease to be conscious of the relation between the two works; he has a clear notion in his mind of exactly which issues he has already settled, and a consistent determination not to be sidetracked into repeating himself, when they reappear in the *De Conceptu Virginali* argument.

He may himself have had a text before him; he certainly intends that his readers should have gone to the trouble of reading the *Cur Deus Homo* first. He says, a little later, in yet another reference to the *Cur Deus Homo*:

De cuius pondere et satisfactione in *Cur Deus Homo* quod mihi visum est, sicut iam legisti, exposui.[3]

('Of the weight [of sin] and of the satisfaction for it, I have said what seems true to me, as you have read in the *Cur Deus Homo*.')

'As you have read' is of course directed in the first instance to Boso, but it is clearly intended to remind other readers, too, that they should read the main work before the 'appendix'. The frequency with which Anselm remarks that he intends to deal: *breviter* with a point already dealt with in the earlier work, when he comes to it again in the *De Conceptu Virginali*, is noticeable. Anselm avoids repeating himself, by making these references; but he also saves himself time, and avoids the risk of being tedious, too.

A second and perhaps more important feature of these repeated cross-references from the second work to the first, is that they help Anselm to link two radically different sequences of argument together at the points where they touch. Just as Anselm never allowed the details of what he had written in the *Cur Deus Homo* to slip from his mind, so he never allowed himself to forget that two distinct sequences of argumentation are involved. In Chapter 21 of the *De Conceptu Virginali*, for example, he again refers to his use of two arguments, when he expressed his willingness to bow to anyone who can produce a better argument than either:

Altiorem autem aliam rationem . . . praeter istam quam hic et illam quam alibi posui.[4]

[1] S 2.158.14. [2] Especially S 2.101.16–17, and cf. S 2.162.17–19.
[3] S 2.162.9–10. [4] S 2.161.3–5.

('But another higher reason . . . besides that which I have set out here, and the one which I set out elsewhere'). It seems that Anselm found neither of his two arguments 'higher' or 'better' than the other; certainly he never says that he regarded them as anything other than straightforward alternatives. But he always distinguishes them carefully, whenever they meet at any point in their sequence.

The technical devices used in expounding the two arguments suggest additional evidence for the view that the *De Conceptu Virginali* argument, although it has every bit as much force as that of the *Cur Deus Homo*, has been envisaged by Anselm as something of an appendix. It is usual in writing appendices to provide a plain, businesslike account of a problem too large for a footnote. That is what Anselm has done; he has not allowed himself any of the literary graces of the *Cur Deus Homo*, any comparably expansive introduction, any preliminary account of his overall purposes. We can infer what these were only from incidental comments and from reading the opening of the *Cur Deus Homo* itself. Above all, in the *Cur Deus Homo*, Anselm has tried to win his readers over by employing every kind of argument, formal and informal. In the *De Conceptu Virginali* the bones of the argument are very much barer. Definition and *divisio*, with the occasional syllogism, present an almost monotonously uniform means of demonstration throughout the work.

Anselm begins by defining his terms:

'Originale' quidem ab origine denominari dubium non est.[1] ('There is no doubt that "original" takes its sense from "origin".') Anselm goes on to look first at two senses of 'original' and then at a third,[2] so as to start a sequence of *divisiones*; he discards one sense at each stage, so that he is left with a single sense as a working principle. He 'defines' 'man' so as to show that in each individual there is a human *natura* and a special *persona*.[3] He is now in a position to see how 'original' sin may subsist in each individual man. In this way, as Anselm exhausts the possibilities of each division he introduces another, so as to lead the reader on to the next 'cross-roads' of *divisio*. There can be no doubt that he deliberately allows the technical framework of his arguments to stand undisguised. At one point he remarks:

Haec igitur pars huius divisionis penitus relinquenda est.[4]

[1] S 2.140.8.   [2] S 2.140.9–11 and 15–17.   [3] S 2.140.18–20.   [4] S 2.148.8–9.

('Therefore we must abandon this part of this division altogether.') Such procedures are never allowed to become conspicuous in the *Cur Deus Homo*, and indeed it seems that Anselm
may have tried to frame his opening statement of the problem
there in such a way that there would be no need for mechanical
definitions of terms at first.[1] The differences between the *Cur
Deus Homo* and the *De Conceptu Virginali* in their modes of expounding their respective arguments are largely differences of
emphasis. Anselm's technical expertise is not any less developed
in the earlier work; but there he has gone to the trouble of
disguising it, and of providing variety, so as to keep his readers'
interest. It is to be supposed that the reader of an appendix will
be prepared to tolerate a plainer presentation, because he has
already proved himself a 'serious' reader.

As to the conceptual devices he has used, Anselm is as inventive and as philosophically daring in the *De Conceptu Virginali* as
he had been in the *Cur Deus Homo*—or indeed anywhere else in
his writings. Reference has already been made to the device of
making 'nothing' seem like 'something' for purposes of argument, so that Anselm can show how God punishes a man for
'something', not for 'nothing':

> Et verum est quia nisi sit *aliquid* propter quod punire debeat
> omnino non punit pro *nihilo*.[2]

('And that is true, since unless there was "something" for which
he ought to punish, he would certainly not punish for "nothing".') Another device characteristic of Anselm in other works
is the use of a 'time-shift'. Anselm has to explain the words of
Scripture which indicate that Original Sin is in every infant
from the moment of its conception.[3] It seems to him absurd to
suggest that every child which is conceived but which is mis-
carried is a damned soul.[4] He suggests that perhaps the tenses
of verbs used in Scripture are not always to be taken at their
face value.[5] It was a notion he was to put forward again in *De
Concordia*, I.4–5.[6] A third principle, equally bold in its conception, is also to be found elsewhere in Anselm's writings. He discusses how the sin of Adam could be passed on to his descendants. We know from a passage in the *De Humanis Moribus* that
Anselm used to tell a story concerning a poisonous herb, which,

[1] S 2.48.2–5.   [2] S 2.147.21–2.   [3] S 2.148.10–15.
[4] S 2.148.5–6.   [5] S 2.148.17–18.   [6] S 2.252–4.

once a man had eaten it, poisoned all his children, too.[1] Anselm
believed, then, that the damage the poison did could be trans-
mitted genetically. If we look at the damage or corruption as a
mutation, this is very much his argument in the *De Conceptu
Virginali*. There, he suggests that, after Adam, a 'mutated'
humanity retains its obligation to be righteous, but that Adam
has passed on the corruption of sin to all his descendants.[2]
Where we find such evidences of Anselm's speculative explorations at work, there can be no question of regarding the *De
Conceptu Virginali* as an undeveloped work, even if Anselm did
not dress it as thoroughly as he did the *Cur Deus Homo* with those
small elegances which are intended to make everything he says
there not only clear, but palatable to his readers.

A final notable feature of both the *Cur Deus Homo* and the *De
Conceptu Virginali*—and one which would link the two works if
nothing else had done so—is Anselm's striking use of concepts
and expressions to be found in the Laon Sentences. In no other
works of Anselm's are such topics so closely crowded together,
or their connection with the Laon material so marked. Anselm's
distinction of *natura* and *persona* in man occurs in the Sentences.[3]
So does his reference to the *propagatio* of the human race from
Adam, a[4] discussion of the reasons why we customarily speak of
the sin as Adam's, not Eve's,[5] the *corruptio* of human nature,[6]
the difference between miraculous and natural events,[7] the
massa peccatrix,[8] even some notion of the role of will and necessity
in the Atonement.[9] The strongest impression these comparisons
give—taken collectively, for they are not individually of great
moment—is that the two Anselmian works and the Laon Sentences all spring from the same stock of currently controversial
issues. The formulation of some of the questions Anselm handles
could hardly have been contrived by truly 'simple' men, unless
a focal point of disquiet had been set in place in their minds,
unless, in other words, they had been shown where some of the
difficulties lay and helped to identify the problems which needed
solution.

---

[1] MA, p. 52.   [2] S 2.141.17–21.
[3] S 2.140.18–20, Lottin, p. 29.8 (28).   [4] S 2.153.6, Lottin, p. 29.7 (28).
[5] S 2.102–4, Lottin, p. 205 (251).   [6] S 2.141.7, Lottin, p. 29.7 (28).
[7] S 2.153.3, 154.4–8, 154.12, Lottin, p. 30.22–3 (28).
[8] S 2.52.16–18, Lottin, pp. 39.37 (43), 42.5 (46).
[9] Lottin, p. 185.25, p. 185 *passim*.

One final aspect of Anselm's view of what he was trying to accomplish in the two works ought perhaps to be considered here. Eadmer points out that the *De Conceptu* was written at about the same time as the *Meditation on Human Redemption*.[1] The *Meditation on Human Redemption* was also written as a companion-piece to the *Cur Deus Homo*, but not with the intention of extending the range of arguments propounded there. Rather, Anselm condenses the argument of the *Cur Deus Homo* there, at least in part, and emphasizes the aspects of the work which have to do with Redemption. Yet there is no companion Meditation for the *De Conceptu Virginali*, despite the scope it would seem to provide for the writing of some sort of sequel to Anselm's three Prayers to the Virgin.[2] Indeed, Anselm's references to the part played by the Virgin in the Incarnation, in both the *Cur Deus Homo* and the *De Conceptu Virginali*, have a detached, almost clinical, character. The Virgin never appears either as a person in her own right, or as an object of veneration there, but only as a factor in the great mechanism of the process of salvation. All this reinforces the impression that the *De Conceptu Virginali* belongs with the *Cur Deus Homo* in its absence of devotional content, and in its view of the role played by the Virgin in the Atonement.

But Anselm evidently saw the *De Conceptu Virginali* not as an afterthought but as an integral part of the work he had begun in the *Cur Deus Homo*. He had, as we have seen, planned to write it while he was completing the *Cur Deus Homo*. In a letter he gives orders for the two works to be copied together.[3] His readers will not come closer to an understanding of divine mysteries through reading it than they would have done through reading the *Cur Deus Homo*; Anselm has nothing different in kind to say about God in the second work. He has merely completed an unfinished task. The *Proslogion* depends upon the *Monologion* in a very different way. Yet the *saepefatum opusculum* of the *De Conceptu Virginali* is readily employed to support the case presented there.

ii: *Anselm's view of sin*

'Dim or indistict views of sin are the origin of most of the

---

[1] VA, p. 122, II. xliv.   [2] S 3.13-26.   [3] S 5.289.21-2.

errors, heresies and false doctrines of the present day.'[1] Anselm cannot be accused of having a dim or indistinct view of sin in either of the senses J. C. Ryle has in mind here. The devotional writings show him to have been overwhelmed at times by his own consciousness of sin, and to have fought a running battle with it of an unexceptionably active kind. But he also thought hard about the nature of sin and developed a view of the doctrines of sin and of Original Sin which would stand up to the strenuous philosophical testing to which he put it. Thinkers of Anselm's day did not need to be convinced of the importance of sin in quite the way that Ryle implies to be necessary in our time. There was much discussion about the way in which God's justice could be reconciled with his mercy, since both are absolute and they seem to constitute opposing forces; but there was no popular feeling equivalent to the view sometimes held today that a God of love cannot be angered for long or very seriously by the misdoings of his creatures. The social code of Anselm's day found the notion of strict justice perfectly acceptable, and there was no need to attempt to blur the consequences of sin so as to make the idea of sin palatable. Nor did Anselm's contemporaries find it difficult to accept that all men are corrupt. Their concept of the rationality of man did not extend to encompass the eighteenth-century view that a reasonable man will respond to reasonable demands by behaving well, and in a reasonable manner. (Unfallen man would have done so, certainly, because his rationality was unclouded by sin.) The fact of Original Sin required no special pleading to establish it in the face of any widespread contemporary arguments for man's essential goodness, God's willingness to take no notice of peccadilloes, or the notion that if a man is treated well, he will behave well.

As is so often the case when we look at Anselm's view of a fundamental doctrinal problem, we find him beginning his thinking from assumptions which did not require questioning in his own day. That does not relieve him of the task of providing definitions, but it does save him the trouble of a vast amount of philosophical endeavour in establishing first principles. His definitions and principles are nevertheless sufficiently universal in their application for us to find them reappearing in modern

[1] J. C. Ryle, *Holiness* (London 1952) reprint, p. 1.

writings on the nature of sin. Ryle's definition of sin comes remarkably close to Anselm's. He emphasizes that sin 'consists in doing, saying, thinking, or imagining, anything which is not in perfect conformity with the mind and law of God.'[1] For 'mind and law' Anselm has 'will', but otherwise the definition could be his. E. H. Askwith says that he regards himself as free only when he can say, 'I prefer to do that which I ought to do. To be free I must find pleasure and delight in doing *for its own sake* that which I see to be good.'[2] The similarity to Anselm's definition of righteousness as the preservation of right willing 'for its own sake' is again striking here. The absence of sin consists not only in acting in accordance with the will of God but in doing so by a free act of the rational will, for the sake of the very rightness of the thing. The Anselmian ingredients in the discussion of sin and righteousness: will, reason, freedom, the notion of goodness preserved *propter se*, appear to be, if not indispensable, still valuable and worth consideration. Again, J. C. Ryle suggests that the infant, although it cannot perhaps be said to sin actively from the moment of its birth, 'carries in its heart the seeds of every kind of wickedness'.[3] The notion of the seed with its genetic endowment of potential sinfulness is to be found in the *De Conceptu Virginali*, too. It would be possible to cite definitions of sin put forward since Anselm's day which would be far more obviously out of tune with his thinking. He did not succeed in formulating definitions which would satisfy later theologians extensively. Abelard had some very different views to put forward less than a generation later.[4] But Anselm was thinking about sin in terms which it is difficult to discard altogether if we are to see sin as an offence against God.

A. Ritschl tries to turn the Anselmian assumptions on their heads: 'It is not our relation of subordination to God, but always some claim born of our freedom, that furnishes a standard for what we call evil . . . evil signifies the whole compass of possible restrictions of our purposive activity.'[5] He sees evil, not as a

---

[1] Ibid., p. 2.

[2] E. H. Askwith, 'Sin and the Need of Atonement' in *Cambridge Theological Essays*, 175–218, p. 209.

[3] Ryle, op. cit., p. 3.

[4] See *Peter Abelard's Ethics*, ed. D. E. Luscombe (Oxford 1971).

[5] A. Ritschl, *The Christian Doctrine of Justification and Reconciliation* (Edinburgh 1900), p. 351.

negation of all the positive goods of God, but as a great brick wall which sets limits to freedom of activity. Whatever the implications of this view may be for the doctrine of sin, it is notable that it cannot be framed at all without employing the concepts of freedom and evil, subordination to the will of God, the idea that freedom can be recognized only by putting it into action—the building-blocks of Anselm's definitions and of those of the majority of his predecessors and contemporaries. The complex of related problems which Anselm sees as germane to the working out of a doctrine of sin are still, it seems, inextricably entangled with it. The questions Anselm tries to answer still require answering. Even if we take the extreme view that the only sin is the sin a man commits against himself, we must begin by defining sin and freedom and will and action and reason, and showing what bearing they have on the problem.

F. R. Tennant argues that 'the existence of sin is the sufficient basis of the doctrines of grace and redemption, quite apart from the further question of sin's origin and mode of propagation.'[1] He poses a question which does not exist for Anselm, for whom both sin present in the world in his own day and Original Sin brought into the world by Adam are given facts. He never questions either the historical truth of the story of Adam or the notion that Adam's Fall brought sin upon the whole human race. His energies are devoted to showing how Adam's sin and his own sin obey the same rules and fit the same definition of sin. What can be argued from experience about the development of sin in any child will thus be applicable to the questions raised by the sin of Adam. What Tennant identifies as the central issue of the question of the transmission of sin from Adam is not a problem for Anselm because he does not perceive the distinctions made by modern science. 'The question [of transmission of sin] turns entirely upon the possibility of the transmission of acquired modifications as distinguished from congenital variations.'[2] When Anselm uses the analogy of the poisonous herb which makes a man sick, he sees no reason why that sickness should not be passed on to the man's children genetically.[3] There are numerous other instances of aspects of the problem of Original Sin which either do not occur to

---

[1] F. R. Tennant, *Origin and Propagation of Sin* (Cambridge 1906), p. 13.
[2] Ibid., p. 36.   [3] MA, p. 52.

Anselm, or do not come within the scope of his treatment, although he would probably have been made aware of them by his reading of Augustine or by contemporary debate. He does not, for example, consider the possibility that the fault of Adam lay in his breaking of God's law; he ignores considerations of guilt before the law in favour of moral corruption; he speaks of sin, not of crime. He does not consider whether Adam was morally innocent—in a state of moral neutrality—before the Fall, or whether he was positively righteous. His concern is with the consequence of the Fall because it made the Incarnation necessary. He infers the nature of sin and its existence from the Fall, not the Fall from the existence of sin, as Tennant seems to be suggesting it is philosophically sounder to do.

There is nothing in Anselm of Leibnitz's distinction between moral evil, physical evil, and metaphysical evil, although he does attempt some classification of kinds of evil in Chapter 12 of the *De Casu Diaboli*. He always looks for the common factor in any definitional problem, even where he makes use of divisions and distinctions in the process of refining his definition. His assumption is that all evil is ultimately one, in that it is the absence of a good that ought to be present. It might be argued that Anselm's conception of the scope of metaphysics is an unusually large one. Working outwards as he does from the pure metaphysical speculations of the *Monologion* and *Proslogion*, he admits little to his arguments which cannot be said to have a metaphysical basis. Much of what Spinoza or Leibnitz or Kant or Hegel have to say about sin and evil arises from their attempt to re-define the range of metaphysical discussions, to determine afresh the point at which we cease to speak of temporal and spatial matters and begin to speak of the eternally and universally true. It is Anselm's boldness as a metaphysician which often enables him to avoid difficulties which beset later thinkers. His ignorance of the conclusions of experimental science is a positive benefit to him here, because it leaves the field of discussion relatively uncluttered. He does not conceive of the difficulties which arise if we try to show how Original Sin could in some sense have evolved with *homo sapiens* from the apes. His system of explanations demands that we take the view that the Fall of man, like the Fall of Satan, happened once and for all, on a single occasion in the past. His freedom as a metaphysician and his limited view of history work together to provide him with an immensely congenial field of speculation, in which the scope of metaphysics is great.

Nevertheless, we have seen Anselm's powers much stretched by the effort to do justice to the claims of other men's views in these treatises of his middle years. If the metaphysics and the history of his day had not forced him into discomfort, the difficulties posed by others had certainly done so. If he assumes in the *Monologion* that if our reasoning powers were unclouded we should all speak the same language and understand one another perfectly, he is obliged in time to come to terms with the implications of the fact that we cannot so so. The factor of sin is therefore of importance for his view of the working of language. It too introduces an element of unreasonableness into the working of the universe, which upsets his metaphysics. To a limited extent, the existence of such random factors is a help to him in working out his arguments. It enables him to set one thing against another so as to make distinctions essential to his task of explaining how God is always a special case. But beyond a certain point the consideration of the respects in which the world is not as God made it is a source both of distress and of philosophical difficulty to him. Anselm is never altogether at his ease amidst forces of change.

9

FORCES OF CHANGE

T HE effects of those forces of change which are already
beginning to make themselves felt in the *Cur Deus Homo*
become more and more obvious as we move beyond the
De Conceptu Virginali to look at the treatises Anselm wrote in the
last years of his life. The last treatises have little to add to what
Anselm has already had to say about the task of talking about
God to his friends. To discuss them at length would be to enter
upon a quite different period of Anselm's intellectual life, where
we should not so easily perceive the direction of his personal
development as a thinker—where, in short, Anselm himself is
not so clearly recognizable.

The interest of what he has to say in these treatises lies elsewhere. He foreshadows some of the most significant developments of twelfth-century theology both in the form and in the
subject-matter of his later writing, but it is clear that this is the
result of external forces working upon him rather than the
natural outcome of the work he had already done. There can
be no question of Anselm's attempting to blaze a trail for others
to follow here. His last treatises were not, as it turned out, regarded as models by his successors; indeed they seem to have
been comparatively little read once the theological movement of
the twelfth century was well under way and those who had
known Anselm personally were few.[1] It seems rather that he
was trying to adapt his writing to a new fashion, and the resulting treatises, full of evidences of his enduring intellectual
power though they are not, in every respect, works which
only he could have written. Besides, Anselm had no wish to
encourage further discussion. His overriding purpose had al-

[1] On the history of the study of the *Cur Deus Homo* in the twelfth century, see
B. P. McGuire, 'The History of Saint Anselm's Theology of the Redemption in the
Twelfth and Thirteenth Centuries', Oxford D.Phil. thesis d.4990 (1970). Honorius'
Elucidarium contains many borrowings from Anselm. See Y. Lefèvre, 'L'Eluci-
darium et les lucidaires', *Bibliothèque des écoles françaises d'Athènes et de Rome*, 80 (Paris
1954).

ways been to settle matters of dispute so that they need cause no further disquiet to anyone.

The first of the developments which affected him was a change in form. Anselm had, hitherto, always chosen either the form of a meditation (for the *Monologion* and the *Proslogion*) or a dialogue-form for his treatises. The single exception among the earlier works is the *De Incarnatione Verbi* which takes the form of an open letter, but the circumstances of its composition meant that its form was to some extent dictated to Anselm, and it cannot be said to reflect his free choice. The *De Conceptu Virginali* is a letter to Boso, written as an appendix to the *Cur Deus Homo* and continuing the conversation which had been held there. But the *De Processione Spiritus Sancti* takes the form of an extended treatment of a *quaestio*. Anselm is particularly anxious to make it plain that he intends to deal only with the single question which has been put to him: 'Because of my limited knowledge, I leave more profound questions to the more knowledgeable', he says, and sets about demonstrating the single principle that the Holy Spirit proceeds from the Father and the Son.[1] In the *De Concordia* he treats three questions (*De tribus illis quaestionibus*),[2] concerning the relation of free will to the foreknowledge, predestination, and grace of God, respectively. Although the *Letters on the Sacraments* take an epistolary form, they, too, deal with a series of questions, as Anselm acknowledges at one point *In tertia quaestione*[3] ('In the third question'). Instead of replying point by point to his pupil's detailed questions, as master and pupil explore the problem together, Anselm has begun to anticipate the objections of his readers with such expressions as: *at inferunt; si quis vult dicere* ('But they object'; 'if anyone wishes to say'). With the change of form has come a change of tone, and the new atmosphere of the treatises resembles that of the twelfth-century schoolroom rather than that of the schoolroom at Bec. Anselm has adopted the form because, as apologist for the official orthodox position, he writes for a readership far wider than the monastic circle to which he had first addressed himself, and a more impersonal tone is indispensable. He has, too, an obligation to cast what he says in a form acceptable to contemporary tastes.

[1] S 2.177.14–17.　　[2] S 2.245.3.　　[3] S 2.231.9.

There is no evidence that he has come to prefer the new form. He says at the opening of both the *De Processione Spiritus Sancti* and the *Letters on the Sacraments* that he intends to do no more than he has been asked to do: that is, to answer certain specific questions. In the *De Concordia* he has nothing to say at all about his reasons for writing. In none of the last treatises has he begun, as he had so often done earlier, with quiet reflections on what he hopes to achieve and a reviewing of the methods he has considered before settling on his final choice. It seems that the new form appeared convenient and appropriate rather than that Anselm discovered in it a congenial vehicle for his thought.

He did not attempt to explore further varieties of form which were in use among his contemporaries and immediate successors. Anselm wrote no Scriptural commentaries, no *Elucidarium* like that of Honorius, in which all theology was brought together in a summary form and systematically arranged. There are no collections of Sentences like those being made at Laon in Anselm's day. It was clearly not his intention to seek out new modes of writing about God. In so far as his last works take a form which was to become increasingly popular in later years, they reflect, not a desire for change on Anselm's part, but the effects of external changes upon him.

Anselm's later works belong to the next age of speculative theology in a second respect: that of their subject-matter. When he had completed the *De Conceptu Virginali*, Anselm had worked his way through a sequence of theological topics which were of deep personal interest to him, and which are the central matters of the Christian faith. He would certainly not have felt it necessary to write a treatise on the Procession of the Holy Spirit if he had not been asked to do so, because the doctrine presented him with no difficulties of acceptance. He never chooses to argue against an erroneous viewpoint in an earlier treatise unless the difficulty has actually been raised, by a friend or pupil. It was never Anselm's practice to look for difficulties in a body of doctrine which he so consistently found entirely reasonable. But the question of the Procession of the Holy Spirit, and in particular, that of the difference between the teaching of the Greeks and that of the Latins, was apparently becoming a focal point of general controversy. When Urban II asked Anselm to defend the Latin Christians' point of view at the Council of Bari in 1098,[1] he was responding to a widely-felt need to take account of the presence of holders of alternative viewpoints in the Christian world. As the twelfth century wore on, attention was more and more often focused upon the need to combat the views of holders of unorthodox opinions. In Anselm's day, *disputationes* with Jews and philosophers and pagans were already being written. Alan of Lille, much later in the twelfth century, was able to put together in a convenient four-part handbook the main points to be dealt with in arguing against Cathars, Waldensians, Jews, and Moslems.[2] Anselm was thus being drawn into the field of theological polemic. In the *De Processione Spiritus Sancti* and in the *Letters on the Sacraments*, which are also chiefly concerned with rebutting the views of the Greeks,[3] he handles matters which are topical because they are in dispute. He was never quite comfortable in writing on controversial issues, if only because in order to settle other men's doubts and to convince the mistaken of their error, he was obliged to arrange his material a little lop-sidedly. He had to choose arguments which would quiet disagreement, and so he could not allow free play to his own thought about the positive aspects of the doctrine in question. In writing works of polemical theology Anselm was entering upon a task which later generations found far more congenial than he. Although he can be seen to be composing treatises which belong to a new age, it is again evident that he was not a leader, but a follower, of the new fashion.

Ever since Augustine's day it has been difficult for theologians to avoid giving some account of what Anselm himself calls 'a very famous question',[4] that of the relation between human free will and divine grace, foreknowledge and predestination. This, too, was to become a topic of renewed interest in the twelfth century. Anselm had already had something to say about it in his *De Libertate Arbitrii*, which opens with a reference to the question.[5] There he had dealt at length with free will, but he had said almost nothing about the three apparently opposing forces. His purpose in the *De Concordia* is to show how

---

[1] VA, pp. 112–13, cf. Eadmer's *Historia Novorum in Anglia*, ed. M. Rule, *Rolls Series* (London 1884), pp. 105–6; Letter 239, S 4.146–7.

[2] PL, 210.305–430.   [3] S 2.223.8 and 12.

[4] S 1.266.25.   [5] S 1.207.4–5.

those forces may be reconciled with that of free will; (its title implies as much). It would not be fair to say that the solving of the problems of the *De Concordia* gave Anselm no intellectual excitement. But the work is altogether the most impersonal of the theological treatises. It has about it the air of a task left outstanding and now conscientiously completed—not entirely mechanically, but without that delight in his discoveries which characterizes Anselm's writing when he is talking about God. It is not impossible that Anselm had only gradually come to realize that there was a need to finish what he had begun in the *De Libertate Arbitrii*, that a clear understanding of the nature of free will was not in itself enough to save his readers from uncertainties about the workings of grace, foreknowledge, and predestination. These topics occur among the Sentences of the School of Laon[1] and they were evidently the subject of active discussion. The existence of something like a public demand, rather than his own wish to settle the questions, may have prompted Anselm to write the *De Concordia*. He says at the end of the work that these were matters over which he himself once had difficulty:

quando in eis mens mea rationem quaerendo fluctuabat.[2] ('When my mind was casting about in search of an explanation of these things'). He thinks now that if anyone had offered him the explanations he has provided for his readers, he would have been grateful. It is clear that these matters have not troubled him personally for some years; the *De Concordia* cannot be compared with the *Proslogion*, which Anselm wrote in excitement because he has himself only just discovered the proof he had been looking for. It is not the product of recent thought, but a setting-out of familiar explanations by a thinker to whom they are no longer new.

Just before Anselm died, Eadmer says, he remarked that he wished he might live a little longer so that he could attempt to solve the problem of the origin of the soul, for he did not know of anyone who could resolve it if he did not live long enough to do so.[3] It is not clear whether this solution was to have formed the subject-matter of another treatise. But Anselm's anxiety to settle the matter before he died may have something to tell us

---

[1] See O. Lottin, *Psychologie et morale aux xii*e* et xiii*e* siècles*, v (Gembloux 1959).
[2] S 2.288.15.   [3] VA, pp. 141–2.

about the frame of mind in which he wrote these last works. Between the completion of the *De Conceptu Virginali* and 1109 when he died, he seems to have given his energies to the tying up of loose ends, rather than to breaking new ground. He was asked to write on certain matters; others lingered in his mind as uncompleted tasks of earlier days. But in both cases it was the external changes of circumstance and the new tastes and demands of contemporary scholarship which encouraged him to write. He was no longer quite free to proceed as his own developing ideas dictated. We cannot see Anselm as a leader of the new thought, but only as a perhaps rather uncomfortable follower, as he experiments with new forms and additional subject-matter.

From a philosophical point of view, forces of change of another kind had to be accommodated in Anselm's scheme of thought. It was necessary for him to emphasize with conspicuous firmness in the *Cur Deus Homo* that he wanted to make his solutions simple and easily comprehensible, if only because the task he had set himself was essentially more complex and involved than that which he had already carried out in the *Monologion* and *Proslogion*. Anselm's discussions there have to do with things which were never otherwise than they are now, with a state of affairs which, throughout eternity, has never been not-so. In discussing such eternally consistent matters there is no room for a consideration of the action of forces which may bring about a changed state of affairs. Anselm emphasizes in the *Proslogion* that God cannot be affected by suffering. He is *impassibilis*.[1] Honorius Augustodunensis makes a similar point in his *Clavis Physicae*:

> Deus non movetur extra se, sed a se ipso in se ipso ad se ipsum.[2]

('God is not moved outside himself, but by himself, in himself and to himself.') No force acts upon God. But in the *Cur Deus Homo* and in several of the later treatises, Anselm has had to account for such events as the Atonement and the conception of Christ in which, it seems, God has been subject to forces of change and has become capable of suffering. In the *De Con-*

[1] S 1.106.5–6.
[2] Honorius Augustodunensis, *Clavis Physicae*, ed. P. Lucentini (Rome 1974), *Temi e Testi* 21, p. 13.5 (18).

cordia he looks at the implications of his philosophy of motion and alteration and necessity and compulsion, which he had found indispensable to the solution of the problems posed by the Atonement, in the further context of the interaction of forces of change in man and in God's purpose for man. In the *Cur Deus Homo*, he notes with regret that he will not be able to deal at length with will, power, and necessity. These seem to him to be intimately interconnected and to have much to do with the problems in hand. Boso proposes that Anselm shall introduce such elements of his thinking about these topics as is necessary as the treatise proceeds, and suggests that that will suffice for the moment.[1] Anselm does indeed have much to say about the freedom of Christ's will in becoming Man, about the fact that no necessity compelled him, although it was necessary for the Redemption to be carried out in that way and in no other, about God's power to redeem the world, and the ways in which he might have gone about it. But, except in some passages of the *De Casu Diaboli*, there is neither room nor need for the development of a philosophical method of handling change in Anselm's thought until he comes to consider why God became Man.

The implicit division in Anselm's writings between those theological topics which involve no consideration of the operation of forces at all, and those which do require force and motion and change to be taken into account, becomes an important explicit distinction in the writings of the next generation, and in the twelfth century at large. It is a focal point of discussion in the 'dialogues' between Jews and Christians that in believing that God became Man, Christians seem to concede that God is mutable. It is also common in twelfth-century discussions of Romans 1:19–20 to find some distinction being made between those eternally true facts about God which observation of the created world should make clear even to pagans, and those details of Incarnation and Redemption which cannot be learned of in that way, as God's goodness, beauty, truth, and omnipotence may. It is difficult to assess the originality of Anselm's perception of the division between these two areas of theological writing. It has been suggested that one of the novelties of Abelard's theology was his inclusion of a variety of topics

---

[1] S 2.49.7–13. Some of these problems are tackled by Anselm in the *Philosophical Fragments*. See MA, pp. 341–3 in particular.

under the umbrella heading of the 'Christian theology'.[1] But in Abelard's day, there was increasing pressure on theological writers to show plainly what they thought their subject-matter included. The Boethian *opuscula sacra* were beginning to attract commentators who could quote Boethius' statement in his *De Trinitate*, that theology does not deal with 'motion', because in God there is no motion:

> theologica, sine motu abstracta atque separabilis, nam dei substantia et materia et motu caret.[2]

Theology proper, in this view, deals strictly with the eternal truths about the divine nature, with the study of God himself, rather than with matters involving change and motion and force. To take one of a number of examples: in the *Lectiones* of the school of Thierry of Chartres we find the following statement:

> 'Sine motu': i.e. sine mutabilitate quia considerat divinam simplicitatem eternitatem que est 'sine motu' i.e. sine mutabilitate.[3]

(' "Without motion": that is, without mutability, for [theology] deals with the everlasting simplicity of God, who is "without motion".') Anselm was most at his ease in such regions. It might almost be argued that the distinctive qualities of the *Cur Deus Homo* as a work of Redemption and Atonement theology lie in Anselm's success in treating such problems as those raised by will, power and necessity by procedures more obviously applicable to the unchanging aspects of God's being. It is not surprising to find that he displays little inclination to explore further an area of philosophical difficulty to which the metaphysics he knew gave him only limited access, and for which he had little natural liking. Will, power and necessity never form the subject-matter for a treatise; Anselm examines them only where it is necessary for him to do so if he is to deal satisfactorily with other matters.

Nor had he perhaps anything further to say about those

---

[1] R. E. Weingart, 'Peter Abailard's Contribution to Mediaeval Sacramentology', *Recherches de théologie ancienne et médiévale*, 34 (1967), 159–178 gives the history of this view.

[2] Boethius, *Theological Tractates*, ed. and tr. H. F. Stewart and E. K. Rand (London 1946), p. 8.14–16 (*De Trinitate*, II).

[3] *Commentaries on Boethius of the School of Thierry of Chartres*, ed. N. M. Häring (Toronto 1971), p. 163.10.

means of talking about God which he had been exploring systematically for more than two decades. Anselm's mind was not, except in the 'lateral thinking' his philosophical discoveries required, an adaptable one, and he could not fit himself easily to these new conditions. But he could and did retain to the end a power of insight which produces frequent hints of the old Anselm in the arguments of the last treatises. Although Anselm himself might have been disinclined to press his last technical innovations so far, he can be seen to be setting out upon the road Robert of Melun was travelling later in the century, when he wrote about the words we use to describe God. He distinguishes the *vocabula*, the names, which are said to apply to God because they are his names, and those which are man's names for God:

De vocabulis que Deo dicuntur convenire ex ipso et ex nobis.[1]

He speaks of *proprietas, significatio*, common and specific senses, the application of words with precision, and the dangers which attend on inaccuracy.[2] Robert has not gone far as yet in the direction of Aquinas. But a line drawn from Anselm's last works to the thirteenth-century scholastics would pass along his way. By contrast, Rupert of Deutz, who owes much to Anselm in his theology, can still write, a generation after Anselm, in a very different tone. In his *De Victoria Verbi Dei* he suggests that only those whom God has taught can worthily speak the words of God:

Solos a Deo doctos, digne verba Dei eloqui posse.[3]

'Happy is he who has deserved to taste the good Word in such a way!'

Felix ille qui taliter meruit bonum gustare Verbum.[4]

Rupert's mode of talking about God was to have its imitators, but not in the Schools. Anselm had been able for many years to speak in both these languages, the language of devotion and the language of hard argument. By the end of his life it was becoming increasingly difficult for one man to encompass both in the same work. Ironically, in view of the fact that Anselm's writings have such a universal and timeless appeal, it seems very

---

[1] Robert of Melun, *Sententiae*, ed. R. M. Martin, *Spicilegium Sacrum Lovaniense*, 25 (1952), p. 19, Book I, 3.
[2] Ibid.   [3] PL, 169.1220.   [4] Ibid.

probable that he himself could only have written them at the time when he did so. Had he been born half a century later, he would have encountered much earlier in life the plethora of objections and technical refinements which so discomfited him, and which increasingly impeded the directness of his vision.

CONCLUSION

IN his later years Anselm moved away from the problems of talking about God. His departure from such matters and his later concentration on other kinds of issue can be explained partly at least by the pressures other people put upon him. But if we are to take the view that the development of his thought had a natural sequence of its own, and that it reflects fundamental aspects of Anselm's own mental make-up, then we must find some other explanation for the changes, within Anselm himself. We must attempt to see him as the author of those changes, and not as their instrument.

Anselm's theory of language was carefully and thoroughly worked out at a very early stage. In the *Monologion* he examined the roots of language in the mind of man, and compared his findings deliberately with what he could understand of the language of God himself, in the hope of perceiving the essential similarities and differences. He had thus confronted the problem of talking about God in his first treatise. By the time he had written the *Tres Tractatus* and the *De Grammatico*, he had also said much of what he had to say about the uses of language by grammarians and dialecticians—about ordinary language and technical expressions as defined by the textbooks of the *artes* with which he was familiar. He did not, in other words, work gradually towards a consideration of the use of language in talking about God. He began from that point. The order in which he composed his treatises shows him again and again beginning with what were to him the most immediately important topics and leaving lesser matters until later. Talking about God is thus for Anselm a point of departure, philosophically speaking, and not a point of arrival.

This habit of never leaving the best till last eventually presented him with two choices: he could either move on to ever less exciting topics, as he followed up the thoughts with which his earlier work had left him, or he could repeat his treatment of a given theme and write about it from another point of view. Anselm was always disinclined to try to re-live past experience by going back over old ground. His habit was to refer his readers back to what he had said before, rather than to try to restate his position. A treatise finished was, for the most part, a subject closed, although it often happened that a topic touched on in one treatise had to be reopened in another because it had a bearing on a new subject. But when Anselm mentions will, sin, or evil again, he does so, not because he wants to write about them in their own right, but because he cannot deal with the subject in hand without mentioning them. This gives a momentary untidiness to his handling of what he tried to make self-contained issues, so that the reader might benefit from reading any single treatise, even if he could not refer to others. The treatises became closely interconnected almost by accident in this way. But Anselm did not intend to risk confusing his readers by writing two treatises on the existence of God or the Procession of the Holy Spirit. His instinct and his usual practice was to give time and thought to the framing of each treatise as he wrote it, so that when it was finished it contained everything he wanted to say about the problem in hand.

That does not argue poverty of invention on Anselm's part. It is very evident that he chose to omit much which had been discussed with friends and pupils, and we frequently see him making the decision to include some point or to leave it out, especially in the *Cur Deus Homo* and the *De Conceptu Virginali*. But it does suggest that he remained remarkably consistent in his views and that once a treatise was done with he rarely saw any need to revise it, even several decades later. The notable exception is the *De Incarnatione Verbi*, but the circumstances of its composition were quite exceptional, and it merely serves to prove the rule that Anselm was not given to *retractationes*. This marked certainty of touch is wholly in keeping with the orderliness of Anselm's progress from one subject to another. He scarcely seems to have envisaged the writing of one work until its predecessor was completed, and there is no evidence that topics for composition crowded upon him urgently at any period of his life except perhaps at the end. He wrote his treatises one at a time, in order, because he found himself ready for the next only as he finished the previous work.

But that leaves us with the inescapable conclusion that he had put himself in a position where each treatise was likely to excite him less than the last, because as he went on he moved away from the direct contemplation of the nature of God, to consider God at work in the world and God's relations with man. That is not to say that he did not find these subjects important and interesting; yet they did not always provide him with quite the pure intellectual pleasures of the *Proslogion* days because of the different nature of their subject-matter. This 'going out of the light' did not happen all at once, or once and for all. The most that can be said is that there is a tendency, after the completion of the *Cur Deus Homo* at least, for Anselm to find it harder to derive the pleasures which came to him most naturally, as he entered upon the treatment of topics which were intrinsically unlikely to yield him the satisfactions he found so readily in his earlier years.

Yet there is much to be learned from the whole body of Anselm's writings about the continuing development of his power of making things clear. This was a skill which never left him. There is no doubt that Anselm's qualities of mind appeared as exceptional to his contemporaries as they do to us. But that did not make of him a man apart. His greater powers of understanding were not such as cut a man off from his fellows, but rather they were gifts of a sort which allowed him to enter into the more limited understanding of others and to open other men's eyes to things they had not perceived before. That was not something Anselm learned to do all at once, as we have seen. In the writing of the *De Incarnatione Verbi* he learned to allow, not only for the limitations of understanding of his young pupils, but also for the enduring limitations of grown men who could not or would not see further. The very years which saw him leaving behind the discussion of the problems of talking about God for other matters also saw him growing in his own power of communicating his thoughts.

Anselm's reaction to criticism, especially if he felt that he had been misunderstood, was to look carefully at his handling of the matter under discussion again; when Lanfranc objected to the mode of demonstration he had used in the *Monologion*, he declined, on reflection, to alter what he had written. But by the time he heard Gaunilo's criticism of the *Proslogion* argument he had come to see that there might be something to be said for meeting the criticisms in an appendix. The *De Incarnatione*

Verbi he rewrote comprehensively, so as to make it watertight against further objections. In the *Cur Deus Homo* he put in the objections at the very beginning of the treatise, anticipating criticism before it came. And so it went on, as Anselm gradually learned more about the workings of other men's minds, albeit in this piecemeal fashion.

But he could only learn such lessons effectively while he had men about him on whose minds he could try out his thoughts. He needed not only the intellectual challenge of simplifying the profoundly difficult for the benefit of beginners, but also the emotional stimulus of having friends and pupils close to him, in actual need of his help. Boso partially filled the gap which was opened up when Anselm left Bec, but he was deprived in his last years of any such contact. Eadmer was a writer of some ability himself, but in a very different line; he learnt much from Anselm about how to write well, but his thinking caught no fire from him. Anselm's theological influence on Gilbert Crispin is more evident. They may have spent some time together in England about the time when Anselm became Archbishop. But Anselm could not always have Gilbert by his side. In any case his acquaintance with Gilbert was of comparatively long standing; it went back to the early days at Bec. Gilbert was no loving young pupil, in whose impressionable young mind Anselm could see, rewardingly, the results of his efforts to help him extend his powers. Even though it seems, to judge from the works he later went on to write, that Gilbert gained a good deal from his talks with Anselm, it is doubtful whether Anselm himself got much in return. Honorius Augustodunensis passed by, and added materials to his own store. But he, too, can have given little or nothing in return. It was not that Anselm needed minds of a capacity to match his own to stimulate him to enjoyment of his thinking; but he did need, very badly, young minds of a naturally philosophical cast, on which he could test the universal applicability of what he had to say. The communities to whom he addressed his pastoral teaching at the end of his life provided a very different kind of audience, for which a different sort of simplification was required. There was no lack of opportunities for practising such skills, as the material collected in the *Memorials* demonstrates. Nevertheless, as a philosopher and theologian, Anselm found himself in a position towards the end of his life where he was forced to draw continually upon his intellectual and emotional capital. He rarely received any addition to his resources.

Thus it is that the works of the later years make their point with clarity; Anselm knew well enough, by the time he wrote the *De Concordia*, how to make himself plain. But the later works rarely possess the conceptual beauty of the earlier, except in moments of especially vivid insight. Anselm rarely recaptures the spirit of excitement in which he had first written, nor the spirit of gentle searching concern for others in which he had composed the *Cur Deus Homo*. Perhaps we should not place too much emphasis on the absence of a Maurice or a Boso in this connection. Anselm may simply have been experiencing, unusually late in life, the fading of intense intellectual and emotional perceptions such as those Wordsworth describes in the *Ode on Imitations of Immortality*.

The impression that Anselm retained this sense of the newness of things well beyond his childhood is reinforced by the fact that, although the devotional works have the ring of a young man's compositions, they were mostly written when Anselm was middle-aged. This provides perhaps the key to the peculiar attractiveness of his thought; he possessed the power to communicate the sheer newness of his intellectual experiences with a childlike openness and simplicity. He could enter into the minds of his pupils because his own was so remarkably unclouded by a sense of his own distance from them in age and experience. It seems to him, not bold, but natural enough to talk about God to his friends. Many of these qualities are those of a saint. But they are also, in the particular circumstances of the learning of Anselm's day, the qualities of an intellectual giant, and in any age, qualities which would have allowed him to speak with great directness to his fellow men.

INDEX